S0-ALA-983

# WAR CRIES

## DIANE GLANCY

## INTRODUCTION BY KIMBERLY BLAESER

HOLY COW! PRESS · DULUTH, MINNESOTA · 1997

CHABOT COLLEGE LIBRARY

PS
3557
.L294
W37
1997

Text ©1997 by Diane Glancy
Introduction ©1997 by Kimberly Blaeser

Cover photography by Joseph Shaffer. Tipi opposite "Brown Bear Trading Post"
on the road between Bonner's Ferry, Idaho, and Kalispel, Montana.

Photograph of Diane Glancy by Tom King

Special acknowledgment to Sara Merz who proofread early versions of this
collection.

First Printing, 1997
10 9 8 7 6 5 4 3 2 1

All rights reserved. No part of this book may be reproduced in any form without
written permission of the Publisher and Diane Glancy. Printed and bound in the
United States of America. Design by Clarity (Duluth, Minnesota).

ISBN 0-930100-54-9

Publisher's Address:
Holy Cow! Press
Post Office Box 3170
Mount Royal Station
Duluth, Minnesota  55803

This project was supported, in part, by grants from the Minnesota Humanities
Commission, St. Paul Companies, the John S. and James L. Knight Foundation Fund
of the Duluth-Superior Area Community Foundation, James P. Lenfestey,
and by other generous individuals.

# ACHNOWLEDGMENTS:

**WEEBJOB**
won the 1984 Five Civilized Tribes Playwriting Competition, Muskogee, Oklahoma, and was produced by the American Indian Theatre Company, April 8-11, 1987, at the Performing Arts Center, Tulsa, Oklahoma. It was published in *Contemporary Plays by Women of Color*, edited by Kathy Perkins and Roberta Uno, Routledge, 1995

**STICK HORSE**
won the 1988 Five Civilized Tribes Museum Playwriting Competition; the 1988 Aspen Summer Theater Award with production in Aspen, Colorado; and the 1990 Borderlands Theater Play Festival Award, Tucson, Arizona

**BULL STAR**
won the 1982 American Indian Theatre Company's Playwriting Award, and was published in the Fall, 1995 *Aboriginal Voices*

**SEGWOHI**
won the 1987 Oklahoma Theater Festival Award and was given a staged reading in Tulsa, Oklahoma

**THE TRUTH TELLER**
was written in part with a 1991 grant from the Minnesota Private College Research Foundation with funds provided by the Blandin Foundation of Grand Rapids, Minnesota

**HALFACT**
was published in Vol. 5, No. 1, Spring 1993, SAIL, Studies in American Indian Literatures, California State University, San Bernardino, California, and was presented at the 1994 MLA in San Diego

I see theater as a tipi with an open smoke-hole
where many voices tell stories of war.

The stories cause the heart to live
with remembrance of bravery.
They cause new bravery to be born.

I see theater as portable. Going anywhere.

The firepit in the center.

Yes. I hear voices speaking against the darkness.

I hear each play as a war cry.

# CONTENTS

# INTRODUCTION

by Kimberly Blaeser

In the stage directions to her play *Weebjob*, Glancy writes, "This scene is the story of how we come from cayos [chaos] into maybe as much light as we can stand. And how we struggle to stay there." Her description might aptly be applied to the whole of Glancy's *War Cries*. These nine plays, though each concerned with their own particular account of Indian lives, all depict a world informed by the chaos of a mixedblood or border culture existence and protagonists who journey out of the dark chaos into some kind of personal or spiritual light. Through her characters' fictional journey Glancy offers her readers or audience inspiration for their own. "The stories," she writes, "cause the heart to live / with remembrance of bravery. / They cause new bravery to be born." Glancy's intentions in this collection are literary to be sure, but like those of many other Native writers, they are also supra-literary. She shares these stories as "voices speaking against the darkness," as "war cries." Each drama contains a spark of healing, an aide to survival.

Indeed the first survival Glancy fosters may be her own. The artistic vision of her characters often reflects Glancy's understanding of the literary arts as a healing force, an understanding previously expressed in works such as *Claiming Breath*. Thus lines from the plays might be read together as Glancy's own *ars poetica*. We hear her voice in that of Sereh from Segwohi who explains:

> I feel these invisible shapes in my head... In my work, I feel I am shaping myself— those dark forms in my head are my fears and apprehensions. I work them into form—useful form.
> ... My life is bound up with my work. It's my pow wow dance. My sweat lodge ceremony. It's where I find soothing. It's where I'm whole.

If Glancy writes out of a personal need for wholeness and balance, this is but part of the impetus behind *War Cries*. The dramas are written as well for the Native community, particularly for the contemporary mixedblood. Indeed two of the plays were written for the Five Civilized Tribes playwriting competition and several have been produced by Native theatre companies. We find many statements in this body of work which characterize the dramas' *raison d'etre* such as the following from Sereh in *Segwohi*: "That's where the battle of our lives is now—shaking off the past—

the defeats—or at least confining them with our art—." Glancy sees her writing as one of the practical methods of dealing with the loss experienced by tribal people. And finally, of course, she writes as well for the larger community, that they might understand more fully the tribal histories and the physical and spiritual conditions of contemporary Indian existence.

The subjects, settings, and tribal affiliations of the characters in the plays vary, but whether set in Salazar Canyon, New Mexico, Tahlequah, Oklahoma, or a "Village in the Far North of the Imagination," whether about Apache, Cherokee, or Cheyenne characters, whether depicting Indian alcoholism, incest, or traditional lifeways, the dramas combine lyrical language and dramatic spectacle to wonderful effect. The plays range from the poetic and surreal *Mother of Mosquitos*, to the dramatic monologue of *One Horse*, to the conflict-based *Bull Star*. Each is stamped with Glancy's singular imaginative vision.

Among the rich and haunting images typical of Glancy's work here is the game of hangman used to underscore Eli's struggle toward sobriety in *Stick Horse*. The author depicts her characters engaged in the child's game, but gives the scene an ominous tone with the knowledge that Eli literally has been slowly losing himself in the progressive disease of alcoholism. His actual physical disintegration is acted out in various scenes and the characters repeatedly allude to the possibility that he might be unable to maintain sobriety. At risk is his very life. Glancy builds tension with a chant-like repetition: "Your head is on the gallows." "The trunk of your body is on the gallows." "Your arm is on the gallows." The protagonist himself is aware of his precarious state and the hangman becomes a symbol to him. At first he feels overpowered: "I try to sweep the letters back. The words I knocked sideways, threw away. They come back to get me now. They make a HANG MAN of ME!! Letters I spilled all lined up. They take my arms and legs." But later, in his decision to achieve sobriety, to reclaim himself, he declares: "The next time I hear them [spirit voices], they will say I'm coming off the gallows— A living Hang Man! Just as one letter comes against another before there is a word— One finger, one toe at a time is taken from the gallows until there is a man—." The images called up verbally are reinforced visually as Glancy's state directions call for the acting out of the game, and for "spirit-dancers" with "giant alphabet letters on their chests" to taunt Eli.

The innovation exemplified in this hangman sequence and the ready intermingling of various realms of being characterize Glancy's dramas throughout. And, also as it does here, her presentation generally offers both the visual and the verbal. The plays contain fine lyrical passages and colorful descriptions such as these lines from the narrator in *Halfact*:

The farmtruck takes off on the dirt road,
blue as slow lightning
with ragged edges of a frayed wire.
The sky still jean blue and worn at the knees.
A hill in its back pocket.

With her evocative language, Glancy sketches vivid images of the landscapes and home places of her characters and traces their history or spiritual investment in those places. In *Segwohi*, for example, she captures the atmosphere with these lines:

A flock of geese rise over the silo into a pale sky. It is autumn. Dried cornstalks rattle in the small field behind the barn. An old truck is parked under a heavy chestnut tree.

Next she locates her primary character in relation to the place: "Segwohi has lived on the land his whole life. He hears the ghosts of his ancestors who camped there during migration."

Glancy uses this same power of expression to fill her plays with mystifying truths and tragic declarations, fit to stand alone, but stronger still when woven into the dramatic fabric. Coyote Girl, a victim of incest in *Halfact*, in taking her dead mother's place knows, "The voice of a woman is a foreign object. / It feels like silence in my mouth;" and the narrator tells us about the girl's mother, "[She] died of untruth. / She was starved of her sense of person."

The plays combine the power of Glancy's language and scene setting with dramatic and symbolic actions. A character who longs for his rodeo days rides an imaginary horse, two characters in a drama, circa 1800, paddle a canoe, make maple sugar, and gather the wild rice. Often the spectacle in the dramas arises from the physical presence of spirit figures. Glancy's works employ masks, mime, dance, music, and chant to give reality to Native visions of another realm of being.

But the creation of stageable spectacle never overrides a concern with speakable language. In fact in Glancy's works, often the visual and dramatic elements are linked to the verbal. In *Weebjob*, the protagonist paints signs of biblical quotations; in *The Best Fancy Dancer the Pushmataha Pow Wow's Ever Seen*, the two young characters are rewriting and performing Columbus's diary; and in *Segwohi*, three characters become involved in drawing pictures and telling the story of those pictures in order to communicate to one another. Indeed, in the hangman scenes, the characters in *Stick Horse* are also acutely aware of the significance of the letters, their tie to the power of words, and Eli speaks of "words stampeding in my head" and "words dancing." He understands that his physical and spiritual alienation is symbolized in his loss of language: "I don't know about words anymore—Sometimes my own name seems strange."

The various conflicts of the plays demonstrate Glancy's own thorough understanding of the role words, voice, and story play. Characters such as Jake (Bullet Proof), the medicine man in *Stick Horse*, expound on the powers and importance of words. Jake claims to create with words a "medicine shirt" for Eli like the ghost shirts worn by warriors and tells Eli, "Here the words riding into your ears. They are strong warriors. They aim their bows and arrows to the voices in your head that lead you to drink." In *Truth Teller*, the woman character desires a dream name for her child and explains to her husband how important this is: "A name is the pine-pitch that holds you together... it's like knowing your history. It's knowing who you are." She likewise emphasizes the importance of story asking, "How can anyone survive without stories?" and claiming, "Our stories carry us like a canoe. That's what stories can do."

Glancy's characters and her plays not only speak about the importance of words and stories, they give us both to live by. Several of the plays contain within them the retelling of a tribal myth: the turtle island creation story in *Weebjob*, a Cherokee story about the killing of a snake in *Segwohi*. Along side the wisdom of these older stories are new words and new stories. In *The Best Fancy Dancer*, for example, Henry tells Jess a story about the placing of the sun in the sky and reminds him to "Listen to our stories." But his advice goes farther: "Healing is creating something. The more you listen, the more you have to tell." In the play Jess finds healing and power following Henry's advice. He listens to Genny read from Columbus's diary and then he creates and tells his own account. He challenges the historical document because he knows all history is merely "human story-telling" and "someone's point-of-view" and that "we need more voices to tell the story." Glancy's collection delivers the same messages as Glancy offers her own as one of the new voices. In *War Cries*, she writes about the importance of storytelling, retells old stories, offers new ones, and finally, encourages readers to enter the storytelling circle because "with stories we will know the way."

Perhaps the most persistent story Glancy tells is the story of beauty and truth and the various forms they take. Nearly all her mixedblood characters struggle with the conception of truth, trying to balance their multiple heritages like young Jess in *The Best Fancy Dancer* who says: "We can't be of the Old World anymore... We can't be the New World either. I'm a mixed blood. I have both worlds in me. I speak for those who have two trails to follow." Some of Glancy's characters come to the mixedblood journey with a painful legacy. Weebjob carries with him boarding school remembrances. Eli in *Stick Horse* expresses his hopelessness in this declaration of destiny: "I'm an alcoholic. Our father was an alcoholic. Our grandfather—." Indeed most of the characters live in a present haunted in one way or another by ghost terrors, by tragic Native American and family histories. But Glancy's *The Best Fancy Dancer* declares this hard truth; "No matter how many rewrites you put on it each day—your past happened. Get used to it." Yet neither the characters in the play nor Glancy's dramas as a whole end with that realization. Instead they claim, "There's ways to survive and not forget your past." Working out the ways of survival is the central concern of the characters in *War Cries*.

Many of the older characters want to continue the life they have known and expect the young to doggedly follow the same lifestyles and traditions. But stasis and survival are shown to be mutually exclusive. Characters like the medicine man in *Stick Horse* instead uphold a tradition of change: "My father said our lives had changed— our magic would also change—and it would still be magic. He would keep our medicine—it didn't matter by which ritual." Living the wisdom of change for many characters means adapting, accepting new visions and new versions of truth, recognizing that perhaps truth has "several headwaters" which still "flow into one stream."

Glancy frequently depicts the confluence of traditions in *War Cries*. In several plays she explores links and crossover between Christian and tribal relations. In *Segwohi*, she dramatizes the debate about turning traditional arts like pottery and song into commercial products. In *The Truth Teller*, she reimagines the earliest conflicts between those family members who stayed with tribal communities and those who ventured into white societies. Whether these plays end in a resolution or a continuation of these mixedblood conflicts, they add a new vision of Indian lives, lives which may follow unlikely paths of survival or search out unlikely sites of truth and beauty. Weebjob may find vision in his squash patch, Sweet Potato in hitchhiking. Each "grows visions" in their own way. What these warriors must remember to survive is what Glancy would have the readers of *War Cries* understand: "There's savages all around. And some of them are us. But we got this message from two Worlds and we're coming into our own."

It's what's wrong with writing—
It kills the voice.
The words written on the page
enter a burial ground.
But speaking brings them back—

# WEEBJOB

13

# CHARACTERS

GERALD LONG CHALK, or Weebjob (Wēeb jōb), age 48, is the main character. His name is a play on the Biblical Job because he is beset with problems, and has a friend, Pick Up, who isn't much comfort. Weebjob is a holy man, a Mescalero Apache. He's stern and unyielding, a little impractical, yet likeable. Weebjob always seems to be at a crossroads in his life. He lets rich land lie fallow. He paints signs and hangs them on his fence. Signs that say: 'He hangs the earth on nothing, Job 26:7,' 'Rodeo / Albuquerque,' 'Behold the behemoth. He eats grass as an ox. He moveth his tail like the pines, Job 40:15,17,' 'Vote / Ofred for Chief.'

PERCY WILLINGDEER, or PICK UP, Weebjob's friend, age 43, is in love with Weebjob's daughter. He is also a Mescalero Apache. He presents Weebjob with his newest disaster when Weebjob finds out that he wants to marry his daughter.

SUZANNE LONG CHALK, or SWEET POTATO, Weebjob's daughter, is 21. She has a mind of her own. She is unhappy with her life because she doesn't know where she belongs. She has run off several times to hitchhike on the interstate to Gallup.

JAMES LONG CHALK, Weebjob's younger son, age 23. He works for the highway department and lives in Socorro with his girlfriend, Hersah.

SARAH LONG CHALK, or SWEET GRASS, Weebjob's wife, age 45. She has a sweet and understanding disposition. She is of Cherokee heritage. When the play begins, she has gone to visit her sister in Hobbs, because she wants to see her, and also, to get away from Weebjob for a while, whom she feels takes her for granted. She is a traditional woman who is just starting to deal with herself as an individual.

WILLIAM LONG CHALK, Weebjob's older son, age 28, a lawyer in Roswell.

MINOR CHARACTERS WHO APPEAR AT THE WEDDING:

    CLEMENT THOUSANDSTICKS, the town buffoon, mid 50s

    MARY JANE COLLAR, Sweet Grass' sister, early 40s

    HERSAH, James' girlfriend, early 20s

    REESAH, William's wife and their CHILD

    WARHALL, Thousandsticks' friend

    MINISTER

    MUSICIANS

    OTHER WEDDING GUESTS

# SETTING

The Salazar Canyon in Lincoln County, New Mexico, is between Roswell and Socorro. Weebjob's house is small, made of mud-brick, with a chimney and low roof, so the flat wind that comes from between the mountains can pass over it. In the background is a grove of mesquites, and farther away, some pines and finally the mountains. A weed-clump marks Weebjob's road, which is nothing more than tire-ruts, that connect with old Highway 380 through the canyon. On the west of Weebjob's house is a squash patch with yellow blossoms. A low cloud hides the mountains at first, but soon lifts.

Weebjob's house is simple. A wooden table and four chairs are on the front porch. Inside the front window is a kitchen-sink full of pots and dishes. A sideboard emptied of its dishes sets along a wall. The floor is covered with Sweet Grass' weavings. Her loom is at a back corner of the house.

# ACT ONE

Scene   i
Scene   ii
Scene   iii
Scene   iv

# ACT TWO

Scene   i
Scene   ii
Scene   iii
Scene   iv

Thou hast fenced me with bones
—Job 10:11

# ACT ONE

## SCENE I

### Weebjob
(WEEBJOB IS IN HIS SQUASH PATCH WHEN HE HEARS A TRUCK. HE TURNS TO THE ROAD, BUT FINISHES DIGGING BEFORE HE WALKS TO THE HOUSE.) It's Pick Up. Mighty Warrior doesn't bark.

### Pick Up
(HE ENTERS.) Ola, Weebjob.

### Weebjob
Ola, Pick Up.

### Pick Up
(THERE'S THE SOUND OF THE TRUCK DOOR SLAMMING.) I've returned with your daughter, Sweet Potato.

### Sweet Potato
My name is Suzanne! (SHE SITS ON THE STEPS OF THE HOUSE.)

### Pick Up
I saw her on the road hitchhiking to Gallup. I told her I would bring her back to her father. (SWEET POTATO SITS ON THE STEPS AND DOESN'T LOOK AT THEM.)

### Weebjob
What have my days come to? (PAUSE.)

### Pick Up
She didn't want to come.

### Weebjob
The young are restless as the pines.

### Pick Up
She says you do nothing but read the Book and sit in the squash patch and stare across the jaundiced hills.

### Weebjob
She overestimates me! And they're mountains, not hills. (SWEET POTATO STILL DOES NOT SPEAK, BUT LIES ON THE PORCH STEP

WITH HER FEET STICKING OFF THE SIDE.) We, who were raised in the old reservation boarding schools, know tolerance, persistence, perspicacity.

### Pick Up
Pardon?

### Weebjob
Discernment.

### Pick Up
Ah! Horse sense. (SWEET POTATO TURNS HER BACKSIDE TO THE MEN.) You learned the Book well at school.

### Weebjob
Every word.

### Sweet Potato
And not a word of it got through. (SHE SITS UP.)

### Weebjob
(LOOKING AT SWEET POTATO.) You misunderstand. I was raised in a different culture—I have trouble understanding—come on, Sweet Potato. Dismount. Your mother is at her sister's, not to return for a few days. I'm hungry. See what's in the kitchen and I will break my fast.

### Sweet Potato
Nothing's in the kitchen if mother's not here. (IMPATIENTLY.) You're busy making philosophy to the pines and religion to the mountains. You print signs and hang them on the fence by the highway. You read the Book. And yet the garden grows nothing but squash vines. Not one word of your Book changes anything!

### Pick Up
I believe the child is bitter.

### Weebjob
(IGNORING PICK UP.) Sweet Potato, my daughter, tuber of my soul, see what's in the kitchen for your starving father, Weebjob. I shall relinquish my fast. (PAUSE.)

### Pick Up
(LOOKING AT WEEBJOB.) She does not move.

#### Weebjob
I see that she does not move!—You need not tell me, Job's friend.
She is stubborn and recalcitrant.

#### Pick Up
You're too kind with your words.

#### Weebjob
I'm grumpy as thunder. Like Mighty Warrior, my dog. Like my wife
two weeks at her sister's and nothing to eat.

#### Pick Up
It must come with age.

#### Weebjob
No, the daughter has it too.

#### Pick Up
And sons.

#### Weebjob
Enough! I'm reminded of my plight. Deserted in the desert. No
loaves and fish.

#### Pick Up
That doesn't sound like you, Weebjob. I've never heard you talk
that way.

#### Weebjob
I'm at a crossroads in my life.

#### Sweet Potato
(RISING FROM THE STEPS.) Mutton. I've heard that all my life.
You're always at a crossroad.

#### Pick Up
You've always lived by the words of the Book you've committed to
memory.

#### Weebjob
I remember nothing. What memory? I can remember nothing but
war.

#### Sweet Potato
(ALMOST RESTS HER ARM AGAINST PICK UP, BUT DECIDES AGAINST
IT.) You've never been in war. You were too young for one, too old
for another.

### Weebjob

To get up in the morning is war. (AS WEEBJOB MAKES THIS SPEECH TO THE HEAVENS, PICK UP BRUSHES SWEET POTATO'S ARM.) To wrestle with the day, and with my work, is war. To have three children with minds of their own is war. (TURNS TO HIS DAUGHTER.) See what there is to eat, Sweet Potato! Your name makes hunger come to me.

### Sweet Potato

I'm going to continue my pilgrimage to Gallup. (SHE SAYS THIS TO PICK UP AS WELL.)

### Pick Up

(TURNS HIS HEAD.) Another crusader in the Long Chalk family.

### Weebjob

I shall continue to meditate on the passages of the Book. I'll stand with my feet on the holy ground of Canaan—(NODS HIS HEAD TO INDICATE HIS SQUASH PATCH.) I will sit in the squash patch—(WAVES HIS ARM TOWARD IT.) see the Thunder Hawk (HE LOOKS TO HEAVEN.)—and fight holy wars. (TURNS TENDERLY TO HIS DAUGHTER.) I need you, Sweet Potato.

### Pick Up

(AGREES WITH WEEBJOB.) Gallup is a long way.

### Weebjob

Three hundred miles.

### Sweet Potato

(SHE WALKS BACK TO THE STEPS. STANDS THERE WITH HER HAND IN HER HIP POCKET.) It's because nothing happens here. You live in the fertile Salazar Canyon, the greenest in New Mexico. (SHE RAISES HER ARMS.) You could have sheep, but you won't fence your land. You could have crops. James makes you an irrigation ditch, but what do you grow? (SHE SLAPS HER HANDS AT HER SIDES.) Nothing! You put up signs where our road runs into the highway. You make more signs. They say, 'Canaan.' Whatever that means. They say, 'The devil and I do not speak'— (SHE LOOKS AT WEEBJOB FIERCELY.) Whatever that means. When I go in to Old Lincoln they ask at the general store if I've come for more paint. (PAUSE.) Once in a while you sell gourds and squash at the roadside stand. You sell mother's blankets in Old Lincoln when we're desperate. What good ever comes from this? (SHE SHRUGS AS THOUGH GIVING UP, AND

STANDS WITH HER HANDS ON HER HIPS AGAIN.)

#### Weebjob
Yes, I have nothing. I'm proud to have nothing! The prophets of the Book had nothing. It's work to have nothing, Sweet Potato. I should have sent you to the Female Seminary where your mother went. Then you wouldn't have these ideas—

#### Sweet Potato
(UNDER HER BREATH.) Shit.

#### Weebjob
Then you would understand that I grow visions—

#### Sweet Potato
(WITH HER HANDS OVER HER EARS.) Heaven above. This is your harvest? I've seen you sitting in your squash patch in some kind of trance. Holy God. You look like you're talking to yourself. Is that the culmination of your life's work?

#### Weebjob
I won't have irreverence on my land. Someday you'll understand what 'Canaan' means. For now, get me something to eat! (MORE DEFINITE NOW.)

#### Sweet Potato
I thought it was your meat to do the will of the Father.

#### Weebjob
It is. And to finish the work I've begun. The fields are white with harvest. This is what I'll do until I hear my name called from beyond the mountains.

#### Sweet Potato
Your fields and desert look brown to me. You interpret the Book to fit your purpose.

#### Weebjob
Not so, Tuber. Indeed, I'm the man you see before your eyes, and I'm not appreciated. There may be things you don't know. I have faith that the desert is white with harvest, and will blossom by faith. I have seen the Thunder Hawk, Sweet Potato, what else can I say to you? (SWEET POTATO WALKS RELUCTANTLY TOWARD THE HOUSE. THE MEN WATCH HER UNTIL SHE ENTERS THE FRONT DOOR.)

### Pick Up
You should beat your sword into a ploughshare and your pulpit into a tractor.

### Weebjob
I don't ask your counsel. You know me, Pick Up. We've been friends many years, though I don't know why. You understand me—

### Pick Up
Not any longer, Weebjob. You can't expect your children to understand your ways. Your sons have already left. William to Roswell and James to Socorro.

### Weebjob
They come back from time to time.

### Pick Up
Your wife's at her sister's.

### Weebjob
(DEFENSIVELY.) Just for a visit. She returns soon.

### Pick Up
Now your daughter is trying to leave. Already she has stayed with James in Socorro more than in Salazar Canyon with you. Now she is trying to leave for Gallup.

### Weebjob
Hush up. She's coming back.

### Sweet Potato
(DISGUSTED AS SHE WALKS UP TO THE MEN.) A turnip and a hard crust of bread. How long has it been since you were at the grocer's in Old Lincoln?

### Pick Up
I don't think he's been.

### Sweet Potato
How long has mother been gone?

### Weebjob
Fifteen days.

#### Sweet Potato
How can you expect me to find something to eat when there's nothing? You're the one who believes in loaves and fishes. You go find something. I'll have to go to town if you want supper.

#### Pick Up
(HE LOOKS UP THE ROAD.) Another car comes.

#### Sweet Potato
A stranger?

#### Weebjob
No, Mighty Warrior is quiet.

#### Sweet Potato
So what does that mean? He's like you. He wouldn't bark if it were Custer.

#### Weebjob
It's James.

#### James
(ENTERS.) Suzanne! I see Pick Up found you. (JAMES LOOKS TO PICK UP, WHO SHAKES HIS HEAD THAT SHE'S ALL RIGHT.) Hersah didn't know where you'd gone.

#### Weebjob
She tried to make her run to Gallup again.

#### Pick Up
Someday she'll make it. Then we'll have to drive three hundred miles to retrieve her. (HE PAUSES, AS THOUGH TO HIMSELF.)— Probably in my truck.

#### Weebjob
James, my younger son. I haven't heard from you—

#### James
I've been busy, Father.

#### Weebjob
It's been a long time.

#### James
My job with the highway department takes me far away. I can't always get back. Hersah and Suzanne keep house for me.

### Sweet Potato
He could have gone to college if you'd let him apply for a loan. And I could have a wool store in Old Lincoln and sell mother's blankets.

### Pick Up
That's six hundred miles by the time we get back to Salazar Canyon from Gallup, Weebjob. I don't think my truck will go that far.

### Weebjob
Hersah is fine?

### James
Yes. I think she's more Sweet Potato's friend than mine.

### Sweet Potato
I'd like for you to call me Suzanne, James. You do when I'm in Socorro. And I think Hersah would be more your friend if you spent more time with her.

### Weebjob
She lives with him, doesn't she?

### Pick Up
Call her Sweet Potato, James. I like to hear it.

### Sweet Potato
Take me to the grocery store in Old Lincoln, James, so I can get us supper.

### Pick Up
I'll take you, Sweet Potato, Suzanne. That way I'll be sure you come back.

### Sweet Potato
If Weebjob would come and see the buildings they've restored, and how they've made it into a town where people can stop, he'd be interested in something other than 'Canaan.' The old brown buildings used to look at one another with blank faces. Now they're painted. Honeysuckle climbs the hitching posts—

### Pick Up
(ALMOST MAKING FUN OF SWEET POTATO.) Old Lincoln has the snap of a jackknife going to its mark. (WEEBJOB SCRATCHES HIMSELF.)

#### Sweet Potato
They asked me about Mother the last time I was there. Weebjob, you could fence off a corner of your land and keep a few sheep and shear them for wool we could sell in Old Lincoln.

#### Pick Up
They were all shepherds in the Book.

#### Weebjob
I've already considered that.

#### Sweet Potato
And he won't do anything about it.

#### James
Let's go to the grocery store.

#### Pick Up
(LOOKS ANXIOUSLY AT SWEET POTATO.) I'll take her! Give me a push, James.

#### Sweet Potato
I'll come back, Pick Up. You don't need to worry that I'll run away to Gallup tonight. The desert gets too cold.

#### Pick Up
(HE STILL LOOKS AT SWEET POTATO.) I need to take my truck. I can't let it set too long in one place or it decides it won't move again. (PICK UP AND SWEET POTATO EXIT. JAMES FOLLOWS. WEEBJOB CHUCKS A STICK.)

#### Weebjob
Fetch it, Mighty Warrior. (HE HEARS PICK UP'S TRUCK COUGH AND START UP. SOON JAMES RETURNS.)

#### Weebjob
I feel badly, James.

#### James
Why, Dad?

#### Weebjob
Sweet Potato told me that you wanted to go to college.

### James
I'm doing fine with the highway department. I'm getting an education from the horticulturist just the same as if I were in school. And I'm getting paid for it.

### Weebjob
When she said that, it made me think how I have stayed here and not helped any of you.

### James
I like my job. Don't worry about Sweet Potato. William has done all right too. Sweet Potato just gets down on everything. Didn't William finish law school?

### Weebjob
Yes, because his wife's family helped him.

### James
(HE TAKES WEEBJOB'S SHOULDERS IN HIS HANDS WITH CARE.) We do what we must.

### Weebjob
What's wrong with her?

### James
I don't know. She can't find anything she wants to do. (HE LETS GO OF WEEBJOB AND PUTS HIS HANDS IN HIS POCKETS.) Weebjob, I could bring you some Spanish bayonet or agave for your garden. I could bring you some vegetables and show you how to care for them, and how to cultivate the squash you already have. Then you could harvest a crop to sell in Old Lincoln each year.

### Weebjob
I don't know.

### James
You've done nothing with the land, Father. You don't even have a fishing license. A driver's license.

### Weebjob
I don't need a license to fish in my own pond.

### James
The land deed—your will—

### Weebjob
I could think I was talking to William. Has he put you up to this?

### James
(SARCASTICALLY.) No, Dad. I actually thought of it on my own.

### Weebjob
I don't seem to know all I need to know either. (THE PUZZLED LOOK RETURNS TO HIS FACE.) What's going on in Socorro that you didn't know Sweet Potato was going to run away to Gallup?

### James
Am I suppposed to know everything she's thinking? I'm gone sometimes several days on highway department work. She and Hersah talk. Ask her. All I know is that I heard them fighting one night.

### Weebjob
The girls?

### James
No, Father. Pick Up and Sweet Potato.

### Weebjob
Pick Up comes to Socorro?

### James
You didn't know?

### Weebjob
Didn't know what? There's nothing to know.

### James
Pick Up comes to Socorro sometimes to see Sweet Potato.

### Weebjob
Pick Up goes to Socorro to see Sweet Potato? He's my friend, not hers! He's old enough to be her father. I expect you to be your sister's keeper and you let something like that happen! He's almost as old as I am. The fool! (WEEBJOB GRABS JAMES' SHIRT.) Why is he bothering Sweet Potato?

### James
(TAKES HIS FATHER'S HANDS IN HIS OWN.) I don't think she minds it.

29

## Weebjob

(PULLS HIS HANDS AWAY FROM JAMES. WEEBJOB HITS HIS THIGHS IN ANGER. HE PICKS UP A STICK AND CHUCKS IT IN THE DITCH OFF STAGE.) Chew it to bits, Mighty Warrior. (HE LOOKS QUESTION-INGLY TO HEAVEN.) WORSE than what I feared has come upon me. (LOOKS TO JAMES.) Why am I not told anything? That old man bothering my daughter! What's wrong with him?

## James

(INTERRUPTS HIS FATHER.) I came for another reason also, Father. Now that I know Sweet Potato is here, I see that Mother is gone. You didn't tell me. A letter came yesterday from Hobbs. She's at her sister's and assumes I know. Why am I not told anything?

## Weebjob

You got a letter from your mother? Let me see it! (JAMES TAKES IT FROM HIS POCKET AND WEEBJOB GRABS IT FROM HIM. WEEBJOB OPENS THE LETTER AND READS.) 'Your father, as you know, is a difficult man to live with.' (WEEBJOB LOOKS AT JAMES.) She writes you this? (JAMES LOOKS AWAY FROM WEEBJOB.) 'He is not a practical man, but is caught up in his ideals. I thought I would stay at my sister's for a month, but I think continually of Weebjob, and how he is getting along without me to cook his meals and clean his house. I think I will finish the visit with my sister soon, and return to Salazar Canyon with Weebjob. I'll ride the bus as far as Roswell and William will bring me home—' (WEEBJOB LOOKS TO HEAVEN.) William knows too! (READS AGAIN.) 'I don't like to be away from Weebjob after all—'

## James

How long has she been gone?

## Weebjob

(REGAINS HIS COMPOSURE.) Fifteen days.

## James

How did she get to Hobbs? It must be two hundred miles—

## Weebjob

I took her to the junction in Carrizozo and she caught the bus.

## James

That was nice of you. Why didn't you make her walk to the junction? I don't like her riding the bus. I would have taken her to Hobbs if I knew you two were quarreling.

### Weebjob

We're not quarreling! She simply wanted to see her sister. And it isn't any business of yours.

### James

Yes, it is.

### Weebjob

The letter she wrote to you is hard for me to accept. I got Sweet Grass at an Indian Female Seminary. She would hardly look at me, much less speak anything to me. Now she tells you all this? (HE READS THE REST OF THE LETTER IN SILENCE.)

### James

I suppose she wrote so that I would understand why she wasn't here when I came.

### Weebjob

Mutton. You used to be too young to know anything. Now you're told all. (HE CRUMPLES THE LETTER AND HANDS IT BACK TO JAMES.)

### James

Things change. (PUTS THE WAD BACK IN HIS POCKET.)

### Weebjob

Not always for the better. (HE SCRATCHES HIMSELF.)

### James

She knew you wouldn't tell me why she wasn't here. What do you ever tell me?

### Weebjob

She leaves your house in Socorro for several days and you don't even call—

### James

She could have come back here for all I knew.

### Weebjob

But you didn't know. How long has she been gone? (JAMES PAUSES.) How long?

### James

Probably a week.

#### Weebjob
And WHAT did you do about it?

#### James
I thought she'd gone off with Pick Up— (WEEBJOB HITS HIS HANDS AGAINST HIS SIDES IN ANGER.) But when Pick Up showed up and didn't know—

#### Weebjob
What else goes on in Socorro that I don't know?

#### James
Nothing, except Sweet Potato was gone for a while. (WEEBJOB TURNS HIS BACK TO JAMES.) —Hersah didn't know anything either, except that Sweet Potato talked about Gallup and the restaurant where she worked one summer—

#### Weebjob
(TURNS TO JAMES.) Why didn't you tell me?

#### James
Probably for the same reason you didn't tell me about Mother.

#### Weebjob
That's different. Sweet Grass is only at her sister's. We ALL hear from her—it's not like Sweet Potato disappearing— (WEEBJOB TURNS ANGRILY TO JAMES AND POKES HIS FINGER AGAINST HIS SHOULDERS.) —I didn't have your advice when I wooed my wife. Why would I need it now to keep her? She'll return. (PROUDLY.) She writes that she can't stay away from me any longer. You read the letter. (CONFIDENTLY.) And Pick Up doesn't have any more chance than an albino squirrel with my daughter. Where are they? (HE LOOKS IMPATIENTLY UP THE ROAD.)

#### James
They've hardly gotten to Old Lincoln. I think if he wanted your advice on how to woo Sweet Potato, he would ask.

#### Weebjob
Mutton. (HE HITS HIS THIGHS IN ANGER).

# SCENE II

### Sweet Potato
(THE STAGE IS DARK EXCEPT FOR A SPOTLIGHT IN THE CORNER
WHICH FALLS ON SWEET POTATO AND PICK UP IN THE TRUCK.)
Why are we stopping? I need to get back to feed Weebjob.

### Pick Up
Let him wait.

### Sweet Potato
I'll hear him bellering in the valley if we don't get back soon—he'll
be painting another sign for the fence by the road— (PICK UP
TOUCHES HER FACE.)

### Pick Up
Where were you for a week?

### Sweet Potato
You already asked me, and I told you I was on the road. (FOLDS HER
ARMS.) Why did you bring me back to him? You know I didn't want
to come.

### Pick Up
You can't run away, Sweet Potato.

### Sweet Potato
My name is Suzanne Long Chalk.

### Pick Up
I'll call you what I please. I can't have you hitchhiking on the road
for anyone to pick up. You shouldn't be out on the road alone. It's
not good. What would you do in Gallup?

### Sweet Potato
Get a job. I can cook, wait tables. I worked there last summer, if you
remember.

### Pick Up
Yes, it's the first time I came to see you—I don't want you to go back
there.

33

### Sweet Potato
You sound like my father.

### Pick Up
It's not as your father that I'm speaking. Work at the Civil War in Old Lincoln if you must have a job. Let the men gawk at you. Wait tables. (HE PAUSES AND LOOKS AT HER.) I care for you, Suzanne. You know that. (PAUSE.) More than as a father. I didn't come to Socorro to see James.

### Sweet Potato
I told you I didn't want to speak of these things.

### Pick Up
I didn't for many years. But now I can't wait any longer. You're more than Weebjob's daughter to me.

### Sweet Potato
Maybe we could be like cousins.

### Pick Up
I want you as a close friend.

### Sweet Potato
We are close friends, Pick Up, my father's friend.

### Pick Up
Yes, I'm his friend.

### Sweet Potato
You wouldn't be if he heard you speak to me like that.

### Pick Up
I know. (HE TOUCHES HER FACE AGAIN.)

### Sweet Potato
I remember you, Pick Up, when you used to have a brown Volks-wagen, and looked like a prune driving it down the road.

### Pick Up
I remember you, Sweet Potato, in a round purple coat, like a plum on narrow legs, with skinny braids sticking out from beneath your cap.

### Sweet Potato
I remember the night you got drunk in the Civil War Bar in Old

Lincoln and came to our house and quoted poetry to the weed-clumps.

### Pick Up
I remember when the faintest bit of snow blew into the valley and you ran into my truck on William's bicycle and sprang the tire.

### Sweet Potato
I remember— (PICK UP PUTS HIS HANDS OVER HER MOUTH.)

### Pick Up
I remember when you fell into the stream. I should have let you drown. (HE KISSES HER.)

### Sweet Potato
Would you call him Father?

### Pick Up
(HE ROLLS HIS HEAD BACK.) I would rather have a buffalo for a father-in-law.

### Sweet Potato
(SHE TAKES UP FOR WEEBJOB.) He's a better man than any I've known.

### Pick Up
I know.

### Sweet Potato
Wise and good-hearted. Quick-tempered. A little harsh with words and his head too much in the Bible, but a good man.

### Pick Up
I don't know what to do, Suzanne. I want you, and I wonder why. I'm almost as old as your father. How could I think of you as a wife? How could you think of me—

### Sweet Potato
Don't talk about it.

### Pick Up
Marry me, Suzanne.

### Sweet Potato
I can hear Weebjob roaring about it now.

### Pick Up

He will be all right. Think about me, Sweet Potato. (HE KISSES HER AGAIN.) Marry me.

### Sweet Potato

Maybe it's what you deserve.

# SCENE III

**Weebjob**
Ah! Here come Rumpelstiltskin and Juliet now.

**James**
Be kind, Father.

**Weebjob**
Why should I be otherwise?

**James**
Because he's doing better with Sweet Potato than you're doing with Mother.

**Weebjob**
Now I am angry, James, and wishing your highway job would take you away again.

**James**
(He laughs.) It might not hurt you to get away. It might broaden you to travel.

**Weebjob**
I get enough broadening here in Salazar Canyon.

**Pick Up**
(ENTERING.) Ola, Weebjob. (SWEET POTATO FOLLOWS, CARRYING A GROCERY SACK. SHE GOES INTO THE HOUSE.)

**Weebjob**
Ola, Pick Up. (IMPATIENTLY.) Where have you been?

**Pick Up**
Old Lincoln isn't just around the curve, you know. If you'd get off your place—

**Weebjob**
It took you longer—

### Pick Up

You know Clement Thousandsticks. (HE JESTURES WITH HIS ARMS.) He waits on the road until he sees us coming, then turns on the highway in front of us and goes slow through the canyon where no one can pass. (WEEBJOB TURNS TO JAMES AND SHRUGS.)

### James

(LAUGHS.) Clement's done that to me too.

### Weebjob

(TURNS BACK TO PICK UP.) And, of course, you had my daughter with you. (SWEET POTATO COMES OUT OF THE HOUSE. WEEBJOB PUTS HIS HAND UP TO HER.) Stay out of this—like you did on your first arrival. I'm going to have a word with Pick Up.

### James

(IGNORING WEEBJOB.) And now that there's one light at the crossroads in Old Lincoln, Clement will slow down until the light turns yellow, then he rushes through and leaves you stopped at the light.

### Weebjob

Step in the house for a moment, Pick Up. It won't take long. (PICK UP FOLLOWS WEEBJOB INTO THE HOUSE.)

### Sweet Potato

(ANGRILY TO JAMES.) What did you tell Weebjob? (SHE BRUSHES THE HAIR FROM HER FACE.)

### James

About what?

### Sweet Potato

James!—what he's upset about! Pick Up and me.

### James

What's there to tell Weebjob? (THE SOUND OF SCRAPING CHAIRS AND LOUD, MUFFLED VOICES COME FROM THE HOUSE.)

### Sweet Potato

There must have been something! (AN INSULT IS HEARD. PICK UP DEFENDS HIMSELF. NOT ALL THE CONVERSATION IS UNDERSTOOD, BUT IT'S CLEAR THEY'RE ARGUING. SWEET POTATO HAS HER HANDS OVER HER EARS.) What could they be doing?

### James

They're too old to hurt one another.

#### Sweet Potato
Don't be sure. I'm going in there, James— (SHE STARTS FOR THE HOUSE WHEN PICK UP BACKS OUT OF THE FRONT DOOR. WEEB-JOB FOLLOWS WITH HIS HAND ON PICK UP'S SHIRT COLLAR.)

#### Weebjob
Mutton if it's all right.

#### Pick Up
Now, Weebjob. (BOTH HANDS ARE UP.)

#### Weebjob
It's not clear to me why I have such a jackass for a friend.

#### Pick Up
Nor do I understand why I put up with you unless it's for your daughter. (WEEBJOB JERKS PICK UP'S SHIRT COLLAR, RIPPING IT.)

#### James
(RUSHES TO THE MEN, TAKES HIS FATHER BY THE SHOULDERS.) Gerald Long Chalk. You're a man of peace!

#### Weebjob
(HE COMES TO HIS SENSES, AND BOWS, FORMALLY.) Forgive me, Pick Up. (STIFFLY.) I forgot myself for a moment and wanted to smash your head.

#### Pick Up
I understand, friend Weebjob. (WEEBJOB HOLDS UP HIS HAND TO PICK UP AS THOUGH PROTESTING THAT HE IS HIS FRIEND, BUT SWEET POTATO INTERRUPTS. SHE LOOKS AT THE TORN PLACE ON PICK UP'S SHIRT, WOULD LIKE TO PULL IT TOGETHER, BUT DE-CIDES TO GO INTO THE HOUSE.)

#### Weebjob
It's too soon to call me friend again, Pick Up. I must go to the squash patch for a while. (WEEBJOB GOES TO THE GARDEN. JAMES AND PICK UP REMAIN ON THE PORCH. PICK UP PULLS HIS SHIRT TOGETHER.)

#### James
Another trip to the Holy Land. (JAMES WATCHES HIS FATHER FOR A MOMENT, THEN HE PUTS HIS HAND ON PICK UP'S SHOULDER TO COMFORT HIM. PICK UP LOOKS AT THE GROUND, SHAKES HIS HEAD. THEY ARE UNCERTAIN AT FIRST WHAT TO SAY TO ONE ANOTHER. WHILE WEEBJOB IS IN THE SQUASH PATCH, THEY TALK, INAUDIBLY.)

## Weebjob

(CHANTS, THEN BEGINS HIS PRAYERS.) Great Spirit. Father of Fathers. Forgive me for anger, and in turn make me forgive Pick Up. Every rock has its flat side. He is taken with Sweet Potato. Maybe it will pass. He has always liked her, but I didn't expect this! Never this! (SHRUGS.) Is it my new burden? Is this the catastrophe that comes even before my wife returns? I need her to soothe me. Bring her back quickly. I'm angry that my son-in-law is nearly as old as I am. I'm angry he's done nothing all his life. More flies than arrows. Wait until Sweet Grass hears about this! Make me forgive him and keep him from marrying my daughter. (HE CHANTS UNTIL SWEET POTATO CALLS HIM.)

## Sweet Potato

(SHE CALLS JAMES AND PICK UP AND HANDS THE PLATES THROUGH THE WINDOW TO THEM. THEN SHE COMES OUT OF THE HOUSE AND CALLS HER FATHER.) How now, Father. Your hamburger is ready. (SHE HOLDS HER ARM FORWARD IN AN INDIAN SALUTE.)

## Weebjob

(WEEBJOB QUICKLY FINISHES HIS PRAYERS, BIDS THE GREAT SPIRIT ADIEU.) Whuoah! (WEEBJOB JOINS JAMES AND PICK UP AT THE TABLE ON THE PORCH.) I see you waited.

## Pick Up

Ola, Weebjob. Have a seat.

## Weebjob

On my own porch? You tell me to be seated. Thank you, kind friend.

## Sweet Potato

Peace, Father. Eat your meal. (THE FOUR OF THEM SIT AT THE TABLE.)

## Weebjob

(ASKS THE BLESSING ON THE MEAL.) Great Spirit, we are grateful for the food which you provide. (SWEET POTATO AND PICK UP LOOK AT ONE ANOTHER.) Now help us to eat this meal in peace. Amen.

## Pick Up

Amen.

## Sweet Potato

(WEEBJOB TAKES A GIANT BITE OUT OF THE HAMBURGER.) Why

are the chairs and table on the porch? (WEEBJOB TRIES TO AN-
SWER, BUT HIS MOUTH IS FULL.) Does Mother know you moved
them out of the kitchen? (HE SHAKES HIS HEAD, NO.) We'll have to
move them back in before she comes. (WEEBJOB SHAKES HIS HEAD,
NO, AGAIN.)

### Weebjob
I'm head of the house. The table stays here.

### James
(TRYING TO AVERT ANOTHER ARGUMENT.) Good burgers, Suzanne.

### Weebjob
I'll be glad when your mother returns. Then I'll eat 'til I'm content.

### Pick Up
(TRYING TO AVOID WEEBJOB.) How's the highway work?

### James
Steady. That's the best part of it.

### Sweet Potato
I had to wash four plates, Weebjob, for our supper. I'll wash the rest
after we eat. It will take me all night to get through that pile—

### Pick Up
(WITHOUT THINKING.) I'll help you. (WEEBJOB GLARES AT HIM.)

### Weebjob
Thank you, Sweet Potato. I can't seem to get through them myself.
(PAUSES AS HE EATS.) Almost as good as Sweet Grass'.

### Sweet Potato
Coffee?

### Weebjob
Yes, thanks. (SHE GOES IN THE HOUSE, RETURNS WITH FOUR
CUPS, THEN GOES BACK FOR THE COFFEE POT, AND POURS IT
WHILE THE MEN TALK.)

### James
We've been landscaping the new section of Highway 25 south of
Elephant Butte. Now we'll move to Mescalero.

### Weebjob
And what are you doing, Pick Up?

## Pick Up

Running Willingdeer's Tow Truck Service, as I always have—are you stuck somewhere, Weebjob? (THEY DRINK COFFEE.) Ah, Weebjob, why don't you go into sheep herding and supply Old Lincoln with wool as well as Sweet Grass' blankets? Why don't you let Sweet Potato and Sweet Grass have their own store? (PAUSE.) I have a letter from Sweet Grass. She mentions it—

## Weebjob

(POUNDS THE TABLE.) MUTTON! (RISES, NEARLY TIPPING THE TABLE.) YOU have a letter from Sweet Grass? (PICK UP PULLS THE LETTER FROM HIS POCKET AND HANDS IT TO WEEBJOB, WHO READS IT WITH DISBELIEF.) I am in Hobbs with my sister, Mary Jane Collar. I don't know how long I will be here. I have not seen her in a long time and she is old and alone. There's much to do. We talk of weaving and clean her small house. We put up cactus jelly for winter and speak of many things. I leave Weebjob to himself for a while. (HE LOOKS TO HEAVEN.) I understand him as a man; sometimes it is easier to bear, sometimes not. (WEEBJOB SITS IN HIS CHAIR. READS MORE QUIETLY NOW.) I've been wanting to write you. I know how hard it is for you to feel about Sweet Potato as you do. Break it gently to Weebjob when the time comes!!! (WEEBJOB'S VOICE RISES AGAIN AS HE FINISHES READING HIS WIFE'S LETTER TO PICK UP.) Tell Sweet Potato I'm fine— (WEEBJOB POUNDS THE TABLE AGAIN, RISES TO HIS FEET.)

## Pick Up

(ANGRY NOW.) Let me ask you something, Weebjob—I've known Sweet Potato since she was a child. I think it was me who first called her Sweet Potato.

## Weebjob

(ANGRY ALSO.) It might have been.

## Pick Up

That was twenty years ago. I've seen her nearly every week since then. I have loved her for years. Tell me, Weebjob, Gerald Long Chalk, holy man of Salazar Canyon—why are you the only one who doesn't know? Are you so buried in YOUR work, you don't know when your friend is in love with your daughter?

## Weebjob

You as a son-in-law. No, by thunder. I won't have it. (BANGS THE TABLE AGAIN.) How old are you, Pick Up?

#### Pick Up
43, and Sweet Potato is 21. It's as though I've always been waiting for her.

#### Weebjob
Bull crackers. You just don't want the responsibility of a wife and family.

#### Pick Up
That might be right. I saw you snorting about it so much through the years, I thought it couldn't be much fun.

#### Weebjob
It's a responsibility to have a wife and raise children.

#### Pick Up
So it would seem, listening to you.

#### Weebjob
Have you asked her to be your wife?

#### Pick Up
Yes, and she almost agreed.

#### Weebjob
She doesn't know what else to do with herself. She hasn't even been able to make it to Gallup again. Maybe that's why she almost gives in to you— (WITH HIS FIST TO PICK UP.) How many young girls are there in the valley? Why my daughter?

#### Pick Up
I would love Sweet Potato no matter what her age. I want her to be my wife and I don't want any old crank standing in the way. (HE PUSHES HIS CHAIR AWAY FROM HIM WITH HIS FOOT. PICK UP AND WEEBJOB STAND FACING ONE ANOTHER.)

#### Weebjob
I'm not having an old Poker for a son-in-law.

#### Pick Up
You will if Sweet Potato agrees.

#### Weebjob
Mutton.

### James
Break it up, Weebjob. How silly to see two old bulls ready to fight.

### Weebjob
Even if one of the old bulls is going to be your brother-in-law?

### James
That's up to Sweet Potato.

### Weebjob
It's up to me to give permission.

### Sweet Potato
It's up to me, Father. I don't have to have your permission.

### Weebjob
(LOOKING UP TO HEAVEN.) My father, Seewootee, never would have believed this!

### Pick Up
Sweet Grass would return sooner if she knew you were close to a wedding.

### Weebjob
There's not going to be a wedding yet! (PAUSE.) I think she wrote to everyone but me—

### Sweet Potato
She hasn't written to me either. I've tried to be like her. But I am not my mother. I can't be her. I know she's sweet and gentle. And I'm not any of that—

### Pick Up
(HE GOES TO SWEET POTATO, PUTS HIS ARM AROUND HER.) Let's walk up the road. (HE DRAWS HER OFF THE PORCH.)

### Weebjob
(LOWERS HIS HEAD, LOOKS AT THEM WITH A SCOWL.) Such patience it will take for me to see him living with my daughter. Maybe they will move to Gallup, James. But I know they won't. I'll probably have them here with me in 'Canaan'—

### James
(LAUGHS.) I doubt that.

## Weebjob

Sweet Grass will return and weave behind my house. I'll watch her make the roaming antelope design, bringing the pattern to a point, a place of finish. Her weaving is resolution. William will come with his wife with their baby, and Reesah will still be unhappy that she's going to have another. She'll cry and I will hear her blow her nose into her handkerchief. (PAUSE.) Pick Up for a son-in-law! (HITS THE TABLE.) MUTTON!

# SCENE IV

### Pick Up
(PICK UP AND SWEET POTATO WALK TOWARD THE ROAD. THE REST OF THE STAGE BECOMES DARK WITH ONLY ONE SPOTLIGHT UPON THEM AS THEY TALK.) Everyone's already thinking of our wedding, Sweet Potato, and you have not actually consented. (SHE IS SILENT.) You're showing such enthusiasm.

### Sweet Potato
I haven't had time to decide.

### Pick Up
I've known you for twenty years.

### Sweet Potato
I don't know if I want to decide.

### Pick Up
Suzanne Long Chalk, will you marry me?

### Sweet Potato
Is this my last chance to answer?

### Pick Up
Probably not.

### Sweet Potato
(THERE'S A LOUD MUTTERING FROM THE SQUASH PATCH. WHEN SWEET POTATO HEARS THE WORD, MUTTON, FROM HER FATHER, SHE TURNS TO LOOK.) I will probably marry you, Pick Up.

### Pick Up
Are you sure?

### Sweet Potato
At this moment, I am.

### Pick Up
When I was your age, you weren't even born, Suzanne. Does that change your mind?

                    Sweet Potato
No.


                    Pick Up
What would change your mind?


                    Sweet Potato
Nothing that I can think of right now.


                    Pick Up
Is it because you don't have any place else to go?


                    Sweet Potato
No. I can stay with James and Hersah in Socorro. Reesah is going to have another baby—I could probably stay with William in Roswell, unless she wants one of her sisters to help— (PAUSE.) I can go to Gallup and work in the restaurant again—it's just that the nights are so cavernous in the desert—


                    Pick Up
I know.


                    Sweet Potato
You don't mind that I'm young?


                    Pick Up
Not as much as having Weebjob for a father-in-law, and him always at a 'crossroads' in his life.


                    Sweet Potato
Can't we get married in the old Indian way?


                    Pick Up
No.


                    Sweet Potato
You could give Weebjob some horses, and I would just move in with you. If it doesn't work, I will put your bedroll by the door and you can move out.


                    Pick Up
No.


                    Sweet Potato
You'd want the horses back?


                    47

Pick Up

I don't have any horses.

Sweet Potato

Your truck, then?

Pick Up

Yes. I don't want to lose my house and truck both. And I don't want you to be able to get out of it that easily.

Sweet Potato

I don't like complications.

Pick Up

You don't want responsibility, Sweet Potato. I am going to marry you by law and in the Old Lincoln Church. And I want you in a dress. I'm going to have you as my wife, Suzanne. I expect you to clean the house, cook my suppers, wash the dishes and clothes. You aren't going to run off whenever you feel like it. You can visit James and Hersah in Socorro. Do what you like. But I will have your attention. Otherwise, don't marry me. You aren't coming to see if you like it. You are making a commitment I expect you to keep. I won't have it any other way. I'm from the old school too.

Sweet Potato

And in trying to get away from Weebjob, I come to someone like him? (SHE SHRUGS HER SHOULDERS.)

Pick Up

I expect you to come to me as a wife who wants to live with me. I expect you to sacrifice your burning ambition to hitchhike to Gallup. I won't have it. I'm old enough to want a wife that I know I'm not going to find on the highway with her thumb up.

Sweet Potato

And what do I get in return for my unending subjection to you?

Pick Up

I'm taking you off Weebjob's hands. He should be giving me the horses. I'm giving you a chance to come where you will have respect as a person, and a chance to be on your own, to do as you want—

Sweet Potato

As long as it isn't making sudden trips?

### Pick Up
That's right. I will give you a chance to open your wool store with your mother in Old Lincoln, if that's what you want. I'd even buy you some sheep. Or you can wait tables at the Civil War if you like. I would rather that you didn't, but you are your own person, Sweet Potato. And I know you're struggling to find something that will satisfy you. I'm not taking you away from that. I'm giving you what you haven't had—

### Sweet Potato
It sounds like 'Canaan' to me. Except— (SHE PUTS HER HANDS TO HER FACE.) Unless I find I don't have any place I belong.

### Pick Up
(HE HOLDS HER.) Then you can be satisfied to be my wife. I'm making a place in my house for you.

### Sweet Potato
One concession, Pick Up.

### Pick Up
What?

### Sweet Potato
No wedding in Old Lincoln Church, and not in a dress. Father's zeal has always made me shudder in church. I want to be married here—in 'Canaan.'

### Weebjob
(HERE THE STAGE LIGHTS COME BACK. WEEBJOB IS IN HIS SQUASH PATCH. JAMES IS IN THE HOUSE WASHING THE POTS AND PANS AT THE SINK.) —Humbleness of mind, meekness, long suffering. (WEEBJOB IS ON HIS KNEES PRAYING.) Forbearing one another, forgiving one another. (HE MAKES A FIST TOWARD HEAVEN.) Could you make this any harder?

### Pick Up
(PICK UP AND SWEET POTATO RETURN TO THE FRONT PORCH.) No—not there. (HE LOOKS TO THE SQUASH PATCH.)

### Sweet Potato
Then the front porch, or outside somewhere—in the pines? But I have always liked the yellow blossoms.

#### Pick Up

Weebjob would never allow a wedding there. That is holy ground to him. I don't want to be married on his place anyway.

#### Sweet Potato

And I don't want to be married in a dress!

#### Weebjob

(LOUDLY.) Huah! Huah!

#### Sweet Potato

He is plugged in again. Yes. I will marry you, Pick Up. I am sure.

#### Weebjob

He cay mo nay. (WEEBJOB FINISHES HIS PRAYER LOUDLY AND RISES. HE STANDS A MOMENT IN HIS SQUASH PATCH. SOON, HE WALKS TO SWEET POTATO AND PICK UP. THEY STILL STAND BY THE PORCH. SWEET POTATO FOLDS HER ARMS AS SHE WATCHES HIM APPROACH. PICK UP HAS HIS HANDS IN HIS HIP POCKETS.) I thought from time to time I would like to have Sweet Potato off my hands. (HE PAUSES.) I thought from time to time I would like to have you off my hands, Pick Up. But in losing her, I gain you. What would be worse.

#### James

What's up?

#### Pick Up

Sweet Potato has consented to marry me.

#### James

(JUMPS UP.) You are going to be my brother-in-law!

#### Weebjob

He has deliberately wormed his way into my family so he can be part-heir of 'Canaan.'

#### Pick Up

You old carp—

#### Weebjob

Minnow!

#### Pick Up

Rudd.

### James
(JAMES HEARS THE SOUND OF A CAR AND HALTS THE ARGUMENT.)
Listen. There's a car coming. (THEY TURN TO THE ROAD.) Mighty
Warrior doesn't bark. It looks like William's car—

# ACT II

## SCENE I

**Sweet Potato**

Look! William comes with Mother.

**Pick Up**

Weebjob! Your wife returns.

**Weebjob**

(WEEBJOB PEERS DOWN THE ROAD.) Sweet Grass returns?

**Pick Up**

Maybe he'll go to roost again and not bother about us.

**Sweet Potato**

I wouldn't count on it.

**Weebjob**

Sweet Grass, my old wife! (WEEBJOB KISSES HIS WIFE WHEN SHE APPEARS WITH WILLIAM.) I'm glad you've returned. Hello, William, my oldest son. (HE KISSES HIS WIFE'S HAND.) How tired it must be from writing.

**William**

(HOLDING A SMALL SUITCASE WHICH BELONGS TO HIS MOTHER.) How are you Father? (WEEBJOB NODS HIS HEAD THAT HE'S FINE. WILLIAM SETS THE SUITCASE ON THE GROUND AND THEY EMBRACE.)

**Sweet Grass**

Ah, the smell of pines! Maybe it does us good to be apart. We know more of what we have.

**Weebjob**

Not so, Sweet Grass. I go hungry, and do not learn. (HE KISSES HER AGAIN.) Your wife didn't come?

**William**

She didn't feel well enough to come. I didn't bring my daughter because I wanted a chance to talk to Mother. The last time we took her for a ride it took Reesah and I both to hold on to her.

### James
Hello, William.

### William
James. (THEY EMBRACE, BRIEFLY.)

### James
Nothing is wrong, though?

### William
No. She's well. Just pregnant and not happy about it at the moment.
She thinks a two-year-old and a baby will be a lot to handle. I don't
help her much, I suppose. My practice takes my time—

### Pick Up
Hello, William.

### William
(HE SMILES.) Hello, Pick Up. (THEY SHAKE HANDS.)

### Sweet Potato
(SHE RUNS TO WILLIAM AND HUGS HIM.) You drove to Hobbs to
get Mother?

### William
No, she rode the bus to Roswell.

### Sweet Grass
I wanted to get back to Salazar Canyon. I didn't want William to go
any more out of his way— (SWEET GRASS EMBRACES HER DAUGHTER.)

### Sweet Potato
We didn't know when you were coming back. After all the letters
you wrote to everyone but me—

### Sweet Grass
I wrote you, Sweet Potato.

### Sweet Potato
It never came.

### Sweet Grass
It's at the General Delivery in Old Lincoln.

### Sweet Potato
(SWEET POTATO HITS HER HEAD.) How could I not think of that? Of course—and we were just there. I've missed you, Mother. (JAMES HUGS HIS MOTHER.)

### Weebjob
Is my letter at General Delivery too? I have a mailbox on the road, you know. The mail truck stops here now and then—

### Sweet Potato
When he can find it among your signs.

### William
I see you have a few new ones, Father. (WILLIAM GOES INTO THE HOUSE WITH HIS MOTHER'S SUITCASE. JAMES FOLLOWS.)

### Weebjob
Dear Wife, you didn't say if my letter was at the General Delivery.

### Sweet Grass
No, it isn't. I didn't write to you, Weebjob. —I didn't know what to say.

### Weebjob
Didn't know what to say! (HE CLAPS HIS HANDS TO HIS SIDE.) You told everyone everything that ever happened!

### Sweet Grass
I didn't know how to write to you—

### Weebjob
Sweet Grass, my old wife back from her sister's in Hobbs. Already things are better. I must make a sign for the fence. How is Mary Jane Collar?

### Sweet Grass
She's fine, Gerald Long Chalk.

### Weebjob
'Canaan' isn't the same without you.

### Sweet Grass
I wanted to get back to my loom behind the house. I even missed Mighty Warrior sleeping under my feet while I weave. I even missed you too, Weebjob.

#### Weebjob
Ah! But not everything is well. We might get a buffalo for a son-in-law.

#### Sweet Grass
I've known it for some time, Weebjob.

#### Weebjob
So your letters to everyone said.

#### Sweet Grass
I was afraid to tell you.

#### Weebjob
You certainly weren't afraid to tell all of Salazar Canyon about it.

#### Sweet Grass
Forgive me, Weebjob. I found that I liked to write letters when I was at Mary Jane Collar's. It made me feel like I was with everyone. I've never been away for a long time.

#### Weebjob
How did you know about Sweet Potato and Pick Up?

#### Sweet Grass
I could tell they were in love. Even before Sweet Potato knew. At first, it upset me too. But now I'm used to it. He might just be the husband Sweet Potato needs.

#### Weebjob
I don't know if I feel more sorry for Pick Up or Sweet Potato.

#### William
(HE COMES OUT OF THE HOUSE WITH JAMES AND CALLS TO WEEBJOB AND SWEET GRASS.) I have to get back to Roswell.

#### Weebjob
(SWEET GRASS TAKES WEEBJOB BY THE HAND AND THEY RETURN TO WILLIAM AND JAMES IN FRONT OF THE HOUSE. PICK UP AND SWEET POTATO SIT ON THE FRONT STEPS.) Yes, I understand. Your job and family. But you'll be returning soon—

#### Sweet Grass
Thank you for bringing me back to 'Cannan.' (THEY EMBRACE ALSO. WILLIAM LEAVES.) I want to speak to you, Sweet Potato. (SWEET POTATO LOOKS AT PICK UP.)

## Pick Up

I'll wait here with James. I need to get back to Old Lincoln after a while—I left in a hurry to look for you— (PICK UP TALKS WITH JAMES ON THE FRONT STEPS WHILE THE WOMEN TALK BY THE FENCE OF WEEBJOB'S SQUASH PATCH. WEEBJOB GOES TO THE SIDE OF THE HOUSE AND WORKS AT PAINTING ANOTHER SIGN TO HANG ON HIS FENCE BY THE ROAD.)

### Sweet Grass

Are you sure, Suzanne, you want to marry Pick Up?

### Sweet Potato

No, I'm not.

### Sweet Grass

Do you love him?

### Sweet Potato

Yes, I always have. I feel like I belong with him. I'm not excited or bored with him. He's just there.

### Sweet Grass

But you can't go running away, as you have from us.

### Sweet Potato

I know. He's said as much.

### Sweet Grass

Is there anything you'd rather do?

### Sweet Potato

Yes, but it's unattainable. I don't like school. I can't be like William and go to college. I barely finished high school. And I wasn't in the right place like James when he found his job. That desert clod-hopper. He just happened to apply for a job and the horticulturist took him!

### Sweet Grass

He always liked the squash patch and cactus.

### Sweet Potato

I've looked and seen things I've wanted, but I could never have them. There's never been any place for me, Mother. I don't want to go to school. I don't really want to wait tables. I'm happy when I'm on my way to Gallup. There isn't any room for me here on 'Canaan.'

**Sweet Grass**

Yes, there is. You're our daughter.

**Sweet Potato**

But I'm not your child any more.

**Sweet Grass**

Just so Pick Up isn't a father to you that you'd resent like Weebjob.

**Sweet Potato**

(SHE LOOKS AT HER MOTHER.) No. He's one of my friends, though he's older.

**Sweet Grass**

He's more like a brother?

**Sweet Potato**

No. He's not like William or James to me. He's not Weebjob to me either. How could they have been friends for so long? They're different from one another.

**Sweet Grass**

They compliment each other somehow.

**Sweet Potato**

Pick Up also asks me why I want to marry him.

**Sweet Grass**

What do you tell him?

**Sweet Potato**

What I tell you.

**Sweet Grass**

You don't know what else to do so you're going to try marriage?

**Sweet Potato**

Pick Up accused me of that also, but it isn't true. I do want to be with him. I think I always did, but was afraid it would look ridiculous. Now I might marry him. We could live in Old Lincoln and drive to Socorro to see James and Hersah on the weekends. Maybe—I could have a wool store. I even have a name for it.

**Sweet Grass**

What?

**Sweet Potato**

'The Spinners.' I might even be able to have sheep on Pick Up's place.

**Sweet Grass**

Will you finally let me teach you to weave?

**Sweet Potato**

Maybe. You'll be supplier of the blankets I sell.

**Sweet Grass**

There isn't anyone else you want to marry?

**Sweet Potato**

There have been others. But they married someone else, or went off, or weren't interested in me. One was so worthless I knew the marriage would never work.

**Sweet Grass**

And you never had a child to shame us. What if someone came—more your age?

**Sweet Potato**

I would still be Pick Up's wife. I do want to be with him, Mother. He's a friend—I want him to be my husband.

**Sweet Grass**

(PUTS HER ARM AROUND SWEET POTATO.) I've always liked Pick Up though if I'd known he would be my son-in-law, I might have kicked about it at first. But now I feel differently. I can see him as your husband. I can understand why he loves you.

**Sweet Potato**

What is it like to be a wife?

**Sweet Grass**

It probably feels differently to every wife. To me it feels right to be Weebjob's wife. I see him as the man he wants to be, even when he falls short of it.

**Sweet Potato**

Which is most of the time.

**Sweet Grass**

No, it isn't. He's a good man. I like to look at him, feel him against me, listen to him. I shouldn't be speaking of these things to you. But

I must be with him. Even if he is in the squash patch, sometimes I go out just to watch him work. Sometimes I hear his prayers, his chants. When he has visions of the Thunder Hawk, I leave him to himself. He's my companion. I don't know what I'd do without him. I suppose I'd go live with Mary Jane Collar and we'd can cactus jelly and paint her back steps. He's all I thought about in Hobbs—

### Sweet Potato
You could live with us.

### Sweet Grass
No. You would be camping out with Pick Up or hiking in the mountains. I would not feel welcome in my son's-in-law house, nor my daughter's-in-law, nor with James either. Do you think he'll marry Hersah?

### Sweet Potato
I don't know. She really doesn't want to get married.

### Sweet Grass
I don't like it. I'm from the old school, like Weebjob.

### Sweet Potato
James knows that, Mother. He might be uncomfortable with it too. He's gone a lot. The highway crews aren't a steady group. They might influence him.

### Sweet Grass
But he knows differently.

### Sweet Potato
I can't answer for him. William is really the only one of us that could endure discomfort for what he wanted. Well, James too, I guess. He reads his horticulture books at night until Hersah gets mad. Sometimes she and I go to the movies, or just into town and talk with the boys. But Hersah didn't like any of the boys the way she likes James. I may have liked some of the boys now and then, but I didn't want to be with them very long. Pick Up makes me feel happy, Mother. He's someone to hold on to when there's nowhere for me, no place I really fit. (SWEET POTATO HOLDS HER HANDS TO HER EARS.) Sometimes I wonder why I was even born.

### Sweet Grass
Sweet Potato. Such talk!

### Sweet Potato

Everyone can do something but me.

### Sweet Grass

You just haven't found your place yet. The Long Chalks have always had God's blessing.

### Sweet Potato

I guess I can have children. But I don't envy William's wife. I probably won't be a good mother either.

### Sweet Grass

I think you will. There's not much in the marriage for her right now but children and housework because William works such long hours.

### Weebjob

(ENTERS AND JOINS THE CONVERSATION.) Daughter, are you marrying Pick Up?

### Sweet Potato

It seems that way.

### Weebjob

Are you sure it's what you want?

### Sweet Potato

Maybe it will be my 'Canaan.' Maybe I will finally understand—

### Weebjob

There's no way marriage to Pick Up could be avoided?

### Sweet Potato

You wouldn't like it.

### James

Dad—

### Weebjob

God's blessing on your marriage, Suzanne Long Chalk. (THEY EMBRACE.)

### Sweet Potato

(AS WEEBJOB STARTS TOWARD JAMES.) —You still seem reserved about it.

#### Weebjob
(TURNS BACK TO SWEET POTATO.) Pick Up has not yet asked my permission to marry you.

#### James
(SWEET GRASS AND SWEET POTATO STAY AT THE FENCE AND TALK A WHILE LONGER. WEEBJOB GOES TO JAMES WHO STANDS AT THE EDGE OF THE HOUSE. PICK UP REMAINS ON THE STEPS.) Do you want me to close your paint cans?

#### Weebjob
At least someone asks something of me. (PUTS HIS ARM AROUND JAMES' SHOULDER BUT LOOKS AT PICK UP.) Yes. How trying to think I will have Pick Up as a son-in-law—

#### James
Weebjob, you're like the Malpais lava pits beyond Carrizozo. Pick Up will be a good husband to Sweet Potato.

#### Weebjob
Maybe before I make my death cry, I will understand it all.

#### James
(THEY CLOSE WEEBJOB'S PAINT CAN.) Sometimes you're like one of the trees in the nursery truck with your roots wrapped in a bag of sand. (THERE'S A NEW SIGN WHICH READS, 'YOU SHOULD LIVE SO LONG.')

#### Weebjob
I guess it's my strict upbringing—

#### James
I'd like for you to be more—'with us.' I'd like to hear the sound of the rototiller on your land.

#### Weebjob
(WEEBJOB IS DISTRACTED BECAUSE SWEET POTATO AND SWEET GRASS WALK PAST HIM FROM THE SQUASH PATCH.) Ah! My wife is back. I will watch Sweet Grass weave—making form out of all those strands of wool, then I can make sense of everything again— (SWEET GRASS ENTERS THE HOUSE. SWEET POTATO REMAINS ON THE STEP TALKING TO PICK UP. THE AUDIENCE CANNOT HEAR THEIR CONVERSATION, BUT IT SHOULD BE EVIDENT WHAT THEY ARE TALKING ABOUT. SHE POINTS TO WEEBJOB. PICK UP SHAKES HIS HEAD. SHE POINTS TO PICK UP THEN WEEBJOB AGAIN. HE FINALLY SHAKES HIS HEAD IN AGREEMENT.)

### Pick Up
Weebjob, father of Sweet Potato, may I have a word with you before I leave?

### Weebjob
(HE AND JAMES WALK TO THE FRONT OF THE PORCH.) You may stay, James.

### Pick Up
I would like to speak to you alone.

### Weebjob
Denied.

### Pick Up
I would like permission to marry your daughter.

### James
(JAMES LOOKS TO THE SKY, EMBARRASSED THAT HE'S THERE.) It's a long drive to Socorro—I need—

### Weebjob
(AS THOUGH HE DOESN'T HEAR JAMES.) Ah! I was waiting for that. In the old days the father was the leader of the family. He was the thinker, the medicine man, the holy man, the elder. He was respected. No decisions were made until HE was asked. He had an HONORABLE place.

### Pick Up
You have an honorable place, Weebjob, father of Sweet Potato, as long as you don't carry it too far and make a burro of yourself.

### Weebjob
So you want to marry my daughter?

### Pick Up
And you consent?

### Weebjob
No, I don't.

### Pick Up
(HE LOOKS AT SWEET POTATO.) I knew he would be obstinate. That's why I didn't want to ask him.

### James

Dad—

### Weebjob

Does this concern you? (SWEET POTATO GETS UP AND EXITS STAGE LEFT.)

### Pick Up

Weebjob, father of Sweet Potato, holy man, prophet of Salazar Canyon, may I have permission to marry your daughter?

### Weebjob

I know you're serious about Sweet Potato. I wondered when my next trial was coming from God. Now I know. Whom He loves He chastens. It doesn't seem I have any choice. Yes, Pick Up, you have my permission to marry Sweet Potato. I wish it could be some other way— (PAUSE.) But I've already given her my blessing.

### Pick Up

Thank you, Weebjob.

### James

Thank you, Father. (PICK UP LEAVES STAGE TO FIND SWEET POTATO.)

### Weebjob

Now maybe he'll stay home.

### James

I have to leave now. Hersah will have supper waiting by the time I get there— (THEY SAY GOODBYE AND JAMES WALKS PAST PICK UP AND SWEET POTATO.) I'll talk to you later. (HE EXITS.)

### Pick Up

Weebjob has consented, and I didn't injure him before he did.

### Sweet Potato

You have shown patience.

### Pick Up

Now, when we can get married?

### Sweet Potato

As soon as you like. But I won't wear a dress.

### Pick Up

And I will NOT be married on 'Canaan.' (HE HOLDS HER IN HIS ARMS.) See that bright spot in the desert where the sun comes through the clouds and makes a ring of light?

### Sweet Potato

When I'm standing on the road with my thumb up, the heat trying to take my breath, the fear of passing cars pounding in my chest, I feel one with the land. The shrubs speak to me like children. The dry river beds maybe without a trickle of water. I wash in the heat and feel alive on Interstate 40 West. Not straining for existence any longer, but filled with meaning.

### Pick Up

But what's in Gallup?

### Sweet Potato

Nothing, I guess, but getting there. I forget I'm a reject of this world. When I'm on my way to Gallup, I'm INDIAN. I like these worn hills with wrinkles like an old man's face, and with sand as brown as our skin. The divided highway is not like 380 through the canyon. Wind plays with my hair and the heat laughs—the terrible heat that pulls one into itself, and windows of the skin are open and we are running with the heat. Not hardly anyone knows but us. I like the morning sun on my back and the long fingers of the evening shadow across the highway. I want to go again across the Cibolo County line to Gallup.

### Pick Up

I believe you do, Suzanne.

### Sweet Potato

Palomino rocks. Mountains and plateaus. Sometimes I sit in the shade of a bush and listen to the cars pass. (PICK UP LOOKS AWAY FROM HER A MOMENT. IT'S HARD FOR HIM TO LISTEN TO PART OF WHAT SHE SAYS, ESPECIALLY WHEN HE REALIZES THERE IS DANGER IN WHAT SHE DOES.) I don't ride with anyone who stops. I look them over first. There are white men who would use me—

### Pick Up

(TURNS AWAY FROM HER.) Indians too.

### Sweet Potato

That's why they can't see and feel the life of the desert, and can't hear the Great Spirit walking in the heat—in the midst of the fiery furnace. See, I know some of the Book too. (HE WALKS AWAY FROM

HER.) What's the matter, Pick Up?

### Pick Up
Go to Gallup. Maybe you have more there on the road than I can give you.

### Sweet Potato
When I get as far as Mesita I know I'll make it. Rock slides where the highway cuts through the plateaus. Payute. Cubero. James goes up into the Piños Mountains, but I have to go farther.

### Pick Up
All the way to Gallup!

### Sweet Potato
What's wrong with hitchhiking to Gallup?

### Pick Up
It isn't for a woman.

### Sweet Potato
It's exactly for me. Every place speaks my name and I know what to call them in return. The cactus and hills and arroyos.

### Pick Up
I don't want you on the highway for another man to see. I don't want you misused, Sweet Potato. You can understand that. I want to protect you— (HE LOOKS AT THE GROUND.) I want to consume you myself.

### Sweet Potato
Last week before I left I kept thinking of El Morro. San Rafael. Quemado. I don't ride with anyone. Sometimes it's like they're dead already when I look at their eyes. They look like a lava rock to me. (SHE TOUCHES PICK UP.) I'm glad you worry about me. It's always been me who saw others look at you. I remember the women who wanted you—why didn't you ever marry after the first time?

### Pick Up
I never found anyone I really wanted to marry. But you've caught me, Suzanne. You have a sweetness too, like your mother. You get a little rusty sometimes, like the desert water in my well—but you're not so tough, Miss Long Chalk. I won't tell anyone, though.

### Sweet Potato
Sometimes the jackrabbits hop right in front of me. (SHE IGNORES HIM.) Pick Up, I'm alive on the road to Gallup.

### Pick Up
It's suicide for you to hitchhike, Sweet Potato.

### Sweet Potato
I've run into the bad ones before— (SHE LOOKS AT PICK UP.) There was a man who tried to pick me up once. He followed me along the highway for a while, but I wouldn't get into his car.

### Pick Up
(ANGRY WITH HER.)  God, Sweet Potato.

### Sweet Potato
I always got away from any trouble.

### Pick Up
But you might not always—how can I let you go? I remember when you had to sit on books to reach the supper table. And now you're hitchhiking? Why do you want to go to Gallup?

### Sweet Potato
For the thrill of passing Ozanbito. The army depot and cathedral. The Outpost Restaurant where I worked that summer on my own. I used to cross the street and eat in the cemetery. The handmade grave markers. A picket fence like a playpen. The little weeds that jumped at my feet.

### Pick Up
The street-corner crowd at Indian capital? The 'No Loitering' sign at the cemetery?

### Sweet Potato
On Sundays I walked up the Cathedral.

### Pick Up
You could teach, Sweet Potato. You aren't too old to go back to school.  The children at Indian missions need teachers—

### Sweet Potato
I don't know—

## Pick Up

I remember you in a little pinafore with the straps crossed on your bare back. They made a big white X and I knew then you were one I could probably wait for— (SWEET POTATO PUSHES PICK UP AWAY WHEN HE TRIES TO KISS HER.) I have to go—I might have some calls for my tow truck. (HE KISSES HER.)

# SCENE II

### Weebjob
(WEEBJOB SITS BY SWEET GRASS AT HER LOOM.) Mutton. All the kissing I see them doing! To be around someone in love is like being in a mountain storm when the sky comes down upon you. The young are restless as the pines. But what's his excuse?

### Sweet Grass
You are muttering against what will make Sweet Potato happy?

### Weebjob
A man serves God, but his reward does not always come at first.

### Sweet Grass
Your problem is that you've never had a problem. God has blessed your life from the beginning.

### Weebjob
Not so, Wife—Sweet Potato running to Gallup. William's unrelenting pursuit of the legal profession, forgetting his spiritual nature. James looking for visions in peyote and drugs.

### Sweet Grass
Just peyote in the Indian church.

### Weebjob
In the reservation and boarding schools as a boy, I first saw the Thunder Hawk vision. I didn't need peyote for it to come.

### Sweet Grass
Weebjob, you don't bend.

### Weebjob
No, Wife. It's by faith we see these things.

### Sweet Grass
We don't all see as you do, Weebjob.

### Weebjob
(HE LOOKS AT HER AS SHE WEAVES.) You never used to contradict

me, Sweet Grass.

### Sweet Grass
Because I express my opinion, you call it contradiction? Haven't I always been free to say what I think?

### Weebjob
Yes, because what you've said always agreed with what I thought you should say.

### Sweet Grass
But if I should want to say something that didn't agree with what you think I should say, then I should be quiet?

### Weebjob
You're not going back to visit your sister.

### Sweet Grass
(LAUGHS.) It isn't her.

### Sweet Potato
(SWEET POTATO JOINS HER PARENTS AFTER PICK UP LEAVES.) Is he threatening to return you to the Female Seminary?

### Sweet Grass
Nearly.

### Weebjob
I can't. It's closed down.

### Sweet Potato
It should have never been opened.

### Sweet Grass
It wasn't that bad, Sweet Potato. There was such upheaval in our lives—it was probably the best place for us. (PAUSE.) Why are you always against school?

### Sweet Potato
Why do you ask such stupid questions? (ANGRILY.) Because I couldn't do it! You ought to know that! (IMPATIENTLY.) I got tired of bad grades—not knowing anything—(PAUSE.) I don't mean to snap at you. But I always failed. Why do you want me to say it?

### Sweet Grass

I'm sorry I brought it up. Yes, I remember your struggle. I don't think you stuck with it, Sweet Potato.

### Sweet Potato

How long does it take to find out you can't do something?

### Sweet Grass

It's not easy for anyone. I remember how hard it was to learn. The days were long—and the nights—memories were frightening as the booger dancers. Those wooden masks with their horrid faces jumped into my dreams. (SHE LOOKS AT WEEBJOB.) There were puzzling times too. I remember the heat under my nightdress where I had not felt a man—

### Sweet Potato

(EMBARRASSED BY HER MOTHER'S SUDDEN FRANKNESS.) I never knew you felt anything like that, Mother. (SWEET POTATO HAS ALWAYS BEEN IN AWE OF HER MOTHER, AND FELT SHE COULD NEVER EQUAL HER. NOW SHE REALIZES HER MOTHER IS HUMAN, AND THEY HAVE SIMILAR FEELINGS.)

### Sweet Grass

I guess it's the thought of you wanting to marry Pick Up—I remember how I felt when I saw Weebjob. I didn't have time to love him. He just decided I would be his wife. But later—those feelings always stayed unspoken.

### Sweet Potato

How could you marry like that? The very thought of it turns my skin.

### Sweet Grass

We didn't know any other way.

### Sweet Potato

You're quiet for once, Weebjob.

### Weebjob

Ah! Yes, I am. I was listening to Sweet Grass, and didn't know what to say. I remembered when I went to the Female Seminary for a wife. I had a friend who I went to see, and all the girls out on the lawn made me think it was a place to get a wife. I was thinking of the boarding school for Indian boys— (PAUSE.) I like this time of evening. I remember the fingers of the sun across the yard of the boarding school from the canyons and arroyos as evening reached from the parched desert. We couldn't ignore it. We woke up in the morning sweating with the heat. It only intensified during the day. We couldn't ignore the poverty of the school. The dreariness of the land. Our heritage was rich with tradition, and it was taken from us. We had to learn a new way, against our will. I longed for Indian ways just as the others. Christianity wasn't enough. And nothing came to fill the particular hunger we felt. Others grew bitter, later drank and wasted their lives. But I have always felt the closeness of the Great Spirit, and that he would manifest himself to me. Why would I have the hunger if there was nothing to fill it? And in the desolation of the nights, when I could hear other boys cry or moan with nightmares, the vision of the Thunder Hawk came, not the vision, for it was the Thunder Hawk himself. A magnificent bird from the spirit world full of light like a blue, stained-glass window in a cathedral. The vine at the window in the winter also reminded me of him. When the land was even deader than it was in summer. The dry vine rattling at the window was like the wings of the Thunder Hawk coming to me right through the walls of the boarding school for Indian boys. It was like the sweat lodge I heard about from the old Indian men before we were taken to school. It seemed to me to be 'Canaan' that was talked about in the Book. And this place too, here where I've lived all these years, where I can do what I want without fear or interference. It is 'Canaan.' I see the Thunder Hawk to this day. He has never left me. Great Spirit, how can you merge with us, who are mortal in our flesh and bound with error and filled with weakness? I must go to the squash patch for a while. I feel the wind over me like the presence of the Great Spirit—like the hot shower in the motel in Roswell when William got married and I stayed until the water ran cold and Sweet Grass called for me to get out. (SWEET GRASS LAUGHS. WEEBJOB GOES TO THE SQUASH PATCH. SWEET POTATO STAYS WITH HER MOTHER WHILE WEEB-JOB PRAYS.)

# SCENE III

(WEEBJOB PRAYS IN HIS SQUASH PATCH. THE THUNDER HAWK COMES TO HIM IN A VISION AGAIN, TWIRLING WITH COLORED LIGHTS, SOMETHING LIKE A MOVING STAINED-GLASS WINDOW IN A CATHEDRAL. BUT THIS IS A NEW-AGE VISION. WHILE THE THUNDER HAWK HOVERS, THE CHARACTERS RISE AND DANCE A GENESIS/TURTLE-ISLAND CREATION MYTH: THEY PULL DRY LAND OUT OF CAYOS. IT SPREADS ON THE GROUND OF THE SQUASH PATCH. THE CHARACTERS DANCE WITH SIGNS FROM WEEBJOB'S FENCE. ONE SIGN READS: SALAZAR CANYON. BUT CAYOS RISES AGAIN AND COVERS THE LAND. THERE'S A 'CIVIL WAR' OF SORTS. THE SOUND OF A TOW TRUCK IS HEARD. SLOWLY IT PULLS CAYOS AWAY. DRY LAND IS ESTABLISHED AGAIN. NOW THE CHARACTERS CONTINUE THE 'SIGN DANCE.' THE SIGN: 'CANAAN HAS A FIELD DAY.' ANOTHER SIGN 'WEEBJOB HAS A MAP' DANCES WITH IT. THE WHOLE SCENE IS A RUSH OF MOVEMENT, A PRELIMINARY TO THE WEDDING SCENE WHICH FOLLOWS. WHAT HAPPENS IN THE SPIRIT WORLD WILL BE ACTED OUT IN THE PHYSICAL. THIS SCENE IS THE STORY OF HOW WE COME FROM CAYOS INTO MAYBE AS MUCH LIGHT AS WE CAN STAND. AND HOW WE STRUGGLE TO STAY THERE.)

# SCENE IV

### Sweet Grass
(SHE IS DRESSED FOR THE WEDDING.) It's a lovely day in Salazar Canyon. Just the day for Weebjob's daughter to marry Pick Up. Already the guests arrive. Come in. Come in. (SEVERAL PEOPLE ENTER CARRYING BOWLS OF FOOD. SWEET GRASS MOTIONS THEM TO THE HOUSE.) Would you carry the table off the porch? (TWO MEN CARRY THE TABLE FROM THE PORCH AND SET IT IN THE YARD. THE WOMEN SET THE BOWLS OF FOOD ON THE TABLE. OTHERS ARRIVE.) Clement Thousandsticks. How nice to see you. Did you have a pleasant drive here? Hersah. James is still in the house. I think he's helping Weebjob get himself ready for the wedding. (SHE GOES INTO THE HOUSE. OTHERS STAND IN CLUMPS TALKING AND GREETING ONE ANOTHER. THERE ARE TWO NEW SIGNS ON THE FENCE: 'BY THE THUNDER OF HIS POWER WHO CAN UNDERSTAND? JOB 26:14' AND 'MISERABLE COMFORTERS ARE YE ALL, JOB 16:1.')

### Clement
(HE SPEAKS TO WARHALL.) Well, I wonder how the holy war was fought in 'Canaan' when Pick Up asked Weebjob to marry his daughter. Bah! Bah!

### Warhall
Hua! (LAUGHTER.)

### Clement
You've got pen stains in your shirt pocket again, Warhall. I see you're still working crosswords in the Roswell Gazette.

### Wedding Guests
(THERE IS THE SOUND OF TALKING AMONG THE GUESTS. AT TIMES SOME CONVERSATIONS ARE HEARD ABOVE OTHERS.)

Been hunting lately?

Jack rabbits run like deer. You shoot when they stop and look back. Though you could almost shoot them at a run, they move so steady.

A cotton tail keeps going until he's gone. He won't look back to see if you're still there.

If they're not careful, Old Lincoln will be under a foot of honeysuckle by next summer.

At least it'll cover those old buildings they painted turquoise.

The Gallup rodeo's big as Albuquerque's.

### Sweet Grass
(SHE COMES FROM THE HOUSE.) William. Reesah. Hello. Thank you for bringing Mary Jane. (THEY EMBRACE.) Such a lovely day for the wedding.

### Weebjob
Uuuuah! (HE MOANS FROM THE HOUSE.)

### Sweet Grass
(WHEN EVERYONE LOOKS TOWARD THE HOUSE.) Weebjob is still getting ready. Don't worry about him. Come. (SWEET GRASS TAKES MARY JANE'S ARM.) I need your help for a moment. (SWEET GRASS GOES INTO THE HOUSE AND GETS A ROLL OF CREPE PAPER, RETURNS TO THE YARD WHERE THEY WAIT.) Wrap this around the fenceposts in the squash patch. We didn't have time to get ready for the wedding. I hadn't seen you in such a long time before I came to Hobbs. Now we've seen each other twice in such a short time.

### Clement
Sarah Long Chalk and Mary Jane Collar. I can remember you two dazzling young sisters.

### Mary Jane
And Clement, I can remember running from you when I came to visit Sarah.

### Warhall
That's probably the wisest thing you ever did.

### Clement
Let's rodeo!

### Sweet Grass
Here now, Clement, the musicians and minister have arrived. Show them the squash patch. When will Weebjob be ready?

### Mary Jane
How lovely the squash patch looks with its yellow blossoms! (SHE

AND REESAH GO TO THE SQUASH PATCH AND WRAP THE FENCE-POSTS WITH CREPE PAPER. THE LITTLE GIRL STANDS WITH THEM.)

### Clement
(HE TAKES THE MINISTER AND THE TWO INDIAN MUSICIANS WITH FLUTE AND DRUM TO THE SQUASH PATCH.) This is where the showdown will take place.

### Mary Jane
I've never heard of a wedding in a squash patch, but Weebjob was never typical. (THE FLUTE PLAYS, WHICH IS THE TRADITIONAL INSTRUMENT FOR LOVE SONGS.)

### Reesah
It was Sweet Potato's idea.

### Mary Jane
That figures.

### Sweet Grass
(JAMES AND HERSAH COME FROM THE HOUSE. THEY TALK TO WILLIAM AND THE OTHER GUESTS. A FEW MORE PEOPLE ARRIVE. SOME BRING BOWLS OF FOOD WHICH THEY SET ON THE TABLE. SOME BRING PRESENTS. SWEET GRASS GREETS EVERYONE.) Weebjob. (SHE GOES TO THE HOUSE.) Our guests are here. James, where is he?

### James
He's taking his time. (JAMES TURNS AND LOOKS AT THE DOOR OF THE HOUSE.) I thought he was behind us. I'll go see what's holding him up now. (JAMES GOES BACK INTO THE HOUSE.)

### Sweet Grass
It would be nice to gather for your wedding too, Hersah.

### Hersah
Not yet. (PICK UP ARRIVES AND THEY ALL MAKE A CLAMOR OVER HIM.)

### Clement
Pick Up!

### Pick Up
Clement Thousandsticks.

### Warhall
Pick Up! You've come to your wedding in 'Canaan.' The old stick is going to make it. He's looking a little pale.

### Clement
Ba-aah! (PICK UP IGNORES THE MEN.) Are you going to Gallup on your honeymoon?

### William
Gentlemen. We're gathered here for a solemn and joyous occasion. Let us respect Pick Up and his new bride.

### Warhall
Hear! Hear! (BOTH MUSICIANS PLAY AND THE WEDDING GUESTS START TO GATHER AROUND THE SQUASH PATCH.)

### James
(HE COAXES WEEBJOB FROM THE HOUSE.) Come, Father, you must greet the wedding guests.

### Weebjob
(HE APPEARS DRESSED FOR THE WEDDING.) For once, I wish Mighty Warrior would bark and scatter this 'assemblage.' (PAUSE.) I cannot believe Pick Up is going to become my son-in-law in my own squash patch on 'Canaan.' Never in all my imagination— (HE LIFTS HIS FIST TO HEAVEN.) I'm at a crossroads in my life.

### Clement
Ah, Weebjob! How grand you look!

### Weebjob
(HE COMES INTO THE YARD.) Mutton!

### Warhall
Weebjob! Father of the Spud who is going to become wife of Pick Up.
### Weebjob
(HE SWATS INTO THE AIR.) As many flies as there used to be arrows.

### Sweet Grass
Weebjob. Where have you been?

### Weebjob
I'm not late. I don't see Tuber yet.

### Sweet Grass
She'll be the last one here, Weebjob. She's the bride. I have spoken to the minister about where to stand. Come, greet the guests. They've brought a lot of food.

### Weebjob
(HE GREETS THE GUESTS AND SEEMS TO FEEL BETTER.) Ofred. Warhall. Kutchell. Clement Thousands of Ticks. (HE SHAKES MANY OF THEIR HANDS.) Reesah. Little One. William. (HE HUGS THEM.) Mary Jane Collar who takes my wife away. Hersah. All. (HE SHAKES THE MINISTER'S HAND.) My Father in heaven. (HE LIFTS HIS ARM TO THE SKY AGAIN.) Squash patch. (HE GREETS HIS BELOVED PLOT OF LAND.) With crepe-paper— (HE LOOKS AT SWEET GRASS.) —on holy ground?

### Sweet Grass
It needed decoration for the wedding. (PAUSE.) Weebjob, there is someone you haven't spoken to—

### Weebjob
I will see enough of him until my name is called from beyond the mountain. Pick Up, my son. (THEY EMBRACE. WILLIAM STANDS WITH REESAH, THE CHILD AND MARY JANE COLLAR. JAMES AND HERSAH AND SWEET GRASS STAND IN FRONT OF THE MINISTER WHO HAS HIS BACK TO THE AUDIENCE, AND THE OTHERS DRAW CLOSE TO THE SQUASH PATCH, LEAVING A MIDDLE AISLE FOR WEEBJOB AND SWEET POTATO. THEY ALL TURN WHEN SHE ENTERS FROM THE BACK. PICK UP SMILES.)

### Sweet Potato
Yes, Father. The desert is white with harvest. I see it now like you always said it was— (THE MUSICIANS PLAY BACKGROUND FLUTE AND DRUM. WEEBJOB AND SWEET POTATO WALK TO THE FRONT OF THE PEOPLE GATHERED FOR THE WEDDING. SWEET POTATO WEARS A DRESS.)

### Weebjob
(MOANS.) How can all this be? (THE FLUTE PLAYS A WEDDING SONG. WEEBJOB MOANS AGAIN SEVERAL TIMES DURING THE CEREMONY.)

### Minister
Relatives and Friends. I want this couple, whose hearts are about to be joined as one, to bless themselves with holy cedar smoke, to cleanse and clear their minds of any bad or negative thoughts for their walk through life. Ah-ho wah-kon-tah. Bless the use of this

cedar for which it is intended. (HE PASSES THE BOWL OF CEDAR IN FRONT OF SWEET POTATO AND PICK UP, THEN THE WEDDING PARTY. THEY WASH THE THIN TRAIL OF SMOKE OVER THEM.)

I want to wish you well, you whose hearts have joined hands to walk the road of life, may your walk be soft and long, always be kind and courteous to each other and may you see many grandchildren and maybe even great-grandchildren. Any way you want it. It will be that way. Ah-ho.

(THE MINISTER HANDS THE TWO-NECKED WEDDING VASE TO SWEET POTATO AND PICK UP. THEY DRINK FROM IT.)

The union of husband and wife in heart, body, and mind is intended by the Great Spirit for their mutual joy. Into this holy union, Percy Willingdeer and Suzanne Long Chalk have come to be joined. If any of you can show just cause why they may not lawfully be married, speak now; or forever hold your peace. (JAMES LOOKS AT WEEBJOB, WHO REMAINS QUIET.) Aho.

### Wedding Guests
Aho.

### Minister
Percy, will you take this woman to be your wife; to live together in the covenant of marriage? Will you love her, comfort her, honor and keep her, in sickness and in health; and, forsaking all others, be faithful to her as long as you both shall live?

### Pick Up
I will.

### Minister
Suzanne, will you have this man to be your husband; to live together in the covenant of marriage? Will you love him, comfort him, honor and keep him, in sickness and in health; and, forsaking all others, be faithful to him as long as you both shall live?

### Sweet Potato
I will.

### Minister
Will all of you witnessing these promises do all in your power to uphold these two persons in their marriage?

### Wedding Guests
(SWEET GRASS LOOKS AT WEEBJOB. THEY BOTH SPEAK WITH THE OTHERS.) We will.

### Minister
Let us pray. O gracious and everliving God, you have created us male and female in your image. Look mercifully upon this man and this woman who come to you seeking your blessing, and assist them with your grace, that they may honor and keep the vows they make; through Jesus Christ our Savior, who lives and reigns with you in the unity of the Holy Spirit, one God, forever and ever. Amen. (WILLIAM'S WIFE WIPES HER EYES, AND WILLIAM PUTS HIS ARM AROUND HIS WIFE.)

### Pick Up
(HE FACES SWEET POTATO, TAKES HER RIGHT HAND.) In the Name of God, I, Percy, take you, Suzanne, to be my wife, to have and to hold from this day forward, for better, for worse, for richer, for poorer, in sickness and in health, to love and to cherish, until we are parted by death.

### Sweet Potato
(SHE TAKES PICK UP'S RIGHT HAND IN HERS AND REPEATS AFTER THE MINISTER ALSO.) In the name of God, I, Suzanne, take you, Percy, to be my husband, to have and to hold from this day forward, for better, for worse, for richer, for poorer, in sickness and in health, to love and to cherish, until we are parted by death.

### Minister
Bless, O Lord, this ring to be a sign of the vows by which this man and this woman have bound themselves to each other.

### Wedding Guests
(WEEBJOB MOANS AGAIN.) Hua! Hua!

### Minister
Now that Percy and Suzanne have given themselves to each other by solemn vows, with the joining of hands and the giving and receiving of a ring, I pronounce that they are husband and wife in the name of the Father, and of the Son, and of the Holy Spirit.

### Pick Up
(ENTHUSIASTICALLY.) And in the name of the sun and wind and moutains and streams— (HE KISSES HIS NEW WIFE. THE MUSICIANS PLAY. THE WEDDING GUESTS HUG THE LONG CHALK FAM-

ILY. EVEN WEEBJOB. THEY CONGRATULATE PICK UP AND SWEET
POTATO. THE WOMEN, MARY JANE COLLAR AND REESAH, GO TO
THE TABLE AND ARRANGE THE BOWLS OF FOOD.)

### Sweet Grass
Do you remember when we were married, Weebjob, and they—

### Weebjob
(HE INTERRUPTS HER.) Yes, and we got away anyway.

### Sweet Grass
But not everyone knew it.

### Sweet Potato
They can speak in half-sentences and know what the other is going
to say—

### Pick Up
May we be married that long.

### Weebjob
You'd be Methuselah by then.

### Clement
Ah, Pick Up and his young wife— (ACTS LIKE HE IS GOING TO
CONGRATULATE SWEET POTATO WITH A KISS.)

### Pick Up
(HOLDS HIS ARM UP TO CLEMENT.) None of you horned toads are
going to kiss my wife.

### Wedding Guests
(THE GUESTS BEGIN TO FORM A TRAIN AND MAKE AN INDIAN
DANCE AROUND 'CANAAN.' THE MUSICIANS CONTINUE TO PLAY.)

### Weebjob
(HE SWATS HIMSELF.) Barking flies!

### Clement
How does it feel to have a son-in-law like Pick Up?

### Weebjob
Go dance with youself, Clement.

### Clement
At least he has Sweet Potato now. She's not your worry any longer.

### Weebjob
She was never that much of a worry.

### Clement
Hoa! A female child who runs off? Tut, tut, Weebjob.

### Wedding Guests
(WHILE THE GUESTS ARE IN THE CIRCLE DANCE, THESE CONVER-
SATIONS ARE HEARD:)

I thought you wanted to dance.

No, I'll sit and talk.

Fine wedding.

Strange though.

Chua. Chua. Whssp.
Yah, a cotton tail keeps going until he's gone.

The Long Chalks always did things their own way.

Good fry bread.

I'll give you my recipe for judenedo.

Yah, there's nothing like cactus jelly.

You voting for Chief?

Not for you, Ofred.

### Weebjob
(TO WILLIAM.) Belief is a matter of will. I choose to believe. Yet I
have seen also in the squash patch when the Thunder Hawk comes
to me. You don't believe because you don't choose to.

### William
I see no evidence of it.

## Weebjob

Because you don't take time. You fill your days with law. But your
rational mind will never explain enough to satisfy you. You have to
admit that God descended into flesh.

## William

I don't see what that's got to do with anything.

## James

Why don't you say those things to me?

## Weebjob

I guess I didn't think you wanted to hear them.

## James

You always talk like that to William and he doesn't want to hear.

## Weejob

Another crossroads in my life.

## William

I have to see how Reesah is doing.

## Weebjob

I have felt Sweet Potato's anger too. I gave her life and made it bitter
for her. But now I want things healed between us. I was always too
serious. And with you, James, I've not been serious enough. (PAUSE.)
I'll make a a new sign for the fence at highway 380: 'I have heard
by hearing, but now I see with my eyes, Job 42:5.'

## Clement

(OVERHEARING.) Another wooden smoke signal? You've got your
fence by the highway nearly covered. What are you going to say
about having Pick Up as a son-in-law? Tut, tut.

## Weebjob

I welcome him to the family.

## Clement

(CLEMENT MOVES TO PICK UP AND SWEET POTATO TO TEASE
THEM AGAIN.) The old war horse and his bride. Where are you
going to take her on your honeymoon?

## Pick Up

What the shit, Clement. We're going to hitchhike to Gallup!

STICK HORSE

# CHARACTERS

ELIJAH (ELI), a 35-year-old Cherokee man, an alcoholic. He wears jeans and a dirty t-shirt.

VIRGENE, his girlfriend. She is in a pink and yellow flowered dress and white ankle-socks and loafers.

QUANNAH, Virgene's friend and Eli's older sister.

JAKE (BULLET PROOF), a friend of Eli's and a Medicine Man who helps Eli in the Indian way. He wears jeans, a ribbon shirt, and a pouch of cedar on his belt. He carries a ceremonial pipe. Also a small drum and rattle to help in the chanting.

FOUR SPIRIT-DANCERS, they wear body stockings and different costumes at various times such as masks, rodeo clown makeup, cowboy hats, banners with letters of the alphabet, hip boots.

# SETTING

June

Tahlequah, Oklahoma

An open garage behind a rent-house on the edge of town. The wide, weathered boards of the back of the old garage are warped and the moon shines through the cracks when the light bulb (which hangs from the ceiling on a cord) is off. The floor of the garage is dirt. On the partial sidewall, a single shelf runs under the window. It is bare except for a small roll of fence wire, several canning jars with nails in them, and a rusty, single-blade garden plow abandoned by a tenant long ago. The sidewall has a single window in it above the shelf. Outside, there is a bush and a clothesline pole with broken clothesline. When the garage light is on, it shines on the bush. The clothesline pole, in front of the bush, makes the shape of a black cross.

(ELI SITS AGAINST THE BACK WALL OF THE GARAGE. VIRGENE STANDS NEAR HIM. SHE HOLDS HER ARMS OUT FROM HER BODY, DANCES THE TWO-STEP SLIGHTLY, AS THOUGH HER MOVEMENTS WERE A SHADOW OF THE POW WOW DANCE SHE IMAGINES. QUANNAH ALSO DANCES THE TWO-STEP. ONE FOOT STEPS FORWARD, THE OTHER FOOT IS PLACED BESIDE IT. THE STEP IS REPEATED. THERE IS A SLIGHT SWAY OF THE BODY, BUT MOVEMENT IS MINIMAL. VIRGENE HUMS TO HERSELF AS SHE DANCES. JAKE SITS AGAINST ANOTHER WALL OF THE GARAGE, WIRED TO A WALKMAN. HIS EYES ARE CLOSED. THERE ARE TWO SPIRIT-DANCERS NEAR ELI WHO STAND WITH THEIR FACES TO THE GARAGE WALL. TWO MORE OUTSIDE THE GARAGE, OPPOSITE THE CLOTHESPOLE, ARE PLAYING CARDS.)

Eli
You should have been driving, Virgene.

Virgene
No. You wanted to.

Eli
My license is suspended—until the end of time.

Quannah
Just think, Eli. The June pow wow. I can see those words dancing on their banner.

Eli
I don't know words anymore—sometimes my own name seems strange. (HE BURIES HIS FACE AGAINST HIS HANDS. HE IS NAUSEOUS AND HAS A HEADACHE.)

Virgene
Hold on. It'll get better. (SHE MOVES CLOSER TO ELI, WATCHING TO SEE IF HE NOTICES HER.)

Eli
You girls go back in the house.

Virgene
We'll stay with you—

Quannah
(STILL DANCING AND HUMMING TO HERSELF.) It's not so bad to be fat.

#### Eli
Now I have to hear it all again. I stand there with the words stampeding into my head—

#### Virgene
(STOPS DANCING AND STANDS NEAR ELI.) This time you weren't drinking. That means EVERYTHING!

#### Eli
They had two police cars and the state trooper at the intersection.

#### Quannah
(SHE TAKES THE ROLL OF FENCE WIRE AND DANCES ACROSS THE FLOOR.) OOOOO—WAH— (SHE KICKS JAKE'S FEET. HE MOVES HIS FEET BUT CONTINUES TO LISTEN TO THE WALKMAN WITH HIS EYES CLOSED.)

#### Virgene
You were sobbing, Eli. You're still weak. They thought they had a drunk Indian on their hands again. Only a few weeks ago you were in the Indian hospital.

#### Quannah
(SHE LETS THE FENCE WIRE FALL.) Only a few weeks ago my brother was nearly dead.

#### Eli
I had to stand there while traffic went by—trying to walk a straight line.

#### Quannah
Like a circus bear on a tightrope. (PRETENDS TO WALK AN IMAGINARY LINE IN THE GARAGE.)

#### Virgene
Those old white women were terrified.

#### Quannah
Two old farm wives on their way to the cemetery on Memorial Day! (SHE LOOKS AT JAKE AS IF HE SHOULD LAUGH, BUT HE CONTIUNES TO IGNORE HER.)

#### Eli
At one time it would have been funny. I remember hog-calling to Sirloin once when he was stopped—but I can't laugh anymore.

### Virgene

They found out you weren't drunk. Quannah and I already dented our fender—

### Eli

You're making excuses for me.

### Quannah

You thought Sirloin was your best friend.

### Eli

I remember when we drove the backroads of Oklahoma—from these northeast hills to the flat prairie—following rodeos and pow wows. I could smell the ripe hay along the road. (THE SPIRIT-DANCERS IN THE GARAGE MAKE SLIGHT UNDULATING MOVE-MENTS.) More wildflowers than I'd ever seen. More than in the cemetery on Memorial Day. (ELI FEELS BETTER AS HE REMEM-BERS.)

### Quannah

We've had nothing but good times.

### Virgene

We've had them for about 20 years. Sirloin was best. Nothing meant anything to him. We were always waiting for court hearings. What else have we done but drink and dance at pow wows and hang around Indian rodeo?

### Jake

We've made our donations to Indian bingo.

### Virgene

Jake, I remember Eli fancy-dancing in the pow wow arenas. I couldn't take my eyes off him. The roach and feather-bustle. The paint streaks on his face.

### Eli

Now I'm not even a pow wow clown. (HE HOLDS HIS HAND UP AS THOUGH A MIRROR.) I see one purple eye. One red ear. I want to creep back under my yellow skin.

### Virgene

No. You got your fire back, Eli. You'll be in the arena again.

#### Quannah

He'll get his firewater back—(VIRGENE LOOKS ANGRILY AT QUAN-
NAH.)

#### Eli

She's right, Virgene. Even when I danced, it was hard. What have
I ever done?

#### Quannah

You hold the record for quitting and getting fired.

#### Jake

That's running on Indian time.

#### Eli

I couldn't be a husband.  A father. I was in jail when my mother
died. My wife left. My children didn't know me.

#### Quannah

That's a record, Eli.

#### Jake

(AS THOUGH SINGING TO HIS WALKMAN.) The old white face of
that clock.

#### Eli

I used to talk instead of going home to them. I had my friends—

#### Quannah

(DANCING AGAIN.) It ain't so bad to be so sad.

#### Eli

At home there was responsibility. My children always needing
something—my wife angry—but my friends suited me. No one
pulled at me. I did what I wanted. And now I got nowhere to go but
in that dark hole ahead of me. That's what you saw me fall into—
(ELI GETS UP, BUT FEELS HIS WEAKNESS AGAIN. THE SPIRIT-
DANCERS HELP HIM HOLD ONTO THE SHELF OF THE GARAGE.)
That's what hurts. Knowing I don't have anything to give. I get the
shudders—  not just from drinking, but to think of the great hole
without drinking. It's worse than living. (HE REACHES FOR VIRGENE
TO SPOOK HER.  SHE STEPS BACK, NEARLY FALLING OVER THE
ROLL OF FENCE WIRE.)

#### Virgene
(RECOVERING HER BALANCE.) No, it's not! It's why you wanted to drive when you shouldn't have.

#### Eli
No, Virgene. I wasn't feeling confident. I wanted to feel free of restraint. Who are they to tell me what to do? Then that old woman stopped in the middle of the street in her Plymouth—a scarf around her head like a helmet. She's the one who ought to be arrested.

#### Virgene
You're not going backwards, Eli. I'm not going to let you. I'm going to see you in the pow wow ring—I may even have someone to dance with again. (SHE STANDS THE FENCE WIRE UP TO HER AS THOUGH IT WERE A MAN, AND DANCES WITH IT.)

#### Quannah
(QUANNAH DANCES TOO.) We're going to punch the clock tonight. (THEY PASS THE FENCE WIRE BACK AND FORTH. THEY FINALLY THROW IT DOWN AND DANCE TOGETHER. THE FOUR SPIRIT-DANCERS DANCE ALSO.)

#### Eli
Shit.

#### Virgene
(WHEN THEY TIRE OF DANCING.) Seriously, Eli, I say you have a start—you got A.A.—

#### Eli
Which don't help—

#### Jake
You got us for community—

#### Virgene
You're dry now—and you got your sister and me cooking your meals—

#### Quannah
(SINGING HER USUAL SONG.) It's not so bad—(SHE KICKS THE ROLL OF FENCE WIRE TO JAKE.)

#### Virgene
(IMPATIENT WITH QUANNAH.) Jake is here for the pipe ceremony—

Eli
I can't see anything without drinking.

Virgene
You heard the doctors. If you don't stop you won't be able to see down the road when you drive. You won't remember what you're supposed to.

Eli
I do that now, Virgene, you have to remind me to take my medicine—my hands shake so bad you have to put the glass of water to my mouth—(HE HOLDS OUT HIS TREMBLING ARM, BRINGS HIS JERKING HAND TO HIS MOUTH AS THOUGH IT HELD A GLASS OF WATER.)

Quannah
Remember when our excursion for the whole day was down the three back steps of the house? Now you've made it to the garage. Think how far you've come, Eli.

Virgene
You don't want to go back.

Eli
(THE SPIRIT-DANCERS COMB ELI'S HAIR.) No. I want to keep these good times we're having right now.

Jake
Why would he want to go back? (WHEN THE SPIRIT-DANCERS MOVE TOWARD JAKE, HE SHUNS THEM.)

Virgene
Remember Sirloin over the loud-speaker when the rodeo-queen rode by? He'd snort and wheeze— (ELI SNORTS AND WHEEZES.)

Quannah
Sherrallee deserved it.

Jake
They finally got the microphone away from him. (VIRGENE AND QUANNAH LAUGH.)

Quannah
They chased him out of the arena that time too.

#### Eli
What did any of us have other than the bottle? (THE SPIRIT-
DANCERS CARESS ELI.)

#### Virgene
I don't know, Eli. You keep asking—I've said before I'll go with you
on Saturdays to pick blackberries.

#### Eli
I'm not having a stand on the highway—I could be an astronaut
easier than I could sit by the road.

#### Virgene
You like to fix cars.

#### Eli
I'm no good at it.

#### Quannah
You could enroll at Northeastern.

#### Eli
I can't read a book. I'm an alcoholic. Our father was an alcoholic.
Our grandfather—

#### Virgene
There's a job somewhere for you—

#### Eli
I been fired by every garage and hardware in town.

#### Quannah
You could raise rabbits again. Anything is better than welfare—
having to report all the time on how we spend the money. I want our
lives to be ours again.

#### Virgene
The church has a job list.

#### Eli
I could preach Jesus on Sunday morning! I could be a crow easier
than—that's IT, Virgene. I'll be a crow. CAW! (HE MAKES A TERRI-
BLE SCREECH.)

#### Quannah
I thought we were Cherokee.

Eli

I feel the wings of the old trickster on my back. I preen my feathers. CAW!!

Virgene

Stop it.

Eli

I jump from my branch. It twangs in the wind. I feel the wind under my shiny black belly. (HE IS STANDING NOW FLAPPING HIS ARMS, JUMPING AROUND THE GARAGE AS THOUGH HE IS FLYING. THE FOUR SPIRIT-DANCERS QUICKLY JOIN HIM IN A FLIGHT-DANCE. HE EVEN TRIES TO CLIMB ON THE SHELF OF THE GARAGE, BUT CAN'T.) I see the fields below me with my blackberry eyes. CAW!! CAW!! (ELI FINALLY TRIPS ON THE ROLL OF FENCE WIRE, FALLS. VIRGENE TRIES TO UNFOLD THE WIRE AND PUT IT OVER HIM, BUT SHE CAN'T. QUANNAH TRIES TO HELP HER. THE SPIRIT-DANCERS PUSH THEM OUT OF THE WAY AND BEGIN TO DANCE WITH ELI, PULLING HIM TO THE EDGE OF THE GARAGE, BUT JAKE COMES TO PULL ELI BACK. THE SPIRIT-DANCERS HOVER TOGETHER OUT- SIDE, ALWAYS OPPOSITE THE CLOTHES POLE.)

Eli

What do I have, Jake? (ELI HOLDS UP HIS JERKING ARM.)

Jake

You can draw lightning bolts in the sky. (ELI JERKS HIS ARM IN JAGGED MOTION.)

Quannah

There's enough of life in plain living, Eli. (SHE HELPS JAKE HOLD ELI'S ARMS TO HIS SIDE TO CONTROL THE SPASMS.) —Even if it's just waiting for the welfare check and commodities. (SHE AND JAKE SIT WITH ELI.)

Eli

Christ. It may be enough for you.

Virgene

We're in No Man's Land. We've lost our Indian heritage. We're not part of the white world.

Quannah

You are if you drink—it's their stuff.

**Jake**
This is our land. It's our power. They're never getting rid of us.

**Virgene**
But we're caught between the two worlds.

**Quannah**
No—we have both worlds to walk in. (SHE LEANS AGAINST JAKE. HE PUTS HIS ARM AROUND HER. SHE LISTENS TO HIS WALKMAN, MOVES HER FOOT TO THE MUSIC. THE SPIRIT-DANCERS REST AGAINST ONE ANOTHER IN THE YARD.)

**Virgene**
Drive a stake into the ground—(ELI SITS UP. HE POUNDS AN IMAGINARY STAKE IN THE GROUND WITH AN IMAGINARY HAMMER.) Get your single-blade plow. (ELI STANDS AND THE SPIRIT-DANCERS PUT THEIR HANDS OVER THEIR EARS.) Borrow a horse. (THEY ROLL ON THE GROUND AS THOUGH WOUNDED.) Hitch it to the plow and walk through the field making one furrow after another. (WHILE SHE IS TALKING, ELI GETS THE ROLL OF FENCE WIRE. HE SETS IT UP, OPENS IT AS THOUGH IT WERE A FENCE FOR HIS LAND, BUT HE STANDS INSIDE.)

**Eli**
It's still the jail I'm going to.

**Virgene**
No—it doesn't have to be that way. (SHE TAKES THE ROLL OF FENCE WIRE AWAY FROM HIM.) We can create something out of nothing.

**Eli**
You sound like Jake.

**Virgene**
Cup your hand. (ELI LOOKS AT HIS TREMBLING HAND.) Cup it like something was in it. What do you see?

**Eli**
Nothing. There's no bottle.

**Virgene**
No, there's air in it. You've got breath, Eli. Now what else do you see?

#### Jake
I see a hand.

#### Eli
I see skin.

#### Jake
(TAKES HIS ARM FROM AROUND QUANNAH TO LOOK AT HIS HAND.)
Two jacks and three aces.

#### Quannah
(SHE STANDS, STILL LISTENING TO THE WALKMAN.) It ain't so bad
to be a fad.

#### Virgene
That's right, Eli. Skin. You've got hands—you've got yourself.
You're the first one out of the chute.

#### Eli
I could be a laundromat. My hand is going around like a dryer.

#### Virgene
You've made something out of nothing.

#### Eli
Just like I was a god.

#### Virgene
I say to you what my father said to me—live.

#### Eli
I say to myself what my father never said to me—live.

#### Virgene
Live.

#### Eli
(BELIEVING.) Live.

#### Jake
(HE BEATS THE DRUM QUIETLY.) Hey ay hey yay. (QUANNAH TWO-
STEPS AROUND THE ROLL OF FENCE WIRE. ELI TRIES TO DANCE
TOO. VIRGENE AND QUANNAH THEN JITTERBUG TOGETHER. THE
SPIRIT-DANCERS MIMIC THEM IN THE YARD. THERE'S A LIGHT
MOMENT WHEN EVERYONE IS DANCING. JAKE PUTS THE WALK-

MAN IN HIS EAR AGAIN.)

#### Virgene
After you serve this time for driving without a license, you can come back here with Quannah and me for good—

#### Quannah
I can just see him planting pansies with us next spring.

#### Virgene
Maybe they'll release you without a sentence.

#### Eli
(HE STOPS HIS ATTEMPTS TO DANCE AND SITS ON THE FLOOR.) I remember jail—(THE SPIRIT-DANCERS CIRCLE THE YARD. ONE ATTEMPTS TO COME OVER THE WALL OF THE GARAGE ON A ROPE.) —laying there on the cot vomiting my guts out—bucking like I was in the rodeo—no, I couldn't ride in the rodeo. I could only be a clown. (THE SPIRIT-DANCER SITS WITH HIS ARM AROUND ELI. ANOTHER ONE COMES OVER THE WALL ON A ROPE.) Not a holy ceremonial clown. No. But one made of grease paint. (THE SPIRIT-DANCER PULLS ELI'S HEAD ON ITS SHOULDER. THE OTHER ONE PLAYS WITH ELI'S FOOT. ANOTHER ONE COMES OVER THE WALL OF THE GARAGE ON A ROPE.) Only Sirloin could stay on a horse. (ANGRILY, VIRGENE KICKS THE ROLL OF FENCE WIRE TOWARD ELI AND THE SPIRIT-DANCERS FLEE.) I could only ride my stick horse. I can't stand it! My body cries for alcohol. Jake—(HE STANDS NOW.) I'm twitching now I want it so bad, I want to fly again. CAW!

#### Jake
You don't fly.

#### Virgene
(SHE PUSHES ELI TO THE GROUND.) You land on your ass in jail. You're not a human being when you drink—

#### Eli
I'd sell anything—anyone—for the times nothing can bring back. (A NEW SPIRIT-DANCER ENTERS. ONE THAT LOOKS LIKE AN INDIAN, BUT WEARS SPURS. HE LINE-DANCES. THE OTHER SPIRIT-DANCERS JOIN HIM.) JESUS—(ELI CRIES OUT IN NEED.) Paste my purple clown eye across my nose—fill my mouth with dirt until I can't breathe. (ELI CALLS OUT.) Sirloin—

#### Virgene
Forget him. He did nothing but coax you back into trouble—Jake—

start the pipe ceremony—

**Quannah**
He's too busy listening to the Boston Pops. (JAKE MOVES HIS FOOT IN TIME TO THE MUSIC WITH HIS EYES CLOSED.)

**Eli**
Do you think the pow wow clown will turn into a fancy-dancer again? Don't you know I wait for Sirloin to come back from the dead so we can play cards? Don't you know I want to see him drive up Main Street again with the Steak House bull on wheels tied behind his motorcycle? What are you hanging around for?

**Quannah**
I live here, Chug-a-lug.

**Virgene**
(STANDS OVER HIM.) I do too.

**Eli**
I'm not going to marry you.

**Virgene**
That's fine with me.

**Eli**
(HE FLIPS THE HEM OF HER FLOWERED DRESS.) Can't you get a man anywhere?

**Virgene**
I got a man.

**Eli**
You're hoping for the day I work again? (HE LIFTS HER DRESS.)

**Virgene**
I don't think that far down the road yet. If I do, I see you driving off to the Anadarko Pow Wow—the rodeo in Elk City or Clinton—with everything you own or borrowed in the backseat of your beat-up car—

**Eli**
I don't even have a car anymore.

**Virgene**

You'd find somebody's to borrow.

**Eli**

I bet you think about me.

**Virgene**

(ANGRY FOR A MOMENT.) What keeps you here? Why aren't you off with your friends again?

**Eli**

They're all dead. Or at Disneyland. Or in the county home.

**Virgene**

Now that's a thought. Quannah and I could bundle you up and drop you at the *Indian Hall of Fame.*

**Eli**

I'm going to get strong as you someday.

**Virgene**

I've never known you strong as me—you can't get your fork to your mouth without dropping green beans all over yourself. Look at your shirt—

**Eli**

(HE STARTS TO GET UP.) I just got no place else to go right now—

**Virgene**

Well then— (SHE PUTS HER FOOT ON HIS THIGH AND PUSHES HIM BACK TO THE GROUND. HE HITS HER AWAY WITH ALL THE FORCE HE CAN MUSTER. SHE IS THROWN OFF BALANCE AND HITS THE SHELF ON THE GARAGE. SHE IS STUNNED FOR A MOMENT. THEN ANGRY.) Watch yourself, Tonto. You will be at the county home. You're here living off Quannah and me—

**Eli**

Don't remind me.

**Virgene**

I can always leave you to yourself. (SHE LEAVES THE GARAGE.)

**Eli**

(ELI SITS FOR A MOMENT WITH HIS HEAD IN HIS HANDS. HE IS WEAK FROM THE EXERTION OF HITTING VIRGENE. SOON HE TRIES

TO STAND. HE WOBBLES ON HIS FEET, STEADYING HIMSELF BY HOLDING TO THE SHELF OF THE GARAGE. THEN HE HOLDS ONE ARM OUT. THE OTHER HAND IS HOLDING AN IMAGINARY REIN. HE STANDS FOR A MOMENT, THEN ROMPS ONCE AS THOUGH ON A HORSE. THE SPIRIT-DANCERS RODEO AROUND HIM. AFTER A MOMENT, HE ROMPS AGAIN. HE KEEPS RIDING, GAINING MO-MENTUM. SOON HE DOES THE IMPOSSIBLE—HE HOLDS BOTH ARMS STRAIGHT OUT FROM HIS BODY—STILL PRANCING AS THOUGH RIDING A BUCKING HORSE WITH NO HANDS—THE SPIR-IT-DANCERS MOTION HIM OUTSIDE.) Spirit Horse—if there is one—(ELI ROMPS SEVERAL TIMES WITH HIS ARMS OUT, BUT DOESN'T FOLLOW THE SPIRIT-DANCERS.) Ah yes—I'm the Great Pretender—(AS ELI KEEPS 'RIDING,' HE CHANGES—FOR A MO-MENT HE RIDES IN THE SPIRIT, SOMEHOW TRANSFORMED, BUT SOON HAS TO TURN AND WALK TO THE BACK WALL OF THE GARAGE, DIZZY. HE STANDS THERE A WHILE UNTIL HE STARTS TO RECOVER.) What am I doing? (LOOKS AROUND.) What does keep me here? (HE STILL HAS TO STEADY HIMSELF AGAINST THE WALL.) Virgene's delightful beaver stew? (ELI LOOKS DOWN AT HIS DIRTY SHIRT. HE STAYS AT THE BACK OF THE GARAGE UNTIL HE FEELS STRENGTH, THEN STARTS TO WALK OUT WHERE THE SPIRIT-DANCERS WAIT FOR HIM. VIRGENE AND QUANNAH INTERCEPT HIS ATTEMPT TO LEAVE.)

Quannah
You're not going anywhere, Eli.

Eli
I don't want you girls telling me—

Quannah
I promised our mother when she died that I would help you if I could. Her last words were about you—YOU! I was with her all the time, but it was ELI— (SHE HITS HER HANDS TO HER THIGHS.)

Virgene
I can't stand to see you go through the DT's again, Eli.

Eli
Afraid you couldn't handle me yourself? You got Quannah on your side. The itinerant horse doctor—is your face-paint yellow too? (HE TRIES TO PINCH HER CHIN, BUT SHE BACKS AWAY FROM HIM AND HE ALMOST LOSES HIS BALANCE.) I'm just going to take a walk up the road.

Virgene
To Factor's or the nearest liquor store.

#### Eli

I don't have money.

#### Virgene

When has that stopped you? (ELI TRIES TO STEP PAST THEM, BUT THEY BLOCK HIS EXIT.) You've already got a court hearing ahead of you, Eli. You're not going to have another disorderly on your record—you haven't got room for any more, chief.

#### Eli

You can't keep me here.

#### Virgene

Just watch us.

#### Eli

There's better looking women—

#### Virgene

(ANGRY.) Then get strong enough so you can walk down the road and go after them.

#### Eli

(TAUNTS HER.) I have before—

#### Quannah

Come on, Eli—'Mother's precious.' Come back in the garage.

#### Eli

No.

#### Quannah

We could go in the house and watch television.

#### Eli

Shit.

#### Quannah

Go to sleep on the couch while we do our beading.

#### Eli

Life doesn't get much better than that.

#### Quannah

The June pow wow is coming. (ELI SHOOTS TWICE AT HIS HEAD.)

**Virgene**
I'm going to tell them I encouraged you to drive.

**Quannah**
They'll let you come home with us again—

**Virgene**
I should be the one going to jail. I wanted you to drive—maybe it was my idea.

**Eli**
Nothing is ever your idea—(HE LEANS ON QUANNAH FOR A MO-MENT)—but to have me here incopat—

**Virgene**
Incapacitated.

**Eli**
Damn—I can't stand this.

**Quannah**
If I can stand my life—always losing—even my own children to my former husband after he straightened out—then you can stand yours, little brother.

**Eli**
(HER TAUNTS ENRAGE HIM.) Get out of my way!

**Quannah**
Not when I posted bail again—

**Virgene**
(QUIETLY.) No, Eli. (SHE AND QUANNAH STAND IN HIS WAY AGAIN. ELI STRUGGLES TO GET PAST THEM. WHEN THEY WON'T MOVE, HE TRIES AGAIN TO STRUGGLE AWAY FROM THEM, BUT HE CAN'T FREE HIMSELF FROM THEIR GRIP. HE GETS ROUGHER, TRYING TO TRIP THEM, FINALLY PUSHING THEM ASIDE. EVENTU-ALLY HE GOES LIMP AND TRIES TO PULL THEM DOWN WITH HIS WEIGHT. ON THE DIRT FLOOR OF THE GARAGE, HE TRIES TO GET UP, BUT THEY HOLD HIM DOWN. HE BUCKS AS THOUGH A RODEO HORSE, BUT HE CAN'T THROW THE WOMEN. WHEN HE TRIES TO STRIKE THEM, VIRGENE STRADDLES HIS CHEST AND HOLDS HIS ARMS OUT FROM HIS SIDES. QUANNAH STRADDLES HIS LEGS SO HE CAN'T KICK.)

Eli
Aaaaahhhhh! (HE GROANS WITH THE EFFORT OF TRYING TO PUSH
OFF THE TWO WOMEN, BUT CANNOT. MEANWHILE, JAKE LOOKS
UP.)

Jake
You need help with your reluctant tenant?

Quannah
Our nightmare made visible.

Eli
Get them off me.

Quannah
Will you be a good boy?

Jake
Come on, Quannah. That doesn't help.

Quannah
Neither does his interruptions in my life. (SHE GETS OFF HER
BROTHER.)

Eli
I'm ready to leave. What have you got going for you anyway—the
Pillsbury Fuck-off?

Jake
She's busy keeping all of them bingo cards she plays at once.

Virgene
(STILL HOLDING HIM DOWN.) You're not leaving, Eli. I care too
much about you—I just wish I knew why. (SHE STAYS ON HIS
CHEST LOOKING AT HIM. HE STOPS STRUGGLING.)

Eli
I could have married you once, but chose my wife.

Virgene
I still care about you, Eli. No matter how it hurts.

Eli
Then you'd better be careful. It may come alive yet. (VIRGENE LETS
GO OF HIS ARMS.) Would you run from me?

>            Virgene
Would you chase me if I did?

>              Eli
Damn. You always got me with your words. (SHE STANDS UP AND
HE SITS AGAINST THE BACK OF THE GARAGE AGAIN, HOLDING HIS
HEAD.)

>             Jake
What's the matter?

>              Eli
Just dizzy again. (JAKE SITS WITH HIM. HE TAKES THE CEDAR OUT
OF THE POUCH ON HIS BELT AND LIGHTS IT ON THE DIRT FLOOR
OF THE GARAGE. WHEN A THIN TRAIL OF SMOKE RISES, JAKE
WASHES IT OVER HIS HEAD WITH HIS HANDS FOR PURIFICATION.
VIRGENE AND QUANNAH DO THE SAME, THEN ELI. JAKE CHANTS.
QUANNAH PULLS THE STRING ON THE LIGHT BULB IN THE GA-
RAGE AND THEY ARE IN THE DARK EXCEPT FOR THE MOONLIGHT
COMING IN THE WINDOW AND BETWEEN THE WIDE BOARDS OF
THE GARAGE.)

>             Jake
We thank you, Great Spirit, for moving among us with your spurs.
Cleanse us from alcohol, purge us with your Drain-O. May we feel
the power of your Spirit which is stronger than drink. (THERE IS A
MOMENT OF SILENCE. QUANNAH SITS DOWN BY JAKE. VIRGENE
STILL STANDS. THE LIGHT FROM THE WINDOW FALLS ACROSS HER
DRESS.)

>              Eli
(HE MOANS.) I can't make it, Jake. I watched the women bead
today. When their steady hands pushed the needle through those
tiny holes in the beads, I shuddered. It was like I was getting the
tremors again. I thought of the holes—they kept getting bigger and
bigger—they swallowed me. I tried to walk through them as if I were
the needle and I shook so bad I couldn't aim myself—

>            Virgene
Why didn't you say something, Eli?

>              Eli
I'm staying with you. I can't tell you what to do.

>             Jake
Yeah. Quannah's got to finish beading her tennis shoes before the

pow wow.

### Virgene
Listen, Bullet Proof—you're supposed to be leading us as a Medicine Man.

### Jake
As usual, Eli, they tell us what we're supposed to do.

### Quannah
It seems to me you need to be told.

### Jake
I want you to sit here, Eli, and tell me what you think of in the dark.

### Eli
Nothing.

### Jake
What is the nothing like?

### Eli
It's a big hole—a dark place in myself I slip through. I can't help it. All the roads point down to it. I try to walk, but slip toward it. And then I'm through the hole, falling in space. I whirl until I'm dizzy, then nauseous. There're dark figures hovering over me—clowns with striped faces. Stick horses spurting sawdust. I feel like I'm going round and around. I feel grooves move under my feet. Then the dark figures again. (THE SPIRIT-DANCERS DANCE.) This time they're things I've never seen—(THE SPIRIT-DANCERS PUT ON MASKS.) They creep down from their ledge where I thrash in space. They take my fingers in their mouths. I try to hit them away but I can't. They eat my arms and legs—(ELI MOANS AS THE SPIRIT-DANCERS CHEW ON HIS FINGERS.) AHHHHHHHHhhhh! (HE TRIES TO STAND AND RUN FROM THE GARAGE, BUT JAKE HOLDS HIM BACK—FIRST HE GRABS HIM BY THE LEG, THEN GETS A GRIP AROUND THE TRUNK OF HIS BODY.)

### Virgene
(SHE HOLDS HER HANDS TO HER FACE.) Oh, God, I can't stand to hear him. (SHE LEAVES THE GARAGE. THE MOONLIGHT COMING IN THE WINDOW FALLS ON JAKE AND ELI. JAKE HOLDS ELI IN HIS ARMS. SOON, ELI CEASES HIS STRUGGLE TO LEAVE. THEN JAKE SWEEPS THE CEDAR SMOKE OVER HIM AND CHANTS. ELI SOBS IN HIS ARMS AND JAKE ROCKS HIM.)

### Quannah

(SHE REACTS BY WALKING OUTSIDE ALSO. SHE STANDS NEAR THE BUSH WITH VIRGENE.) I'm taking care of him—just like mother asked. Do I have children? They are with their father and step-mother. Do I have anyone calling me? No. I have a brother who has slipped over the edge of the earth. I can't bring him back. What can anyone do? Is there anything?—(PAUSE.) I will be like you, Virgene, and say he will make it back to us. I will watch him tumble in the sky and say he is with us. I will speak words I don't know. Words of hope to him. (SHE LEANS AGAINST THE CLOTHESLINE POLE AND HUMS TO THE SPIRIT. MEANWHILE IN THE GARAGE, ELI HAS STOPPED CRYING AND JAKE NO LONGER ROCKS HIM. ELI IS ALSO HUMMING NOW AS HE TRIES TO HOLD ONTO THE PRESENT WORLD.)

### Jake

Ask the Great Spirit into your hollowness. He created the earth out of nothing. That's what your name means, Eli. Elijah—the Great Spirit is God. (QUANNAH HOLDS TO THE CLOTHESLINE POLE IN THE YARD. VIRGENE STANDS BESIDE HER.) Elijah was the one who called fire down from heaven. Then he left in a chariot of fire! Look around you at the spirits hovering in the garage—the prophets—Christ himself is behind you—

### Virgene

(PUTS HER HAND ON QUANNAH'S SHOULDER.) He may make it tonight. (QUANNAH NODS.) This's hard for me—

### Quannah

Well, it's hard for me too. I grew up with him. He was always getting in trouble. I behaved myself. When is it going to be my time to stomp my feet and throw fits and have everyone rush to me? Why is he more important than me?

### Virgene

He's not, Quannah.

### Quannah

I think I'll decide to go off and drink. Yes, that will be the outcome of Bullet Proof's ceremony this night—

### Virgene

Then go.

### Quannah

What a waste it is. And the only men you get is the kind hanging on you for one night—

### Virgene

Jake comes in your back window more than one night.

### Quannah

You don't have to worry about Eli going anywhere—he can't climb up a step much less the back window. You pick such lost causes—

### Virgene

He's not lost—

### Quannah

You have such noble goals. I've never found anything to be noble about.

### Virgene

Eli's had no one to follow like Jake has—only Sirloin always stealing that Steak House bull—or riding up Main Street with those wigs tied to him as if they were scalps—

### Quannah

What are you holding out for?

### Virgene

Leave me alone. I could go off and leave you and that Holy Man who climbs in your back window. Then who would help you pay the rent? I could leave you with Eli hanging by a thread—

### Quannah

Why don't you look for a man who suits you?

### Virgene

Eli will—when has Jake taken you out to eat?—or asked you to dance?

### Quannah

I haven't expected him to.

### Virgene

I haven't expected much from Eli either. I just remember the fun we had before it all changed. Before Sirloin was killed—when all of us were together. What happened to all those years? I'd work all day at the dress store. My biggest worry was finding something pretty to wear that night. We'd stomp-dance at the pow wows. Or we'd drink at Factor's. You and your former husband. Sirloin and me. Jake and me. Eli and me. Eli and his former wife. Everyone and me. No one and me. We'd sit at Sirloin's cabin while the men played cards and you and I and the other girls talked on the front porch until the men came out—

Quannah

Usually drunk—tripping over the pointed toes on their cowboy boots.

Virgene

And now Sirloin is dead and others have disappeared—and Jake is out in the garage trying to pull Eli through another night. This time Eli is going to make it.

Quannah

How do you know?

Virgene

It's his last chance. He wouldn't stop before that. He'd live every minute he could.

Quannah

It's been his last chance since he was born. I remember how he tormented me—he'd hide my doll or ride his stick horse through my jacks game. That broomstick horse—maybe it was from a rummage sale or the church gave it to him—they were always coming out with coats or shoes that didn't fit—but this stick horse—it probably made him want to ride in the rodeo. He didn't get far—I can remember him stiff as the stick on his toy horse the next day. Always without money to pay his next entry fees. He ended up as a clown—

Virgene

I don't want to hear what Eli did 20 years ago—

Quannah

Come on, Virgene, hang it up. You're holding out for something that won't ever happen—

Virgene

No. Then I'd be like you.

#### Eli
Ahhhhmmmm.

#### Virgene
Eli's riding again. Aren't you going to run to him? (VIRGENE LEAVES QUANNAH AT THE CLOTHESLINE POLE AND GOES INTO THE GARAGE. SHE TURNS ON THE LIGHT.)

#### Jake
(QUICKLY.) Turn off the light!

#### Eli
No. I want the light for a moment. (HE RUBS HIS EYES.) —The days and nights fly past. They flash a few times like a light bulb and then they're gone.

#### Jake
Sitting here in the dark, I saw the spirits in the garage.

#### Eli
I saw little pieces of light flying through the garage. I saw hollow crates like letters that could make words. There were so many of them—

#### Virgene
There's nothing wrong with the sober life. You can get a driver's license—

#### Eli
I've spent 20 years getting tickets and staying in trouble. They'll never give my license back.

#### Virgene
When you've got your head back they will—

#### Eli
The spirits were dancing like snow across the road. There was a dry snow last winter—it waved back and forth across the pavement behind the cars—it was the spirits in their white dresses—(ELI SEES QUANNAH ENTER THE GARAGE)—dancing in beaded tennis shoes.

#### Quannah
If you passed up one chance to make fun of me—if just once—

#### Jake
Leave him alone, Quannah.

## Quannah

(SHE TURNS ON HIM.) And you, Medicine Man—you got just as much of the human in you—maybe more because I don't pretend to be any holy woman. I let my husband have the children because he wanted them—

## Jake

Quannah, you were having trouble taking care of them. Nathan was always running off. You were sick. They were sick—hungry. Howard's got a wife now who wanted them. They can take better care of them—

## Quannah

Than me! Their own mother! What do you know? You haven't had children. None of you—Eli never took care of his—it was the same as not having them—you're all busy getting drunk and trying to pull one another through the knots you make for yourselves.

## Jake

When do the children bother you, but when you're mad at something else—mainly yourself?

## Quannah

So now I've got the child back that I've always had. (SHE TURNS TO ELI.)—Only now he's getting more of a burden than I can handle—why don't you take him to your house, Jake, since you have such a gift for caring—(QUANNAH LEAVES THE GARAGE AND STANDS AT THE BUSH WITH HER ARMS FOLDED.)

## Eli

She's right. I've wanted to be like her. The Silver Pullet. Buck-buck. (HE IMMITATES A HEN.) Yes. She can live life. She can get right out of bed every morning and eat her Shredded Wheat with four spoonfulls of sugar on it, and get to her job on time. It means something to her! What could it mean to me? I stay awake thinking about it. (HE HOLDS HIS HEAD.) How can she do it?—my own sister. How can you, Virgene?

## Virgene

There's nothing else but this, Eli—until we're angels flying around in heaven. It isn't so bad here, Eli. You get up. You work. It's dinner. You watch television. Sleep. Then it's another day.

## Eli

My God! What pulls you on? Where's the meaning? Our land and our way of life was taken. Our language. The words that come to replace it are dead! I see cemetery flowers when I smoke the pipe— I'm supposed to speak another man's language. I'm supposed to read and know how to write it!! I'm supposed to stand in court and listen to their words as though they were law?

### Virgene
They are, Eli.

### Eli
No! They're meaningless. I'm supposed to live without my life, but someone else's idea of what life is? This isn't my culture. These aren't my rules.

### Virgene
So you're going to jump into your clown-barrel and suffocate? That shows what power they have—and what little you have— (JAKE GOES TO THE WINDOW AND SEES QUANNAH STANDING OUTSIDE AT THE BUSH. HE GOES TO HER. MEANWHILE VIRGENE AND ELI TALK, THOUGH THE AUDIENCE CAN'T HEAR THEIR WORDS.)

### Quannah
When have you ever done anything for me except crawl in my bed and the next day I see you in the cafe and you don't even buy me a cup of coffee?

### Jake
I don't want everybody knowing your bed can be crawled into.

### Quannah
That's a lame excuse.

### Jake
Quannah, you always got a mouth full of barbed wire.

### Quannah
And you always got five roads out of every situation you get yourself into. You could let them know you're the only one—

### Jake
How can I be sure of that?

### Quannah
Nobody else comes around. Who'd want three kids to take care of?

Jake

You don't have them anymore.

Quannah

And still no one comes but you.

Jake

You give everybody so much guff.

Quannah

I don't want anybody else here but you.

Jake

You got a strange way of showing it.

Quannah

Maybe if something went right. Maybe if I had something to feel good about—even myself.

Jake

(HE TAKES HER IN HIS ARMS.) It's true. I can talk to the spirit world in the pipe ceremony and think what a Holy Man I am, and the next night I'm crawling to you—

Quannah

Isn't that what it's like to be human? Didn't we all crawl out of the same log? You just think you're up there above us all. (SHE BACKS AWAY FROM JAKE.) That's why you get mad at me sometimes. That's why you ignore me at the cafe. I'm the reminder you're not only a Holy Man—

Virgene

(SHE COMES OUTSIDE.) Eli is restless again, Jake.

Quannah

—Always him. (SHE GOES INTO THE GARAGE, LOOKS AT ELI WHO SITS WITH HIS HEAD IN HIS HANDS AND DOESN'T SEE HER. SOON SHE GOES TO HIM AND SITS BESIDE HIM ON THE GARAGE FLOOR.)

Virgene

(SHE STAYS OUTSIDE A MOMENT WITH JAKE.) You use Quannah—

Jake

She enjoys it too.

### Virgene

But it still seems to be to your benefit. She comes away feeling used —and you crow.

### Jake

Who's crowing?

### Virgene

—Until, of course you have to bring around the pipe and then you're humble but the spirits still talk to you. You tell us where to go. You show us the road and remind us of the visions of the Fathers, the earth longing for its healing—you can even make sense of Christianity. You tie it up with the fragments we got left of our own religion—maybe that's the new ground we start from—you really are bulletproof—you always make it through without wounds—

### Jake

We're ALL in pain because the earth is.

### Virgene

I've always looked up to you, Jake. I don't care how many times you crawl into Quannah's window. I just wish you'd knock on her front door for a change. Why don't you buy her a cup of coffee? Why don't you come and sit down by us in the cafe? Why, you could even buy her a chicken-fried steak one night.

### Jake

It would become a habit. Then how would I not do it the next night?

### Virgene

We're all on our own here—when we get to economics. But it's when we get to the spirit—oh, that's when the men are superior—

### Jake

You sound like Quannah.

### Virgene

I've lived with her too long I guess. In fact— (VIRGENE STARTS TO SAY SOMETHING, CHANGES HER MIND, THEN STARTS TO SPEAK AGAIN.) How many times have you eaten with us, Jake? I mean, sure, you bring Eli home and we'd be sitting there at the table, and ah, come on, sit down it's no trouble and when the food was gone you quit eating. I mean, both Quannah and I work. There's not much rent to this place on the edge of Tahlequah. I don't rely on church clothes anymore. I don't have to go to the hand-me-down store though I like the clothes there. In fact, I got this dress there— (SHE SEEMS IN A QUANDRY AS TO WHAT TO SAY.) I need to shorten it a bit. I don't know—(SHE GETS ANGRY WITH HERSELF IN GETTING SIDETRACKED FROM THE POINT SHE WANTS TO MAKE.)— then you and Eli come along again—when you need us—who are we to you? (AT THIS POINT, ELI LOOKS UP. HE HEARS VIRGENE'S ANGER AT JAKE. HE HOLDS HIS HEAD AGAIN. THE SPIRIT-DANCERS TRY TO SEDUCE HIM INTO FOLLOWING THEM AGAIN.)

### Eli
I got to get out of here. (QUANNAH REACHES TO HIM, BUT HE JERKS AWAY.)

### Virgene
We're not a motorcycle sidecar to your antics—what do I get from having a drunk on my hands—what does Quannah— ?

### Eli
(HE JUMPS UP OFF THE GARAGE FLOOR, RUNS OUT.) AHHHHHH-HH! (HIS WAR CRY.) I can't stand it—

### Quannah
JAKE!! (THEY RUN AFTER HIM AND DRAG HIM BACK. THE SPIRIT-DANCERS HAVE A TUG-OF-WAR WITH THEM.)

### Virgene
Where does he get the strength?

### Jake
It's his will to break from this world.

### Quannah
(THEY HOLD HIM DOWN ON THE GROUND.) I can't hold him.

### Virgene
Here, tie him to the clothesline pole. (THEY RAISE HIM TO THE CLOTHESLINE POLE. HIS BODY IS STIFF AS THEY LIFT HIM FROM THE GROUND. THE SPIRIT-DANCERS LEAVE. VIRGENE GRABS THE LOOSE END OF THE CLOTHESLINE. JAKE HOLDS ELI TO THE POST. QUANNAH LIFTS HIS ARMS TO THE CROSS-SHAPED POLE. VIRGENE WRAPS THE LINE AROUND HIS BODY AND OUTSTRETCHED ARMS.)

### Eli
I have to have a drink—(HE STRUGGLES, BUT CANNOT FREE HIMSELF.) AAAAhhhhhhh! (HE LETS OUT A CRY OF ANGUISH.)

Let me GO!! (HE JIGGLES UP AND DOWN.) EEEEEEEEEaaaaaa!

### Quannah
(PLEADING.) Jake—

### Eli
CAW! CAW! (HIS TERRIBLE CROW-VOICE AGAIN.)

### Jake
Hold on, Quannah. (HE HOLDS HER BUT SHE SINKS TO THE GROUND.)

### Quannah
He's gone too far—

### Eli
ELA SABAK TAAAAAMI! (STILL STRUGGLING TO GET LOOSE FROM THE CLOTHESLINE POLE.)

### Virgene
(PANICKED.) Jesus. Why don't we let him go? I'll drive him to Factor's myself and let him drink himself to death. Tonight if possible—then he'd get it over with.

### Jake
No, Virgene.

### Eli
I don't want to go into that black hole. (HIS BODY JIGGLES UP AND DOWN AGAIN.) EEEEEooooo! Giddy-up, stick horse. EE-EEEEEEOOOOOOOOOOOO!!!!!

### Virgene
Don't let him fall, Jake.

### Jake
He's not leaving—

### Eli
I have to GET OUT of here!!!!!!

### Quannah
I could just get my pistol and shoot him. (SHE HOLDS HER HANDS TO HER FACE BECAUSE SHE CAN'T LOOK AT ELI STRUGGLING.)

#### Jake
(HE CHANTS CALMLY TO ELI.) Hey oo oo oo. Hey oo oo oo.
(VIRGENE JOINS HIM. SOON QUANNAH IS HUMMING ALSO.)

#### Virgene
Hey cah hey oo.

#### Quannah
Ah mey ah mey.

#### Jake
The cedar smoke is washing over you, Eli. Feel it on your head. (HE
BRUSHES HIS HAND ACROSS ELI'S HEAD.) The spirits are holding
up your arms. Your back is straight as a post. You are strong. (THE
WOMEN ARE STILL CHANTING.)

#### Eli
Aaaahhhh yay yay—(HIS CHANTING AT FIRST IS LIKE A GROWL IN
HIS CHEST.) Aahhhh—(HE GROWS CALMER AS HE LISTENS TO
JAKE.)

#### Jake
You're not going to fall—not right now, anyway.

#### Virgene
(SHE BEGINS THE TWO-STEP AROUND THE CLOTHESLINE POLE.
JAKE IS CHANTING AGAIN, MOVING HIS HANDS AS THOUGH HE
BEATS THE DRUM. JAKE'S MOVEMENTS ARE MORE EXAGGERATED
THAN THE WOMEN'S. VIRGENE STILL CHANTS.) Hey cah hey ho.
(SOON QUANNAH STANDS AND JOINS HER, BUT SOON DANCES
NEAR JAKE.)

#### Jake
Hey yey yey yey.

#### Quannah
Hey yey yey yey.

#### Eli
AH YAY AHH AHH!

#### Virgene
Hey yey yey yey. (THEY CONTINUE THEIR DANCING AND CHANT-
ING FOR A MOMENT. THEN JAKE LOOKS AT ELI.)

### Jake

By the powers from the north and south and east and west—you are
Eli, a warrior. Come down from your pole and live among us.
(VIRGENE, JAKE AND QUANNAH DRAG ELI FROM THE CLOTHES-
LINE POLE BACK INTO THE GARAGE. HIS BODY LIMP AS THEY LAY
HIM ON THE DIRT FLOOR. THEY SIT QUIETLY FOR A MOMENT,
THROUGH VIRGENE STILL HUMS TO HERSELF. SOON JAKE LOOKS
STRANGELY AT QUANNAH.) You have a gun, Quannah?

### Quannah

Yes. I keep it under my bed in a pink beaded case.

### Virgene

We live here by ourselves. Don't you think it's a good idea? (SHE
LEANS DOWN TO PUSH THE HAIR BACK FROM ELI'S FACE. JAKE
SHAKES HIS HEAD.) Eli—can you hear me? (ELI GROANS.) You're
going to make it tonight. The worst is over—(JAKE MOANS AGAIN
AND PULLS UP INTO A BALL TO AVOID VIRGENE.)

### Quannah

The worst is never over. The worst is always waiting like a row of
aluminum cans on the fence.

### Virgene

Some nights we're sitting out there on the back steps. (SHE MO-
TIONS TOWARD THE HOUSE.) The bugs chirp in the woods. The
twigs snap with the footsteps of a rabbit or opossum. The stars are
wide-eyed—but that road still disappears into the dark. Sometimes
you think you hear a car stop somewhere. You think they're getting
out and crawling up the road in the dark. About the time you get up
to go in the house, they jump from the bush—

### Quannah

Except I have my pistol tied against my leg—right above my beaded
tennis shoe. (SHE LOOKS AT JAKE.) Then pow. POW!

### Virgene

And I say to Quannah, I think you got 'em. Yes, even when Eli is
here, we live by ourselves. Unless he comes back to himself—and
I see him like he was before—years ago—when I thought there was
no man like Elijah. Even when you're in Quannah's room for the
night, Jake—it still feels like we're here by ourselves.

### Jake

You haven't known when I've been in Quannah's room—

### Virgene
(SHE IGNORES HIM.) Yes, we're here on the end of this road by ourselves—

### Jake
Have you ever used that gun, Quannah?

### Quannah
I'm going to get it out sometime. Just for practice. (ELI TRIES TO SIT UP, AND VIRGENE HELPS HIM.) Then I'll be ready for the next thing that creeps up the road. Some spook wearing a headband or—

### Jake
I'm going to keep coming to your house.

### Eli
You don't know what a spook is, Quannah. Neither of you do. (HE BRUSHES THE HAIR OUT OF HIS FACE.) You don't know what it's like having them in your head where no gun can get to them. Each night they crawl up the road with their headlight eyes. They go right into you and there's nothing you can do. You hear their voices call you—you feel their fingernails scratching the inside of your eyes— making their cave drawings on your skull.

### Quannah
Shit—I'm tired of your spook stories. (SHE PACES THE GARAGE.) It's how you get out of living. You can't be responsible for anything because the spooks got you. You're the spook! Eli in his chariot going off to heaven. Elijah on his stick horse—

### Virgene
How can you talk like that after—(SHE HOLDS HER ARM OUT TOWARD THE CLOTHESLINE POLE.)

### Quannah
(QUIETLY.) He was always busy with the next world. So I got to do everything he should have been doing in this one. He could clown his way out of anything. Or put on such a horror show you didn't ask anything of him. He's the space man, all right. He's sure not made for this world. (SHE SLAPS HER HANDS TO HER THIGHS IN BOTH ANGER AND DESPERATION FOR HER BROTHER.) I can do things like cook his meals and wash the vomit off his shirts. I can leave my child's birthday party and visit Eli in the hospital where the police have just taken him. What matters other than Eli's condition? He's just like old Norvall, our father, was. I know what it is to lose

everything too. Does Eli ever rush to me? (ELI MOANS AGAIN.) When Sirloin died, Virgene and I had to go to the funeral parlor with his clothes. We had to hold up Eli to walk past the casket. We had to—

#### Eli
Slobber on, sister. You've always held up a horror mask as a mirror for me. Remember the brown paper sacks we used to paint in school?

#### Jake
Yes, the war masks—we'd cut holes for eyes—

#### Eli
I'd have trouble getting mine spooky enough, but Quannah, she was an artist at it—a medicine woman.

#### Quannah
Piss on yourself, Eli.

#### Eli
I'd rather be drunk than here with you—

#### Quannah
I'd rather have my former husband bothering me than be here— (SHE LOOKS OUT THE WINDOW.)

#### Virgene
(INTERRUPTS.) Jake, light your pipe before we have an uprising— what did you come here for? Just to watch them so the heat is off you? (SHE PULLS THE LIGHT CORD OFF.)

#### Jake
(HE PULLS IT ON AGAIN.) The pipe ceremony isn't a hoedown we're doing. The air has to be right—(PAUSE.) Right now the garage is full of our doings.

#### Virgene
Like pigeons, I guess. If we waited until we were perfect, we'd have no need of your spirits.

#### Jake
They aren't my spirits and they don't hang around all the time.

#### Virgene

You said you saw them before—jumping in their little white dresses like popcorn. (SHE STANDS NEAR THE WINDOW WITH QUANNAH.)

#### Eli

Snowflakes.

#### Jake

They've got to be spirits if they stick with us—

#### Quannah

Isn't our weakness their strength? Don't they just love it when we're hanging by our toenails—about to go off the edge of the earth in our Volkswagon—screaming our little lungs out?

#### Jake

Great Spirit—forgive us this night. (ELI ROLLS UP IN A BALL AGAIN— THIS TIME VIRGENE GOES TO HIM AND HE RESTS HIS HEAD IN HER LAP. ONCE IN A WHILE SHE STROKES HIS HEAD.)

#### Eli

Make me satisfied with NyQuil.

#### Jake

You remember, Eli, after that snow last winter—when the wind blew it all over the road. After that, there was an ice storm—and I was driving too fast to Virgene and Quannah's and the car skidded off the road and down the embankment.

#### Eli

And you were screaming, 'Jesus.' You were screaming, 'Stone man, old giver of our medicine.'

#### Jake

I had our ass covered.

#### Eli

Forward and backward.

#### Jake

Yo. And I tried to stomp-dance the car out of the ditch, but finally had to walk back up the road to the highway to get a tow truck. It didn't spin and spin its wheels to pull us out, Eli. No, the tow truck had a crank on the back of it, and the man hooked a chain to our car and the crank turned and the chain pulled our DeSoto out of the ditch. (JAKE TURNS OFF THE LIGHT IN THE GARAGE. THE BRIGHT

MOON SHINES IN THE WINDOW AND BETWEEN THE OLD BOARDS OF THE GARAGE MAKING STRIPES ACROSS THE FLOOR. THE SPIRIT-DANCERS SAUNTER AROUND THE GARAGE.) Before you know it, Eli, the Great Spirit's going to pull you out. But you got to hang on. You had to wait in the car until I came back with the tow truck.

### Eli

I was drunk, Jake. I hardly remember. (HE BRUSHES VIRGENE'S HAND AWAY WHEN SHE STROKES HIS HEAD.) Yeah—I remember the snow—we don't get enough of it in Oklahoma to fill Quannah's bird bath. But the ice—it seems like words to me—words that move around it in the snow. Sometimes I hear words, Jake, but I don't know what they're saying—they're not talking to me, but go right by—like cars when I'm drunk and trying to hitchhike back to Virgene.

### Jake

You do remember the ice. The truck went by the car at first. It was so far down in the ditch I didn't see it, and had to tell the man to back up. (VIRGENE STROKES ELI'S HEAD AGAIN WHILE JAKE TALKS.)

### Eli

How'd we pay for it?

### Jake

I don't think we did.

### Quannah

You both got bills lined up to Texas.

### Eli

(ELI TAKES VIRGENE'S HAND TO KEEP HER FROM STROKING HIS HEAD.) Don't, Virgene. I'm strung out—that makes the quivers run through me. I got enough of them already. (VIRGENE GOES TO THE WINDOW AND STANDS WITH HER ARM AROUND QUANNAH. JAKE SITS ON THE FLOOR WITH ELI.) I want a drink, Jake. I might forget for as long as it takes your voice to reach my ear, but it comes back on me again—(THE SPIRIT-DANCERS RETURN. THEY CRAWL QUIETLY ALONG THE BACK OF THE GARAGE.) It's coming now.

### Jake

(JAKE IGNORES HIM AND BEGINS TO CHANT.) Hey ay ay ay. Hey ay ay ay. (THE SPIRIT-DANCERS DANCE, FACING THE BACK OF THE GARAGE AT FIRST, WHICH MAKES THEM BLEND IN WITH THE GARAGE WALL, ALMOST INVISIBLE, THEN THEY TURN AROUND IN THEIR HORROR MASKS.)

#### Eli
EEEEEEeeeee! (HE STRUGGLES AGAINST JAKE, BUT JAKE WON'T
LET GO.)

#### Jake
Great Spirit, bless us. Don't wipe us out like Quannah hosing the
turds out of her bird bath.

#### Eli
I got to get out of here—it's like I'm in jail—(THE SPIRIT-DANCERS
TOUCH ELI'S FACE, HIS HANDS. ONE KISSES HIM.) EEEEooooww-
ww! (THEY STILL CAN'T PULL ELI AWAY. VIRGENE AND QUANNAH
BOTH COME TO HELP JAKE HOLD ELI.)

#### Jake
Hey ay hay ay. (THE WOMEN JOIN IN HIS CHANTING. THE SPIRIT-
DANCERS LEAVE ELI ALONE.)

#### Virgene
Hey ah a hay.

#### Quannah
Cau mah cay mah.

#### Eli
(WHEN HE'S CALMER, HE SPEAKS AGAIN, AND THEY STOP CHANT-
ING.) I see a line of light down my face, and another line across it.
My face is in four sections. The four quarters split. My face separates.
(HE HOLDS HIS HANDS TO HIS HEAD.) My left eye moves away from
my right eye. (ELI CRIES OUT.) One side of my mouth leaves the
other. EEEEEooooWWWWW! (ELI STRUGGLES AGAIN, JERKING
HIS LEGS. THE SPIRIT-DANCERS CIRCLE ELI AGAIN.)

#### Virgene
Aaaaahhhhh! (VIRGENE SCREAMS WITH HER HANDS OVER HER
EARS.) Stop him.

#### Jake
Leave him alone. He'll come out of it.

#### Quannah
I can't bear this. My mother used to protect me from Eli. I never saw
his ravings. If I heard them, she'd tell me they weren't as bad as
they sounded—but they are—(VIRGENE HOLDS QUANNAH AGAIN.)

### Eli

I'm four horses running away from each other in the arena. (HE MOANS AND HOLDS TO JAKE, SILENT AND NO LONGER STRUGGLING.)

### Jake

(JAKE LEANS OVER HIM.) I see the Great Spirit over us. Eli—I make you a prayer which is a medicine shirt—like the shirts the ancestors made in the Indian wars. Holy shirts. Ghost shirts painted with hands which made the warriors bulletproof. You know how the plains warriors rode into battle, and the bullets of the cavalry went by them. You hear the words, Eli. They work for you too. (ELI LAYS ON THE FLOOR, HIS ARMS OUTSTRETCHED FROM HIS BODY, HIS LEGS TOGETHER.) I hold my hands over your ears. I push the parts of your head back together. I hold your ears shut with my hands so the words do not roll back out. Be silent, Eli. Hear the words riding into your ears. They are strong warriors. They aim their bows and arrows to the voices in your head that lead you to drink. EE-EEEchow. The arrows strike the voices that bother you. They are dead, Eli. They are dead. I bind your head together. The four sections come back. You are inside that head. Eli—you are whole.

### Quannah

Ey mey mey mey.

### Virgene

Hey ey ey ey.

### Jake

We come to you, Great Spirit. We thank you for life. It's a full house you give us. (THE SPIRIT-DANCERS FACE THE BACK WALL OF THE GARAGE AND BECOME ALMOST INVISIBLE AGAIN.)

### Eli

Hay cah yey ha.

### Quannah

Hay cay yey ha.

### Virgene

Hay cah yey ha.

### Jake

I feel the spirit of peace—I felt it long ago when I was with my father in our ceremonies. The medicine men argued over which way to sit in the lodge. They argued over the old ways—they didn't want to change. My father said our lives had changed—our magic would also change—and it would still be magic. He would keep our medicine—it didn't matter by which ritual. It was faith in the magic that kept it going. I remember sitting by my father in the lodge. I felt his spirit press into me. I feel his spirit of peace to this day.

### Eli
Mah to cah ha. (THERE IS SADNESS AND LONGING IN ELI'S CHANT.)

### Quannah
(SHE CRIES.) I understand that my children are happy with their father. But I see a hollow place for me. The size of a bird bath. Fill it, Great Spirit, with your rain. I wasted my life. I sat in Factor's until he pushed me out to close. I didn't know what my children were doing. I wouldn't hold up my end of the stick. I was jealous of Eli. I let everything fall—

### Eli
I see Virgene and Quannah dancing together on Sirloin's porch while we played cards in his cabin. Then I lost my cards because I couldn't keep my eyes off Virgene's skirt. Her hips jiggled when she danced—

### Quannah
He's back to himself.

### Virgene
It's like the fairgrounds in Tulsa in this garage when I close my eyes. Somewhere in the back of my head, the lights still climb to the sky.

### Quannah
I think of the pow wow banner waving—the grand entry.

### Virgene
Now I'm thinking of the trip we took to California. (SHE LOOKS AT HER HANDS, TALKING MORE TO HERSELF THAN ELI, WHOM SHE ADDRESSES.) You remember, Eli, how Sirloin and you and I and one of Sirloin's girlfriends would be talking on the steps of his cabin, and all of a sudden someone would get an idea to go somewhere— and we'd get in the car and go—Chickasha, Oklahoma—Anadarko. Sometimes Texas or New Mexico. I remember the trip we took across the desert to California, and the 'Last Chance' Texaco station. I remember Sirloin in his bare feet dancing on the hot pavement.

### Eli

I see the 'Last Chance' sign too. I'm too near the hole. If I don't stop, the NOTHINGNESS will fill my head and I won't be able to come back to myself. I won't be able to think. I can almost feel it now. Jake—(HE STANDS AND JAKE STANDS THEN TOO SO ELI CAN LEAN ON HIM.) I break out in a sweat—I see a border of white flowers around the dark hole. Is it my grave?

### Quannah

Don't talk that way, Eli. (SHE HOLDS HER HANDS OVER HER EARS.) I want to think about dancing at the pow wow—

### Eli

Am I dying?

### Jake

I think you will if you keep drinking.

### Eli

Am I already dead?

### Jake

No. What does your name mean, Eli? (HE SITS DOWN BESIDE VIRGENE AND QUANNAH, LEAVING ELI STANDING BY HIMSELF IN THE GARAGE.)

### Eli

The Great Spirit is God. That's what my name means. That's what I mean. I take the white flowers I see and hold them to my chest. (PAUSE.) They are gone. But once—(HE HOLDS HIS SIDES AS THOUGH NAUSEOUS.) I was a boy—the flowers bloomed— delicate and white—I wanted to ride a horse in a rodeo. Round and around the arena. People clapping. My father smiling. Quannah playing some game.

### Quannah

Hang Man. You have to say the letters to spell the word I'm thinking of.

### Virgene

M.

### Quannah

No. Your head is on the gallows. (SHE DRAWS A CIRCLE ON AN IMAGINARY PIECE OF PAPER.)

Virgene

A.

Quannah

Yes. (SHE WRITES AN A.)

Virgene

V.

Quannah

No. The trunk of your body is on the gallows. (SHE DRAWS A STRAIGHT LINE DOWN FROM THE HEAD ON THE IMAGINARY PAPER.)

Virgene

H.

Quannah

No, Virgene. Guess the letters you use more often. Your arm is on the gallows. (SHE DRAWS A LINE OUT FROM THE TRUNK OF HER BODY.)

Virgene

S. (ELI BEGINS TO RIDE HIS STICK HORSE WHILE THEY PLAY.)

Quannah

Yes. (SHE WRITES AN S.)

Eli

Giddy up. (DEEP IN HIS THROAT.) Guddy up—up—up. (HE MAKES A COMIC RODEO RIDE.)

Virgene

(ELI STILL RIDES.) Ah—(SHE IS THINKING.) B.

Quannah

No. Your other arm is on the gallows. (SHE DRAWS ANOTHER LINE.)

Eli

Vowels, Virgene. Guess vowels—HOWELS from the bowels. (HE MAKES A WAR CRY. WAKES THE SPIRIT-DANCERS.) IIIIEEEEEEEE! I'm riding in the rodeo.

Quannah

You sound more like the rodeo clown. (ELI RIDES HIS STICK HORSE

THROUGH THEIR GAME.) Not a ceremonial clown who could help us laugh and understand—no, you're a barrel clown—

### Virgene
Quit it, Quannah.

### Quannah
You're telling me to quit? He's the one—

### Eli
I'm on my stick horse. The dimestore *harse*. The rodeo rodeo-er. I'm a jangling buckeroo. The Steak House bull on roller skates. Rohm. Rohm. (HE CLOWNS NOW AS IF THE STICK WERE A MOTORCYCLE.)

### Virgene
You're a real cowboy, Eli.

### Quannah
Your teeth glitter with rhinestones and you twang like a tin guitar. All you can do is guzzle firewater and snag girls behind the rodeo arena at night—

### Eli
(HE MOCKS THE GAME THE WOMEN PLAYED AS GIRLS.) Let me write something on a paper and fold it over and pass it to Virgene. Let her write something without seeing what I wrote. Then she folds the paper and passes it to Quannah. Quannah writes something without seeing what Virgene wrote. Then we'll unfold the paper and read what we've written. (HE PRANCES ON HIS STICK HORSE, STOMPING HIS FEET CLOSE TO THEM. THE SPIRIT-DANCERS RIDE TOO. THE WOMEN SCREAM AND BACK AWAY FROM ELI. QUANNAH HIDES UNDER THE SHELF. VIRGENE RUNS AND HOLD THE FENCE WIRE IN FRONT OF HER. ELI CHASES HER ON HIS HORSE.) Gitty up. Yup. Yup. Come on, Silver.

### Virgene
There's a word that comes to mind for you, Eli.

### Eli
(STILL ON HIS HORSE.) Does it start with a B?

### Virgene
No, an A. A vowel—think of the letters you use the most.

### Eli
A crow.

                    Quannah
Asshole.


                    Jake
Quannah. (HE TAKES HER ARM.)


                    Quannah
What did he ever do but mess up my games?


                        Eli
Mess up her games.


                    Quannah
On that stupid horse. A broomstick donkey.


                        Eli
Giddy up, Buckeroo.


                    Jake
You're not a girl anymore. (HE TRIES TO HOLD QUANNAH IN HIS
ARMS AS SHE WATCHES ELI, ANGRILY.)


                        Eli
CAW!! (THE SPIRIT-DANCERS CIRCLE IN HORROR MASKS. ELI
DANCES WITH THEM. VIRGENE TRIES AT TIMES TO PULL HIM
BACK. FINALLY HE STANDS WITH HIS ARMS AROUND HER.)


                    Quannah
(PUTS HER HANDS TO HER EARS.) It's not so bad to be so mad.


                    Jake
(LOOKS AT HER WITH SYMPATHY.) If I brought you some flowers—
what would you like?


                    Quannah
What would I do with flowers?


                    Jake
What do you want, Quannah? When you're through complaining?
When you're by yourself and everything is quiet?


                    Quannah
I want my children. I want my brother's howling to go away. I want
to be young again—I had a white dress once—a white buckskin
jingle dress. I remember walking with Eli in the entry parade at the

pow wow. My mother and father with us—when they weren't drunk. We were real people then.

### Eli
I see the demons in their beaded faces. (THE SPIRIT-DANCERS CONTINUE THEIR SEDUCTIVE DANCE.)

### Virgene
Ey mey mey mey.

### Eli
Don't leave me alone, Virgene, even at night.

### Virgene
I can't sleep with you, Eli. You thrash all night. Sometimes I smell the stagnant creek.

### Eli
When I was in the hospital I saw the drunks with their bellies swollen up like rotten fish on the bank.

### Virgene
I can almost see the spooks coming for you, Eli.

### Jake
What else do you want, Quannah?

### Quannah
I want you, Jake. But you're always slipping away.

### Jake
I'm always slipping back into your window, you mean.

### Quannah
I want to tell you to stay away. You'll always be leaving me, Coyote Man. I want to put the picture of your parents on the mantel with mine. I want your tobacco pouch there—your pipe.

### Jake
Hey—I got to keep moving around some, Quannah. You know a medicine man's got places to go.

### Quannah
How can you stay in your boundaries, Jake, when Eli's spilling over his?

**Jake**

Pretend I have some white flowers in my hand, Quannah, and I'm giving them to you.

**Quannah**

And some candy?

**Jake**

Some white flowers and a bag of Jolly Ranchers.

**Quannah**

Yes, my favorite.

**Jake**

Hard rock candy. Pure sugar.

**Quannah**

I used to love apples too. The white blossoms of them in spring.

**Jake**

Then I'm bringing you a bag of apples too.

**Quannah**

About the time I got used to you, you'd be gone.

**Jake**

You can't hold something all closed up in a plastic bag. You got to let things breathe.

**Quannah**

I would have trouble, Jake, with your kind of breathing. I remember when your mother and father had sweat lodge ceremonies. I remember other ceremonies—don't you want a place, Jake? We could have garage sales on Saturdays. Go bowling on Friday nights.

**Jake**

Sometimes I like to be on a bus, Quannah, riding through the country not knowing anyone. Not feeling connected. If I reach to you, Quannah, I might be like our car stuck in the ditch.

**Quannah**

We're getting older, Jake. You might not always want to ride the bus. You might like the ditch. We're the lawnchair club at the pow wows now. The slow dance at Factor's. (JAKE HOLDS HER IN HIS ARMS.)

#### Virgene
I want someone to hold me too, Eli. I don't know where we're going.

#### Quannah
You don't want to go with Eli.

#### Eli
The stick horse prances in the arena. His tail braided tight as a papoose on a cradle-board. His mane waves like tall cornstalks. *Sou-tache.*

#### Virgene
I feel like I'm with my father.

#### Jake
A spirit horse rides above the stick horse. The spirit horse paws the air. (HE LETS GO OF QUANNAH.) I see the sky above him. How bright the stars shine, Quannah. A lighted marquee! I see the end of the ages!! AHHHH! (HE MOANS.) The mountains pulled up by their roots. The oceans flopped on a spatula.

#### Quannah
And there beyond the planets—our hunting grounds with neon lights and a fry-bread booth.

#### Virgene
I want to see the ones in the hunting grounds—my mother and father. My father fishing.

#### Quannah
They're gone for now, Virgene. We have to live without them for a while.

#### Jake
But not forever. We'll see them again. I know Sirloin's there wearing a blonde wig and a 'rent-a-tux.' Yeah, even the bull on wheels has a halo. And the motorcycle with a coon-tail and mudflaps—now it's got retro-rockets.

#### Eli
Remember when we stole Sirloin's motorcycle and left a bicycle in his yard with playing cards clothes-pinned to the spokes.

#### Jake
And he rode it down Main Street and left it at the church for the

preacher's 'wheels.'

Virgene

Can a man eat fire and live?

Quannah

How far can he go and come back?

Virgene

Can a man be crucified and live?

Quannah

Eli does.

Eli

I'm thinking what I've done. The people I've let down. I want forgiveness.

Quannah

Ask your wife. Your children. The beaded rabbit queen.

Eli

Don't say that, Quannah. I see the spirits in their beaded masks. They're asking me to come. Their arms are outstretched to me. My crooked eye. My mouth filled with dust. I try to sweep the letters back. The words I knocked sideways, threw away. They come back to get me now. They make a HANG MAN of ME!! Letters I spilled all lined up. They take my arms and legs. (HE BEGINS TO PANIC AGAIN. HIS ARMS THRASH. THE SPIRIT-DANCERS HAVE GIANT ALPHABET LETTERS ON THEIR CHESTS. THEY LEAN DOWN TO ELI AGAIN. THEY KISS HIM, TOUCH HIS CROTCH. MOVE SEDUCTIVELY AROUND HIM.)

Virgene

Hold on, Eli.

Eli

Sirloin. Sir. Sir Loin. How does it feel to have the flowers over you? Pow. Pow. Old women in a Plymouth. Eeeeooowww.

Virgene

Sirloin wanted to be in the cemetery more than any of us.

Jake

Sirloin's not in the ground. No. He flew.

131

                              Eli
I'm flying out of here too.


                            Virgene
You won't come back. I'll be alone.


                              Eli
Jake and Quannah are with you. (THE SPIRIT-DANCERS MOVE
AROUND THE GARAGE. ONE PUTS HIS MOUTH ON ELI'S CROTCH.
QUANNAH CRAWLS TO THE SIDE OF THE GARAGE BEHIND THE
ROLL OF FENCEWIRE.)


                            Virgene
I want to share your wire quilt.


                              Eli
They're pulling me away, Jake.


                             Jake
Not yet, Eli.


                              Eli
Yes, I'm all jacked up—


                             Jake
Let them come. (JAKE HOLDS ELI DOWN. VIRGENE AND QUANNAH
HELP HIM. JAKE HOLDS HIS HEAD. QUANNAH HOLDS ONE ARM
OUTSTRETCHED FROM HIS BODY. VIRGENE HOLDS THE OTHER.)


                              Eli
There's nothing you can do. (THE SPIRIT DANCERS ARE ON ELI
SUCKING HIS EARS AND NECK AND OTHER PARTS). AAAAaaaaah-
hhheeee!! (ELI THRASHES.)


                            Virgene
We won't let them have you.


                            Quannah
Eli, hold on—


                              Eli
The dark hole! (ELI STILL THRASHES.)


                             Jake
Go down into it to come back—

#### Virgene
I can almost see them.

#### Quannah
Hey yey hey ho.

#### Eli
They gnaw my fingers. Eat my knuckles. My wrists. Up my ARMS!! O GOD!! The stick horse grazes my chest like grass. My heart. LUNGS!! My spine is open to the sky. My blood runs over the grease-paint on my rodeo clown face.

#### Jake
The spirit of peace leaves the hunting grounds to travel back to the earth. The spirit horse touches your legs and they are strong. It calls the blood back under your skin.

#### Virgene
Hey yey hey ho—

#### Quannah
It sews up the teeth-holes in your chest.

#### Eli
Savior horse—

#### Jake
Your wounding stick has become your healer.

#### Eli
(CALMER NOW. THE OTHERS LET GO OF HIM.) The stick horse touches my legs—it calls the blood back into my arms—glory horse. (THE SPIRIT-DANCERS LEAVE ELI ALONE FOR A MOMENT.) I see into my hand as though it were a field, far away. (ELI CUPS HIS HAND.) I'm a crow looking down at the earth with my black, shiny eye. I see lines in my field. (ELI OPENS HIS HAND AND LOOKS AT IT.) The furrows run all different directions—it's not an ordinary field. No, this is not a field I've seen before.

#### Quannah
Plant the furrows, Eli.

#### Eli
An Indian who plows!

### Virgene
Our Cherokee ancestors were corn farmers. You'll live.

### Eli
Even if it's only to feel the air wash in and out my lungs. I will visit my children. I will tell them to live. I will be like Jake's father was to him. Like Virgene's father was to her.

### Virgene
My father told me not drink. (VIRGENE TRIES TO HOLD ELI'S ATTENTION.) He told me not to fish for men. We marched up the backroad in the muck of history. Now we'd take responsibility and turn every page.

### Quannah
He ho hey ho.

### Virgene
I read the fisherman's catalogue at the laundromat—while Eli's hand went round and around like a dryer in the Indian hospital when he was drying out. I remember my father in his Sears & Roebuck hip-boots and tackle box. How we laughed at him. How I hated fishing, shoving the sharp hook through the worm like a rod into the spine. I read the names of the bait and lures: Fire Claw. Hula Popper. Slider Worm. Hot afternoons and dark nights until mosquitos raised slaps of a ruler across the hand. (HERE THE SPIRIT-DANCERS ENTER LIKE FISHERMAN AND LURES. VIRGENE AND QUANNAH UNFOLD THE FENCE WIRE AGAIN AS THOUGH IT WERE A QUILT. THEY SHAKE IT OUT BETWEEN THEM.) The quilt pops when I pull it from the dryer. Eli's socks stick to it—(VIRGENE PULLS IMAGINARY SOCKS FROM THE FENCE WIRE. ELI WATCHES THEM.) Then my father died and left me holding these pages snapping with Jelly Wigglers and Hot Chunks. (THEY ROLL UP THE FENCE WIRE AGAIN.)

### Quannah
Chartreuse Shiners and Smelly Night Crawlers. (SHE WALKS TO ELI.)

### Quannah
Hey ho hey ho.

### Jake
Ho hey ho hey.

### Eli

I'm writing words I never knew. (HIS ARMS AND HANDS TREMBLE AS HE HOLDS THEM OUT TO VIRGENE.) I'm writing in a night-program somewhere.

### Virgene

I'll go with you, Eli.

### Eli

I may even read—*The Farmer's Almanac, The Wallstreet Journal, The National Inquirer.*

### Virgene

I've got a fisherman's catalogue—

### Eli

I've got a hundred fragments and broken pieces to sweep back together—

### Virgene

Maybe you could work in the Indian hospital again—sweeping floors—(ELI PULLS INTO HIMSELF AGAIN.)

### Eli

I'm still nowhere, but I make a corral for my stick-horse. (THE SPIRIT-DANCERS KICK THE FENCE WIRE SO IT ROLLS ACROSS THE FLOOR.) I fill the black hole with sawdust. I will talk to the metal tumbleweed and say 'peace' to the uprisings in my head. I will sing the songs our old healer, the Stone Man, gave us.

### Jake

Hey ho ho.

### Quannah

Covered in all directions.

### Eli

(ELI HITS THE FENCE WIRE BACK ACROSS THE FLOOR.) I hold my nothing as though it were SOMETHING! I paste my fragments together and call my hand my house in air. (HE HOLDS HIS HAND UP.)

### Virgene

Hi yey ho ho. (SHE TWO-STEPS AROUND ELI AS HE TALKS.)

## Eli

I will build a tree for my crow. I'll survive jail this time. I'll nail the clothesline back to the pole for you and Quannah. I'll say Christ and be healed. I look at this emptiness and say YOU ARE SOME-THING! I look at my stick horse and say you are WAR HORSE! I'll make a war-mask for him.

## Quannah

*I'll* make a war-mask for him.

## Eli

Sometimes I wonder what it was like to be us.

## Jake

Sometimes I have that thought too—when the sun weaves its old patterns on the wall—I think we were once whole—like a dream we had in the night and can't remember when we wake.

## Quannah

There's as much difference as there is between the plastic Steak House bull and the real one in the rodeo.

## Jake

We're not really visible. Our heritage has been erased and we live without a sense of who we were. We're the people who live without our lives—whose arms and legs move at times without our bodies—whose thoughts move without the heart and mind.

## Eli

I told our father once I would be different. But I wasn't—what an asshole I was—I wish he were here now—last of the 49'ers—Old Norvall—I'd tell him—

## Virgene

I'd tell him you're sober—and standing in this garage without us HOLDING you, or locking—(SHE DOESN'T SAY WHAT SHE'S THINK-ING.) Light the pipe, now, Jake—

## Jake

They're always nagging, Eli—

## Virgene

I feel it too—the peace you say comes like hummingbirds in a tornado.

**Quannah**

You're quiet, Jake—

**Jake**

I was listening to the ancestors. I heard their Cherokee voices in the corners of the garage—and over the roof—Mother Earth, we've made a garage floor of you—(HE PATS THE GROUND.)—And yet I feel your presence. (JAKE LIGHTS THE PIPE. HE PUFFS IT, THEN HOLDS IT UP. THE OTHERS SIT WITH HIM. THEY FORM A CIRCLE, EACH REPRESENTING ONE OF THE FOUR DIRECTIONS. JAKE POINTS TO EACH ONE WITH THE PIPE, THEN HIMSELF.) To the four directions.

**Eli**

Hey bo cah may.

**Virgene**

Ah hey ah hey.

**Quannah**

To bay ah meh.

**Jake**

Ehy cah may may. (HE PUFFS THE PIPE, PASSES IT TO ELI. ELI PUFFS AND PASSES IT TO VIRGENE. VIRGENE PUFFS ON THE PIPE AND PASSES IT TO QUANNAH. WHEN QUANNAH HAS HER TURN, SHE RETURNS IT TO JAKE.)

**Virgene**

What did the ancestors say? (JAKE PUFFS ON THE PIPE AND SETS IT IN THE MIDDLE OF THEIR CIRCLE.)

**Jake**

For Quannah to get her beaded shoes ready. We're going to a pow wow.

**Quannah**

Ah-ho. (QUANNAH LAUGHS.)

**Jake**

They said for Eli to get a job at the bait farm—

**Virgene**

Ah-ho.

Jake

They said for you and Quannah to park your Volkswagon in the garage instead of leaving it in the yard all night. A raccoon jumped out when I drove up tonight—

Virgene

It was probably after one of Quannah's stale peanut butter sandwiches.

Quannah

I think the squirrels bury their nuts in there too.

Virgene

Do you still hear the voices, Jake?

Jake

Yes. Sometimes they say things which are not for now.

Eli

The next time I hear them, they will say I'm coming off the gallows— a living Hang Man! Just as one letter comes against another before there is a word—one finger, one toe at a time is taken from the gallows until there is a man—I'm starting backwards from a child's game—(THE SPIRIT-DANCERS REASSEMBLE.) Living sober can't be worse than the black hole—

Jake

Yo, Eli—you've done the hard part—you've been an alcoholic first.

Eli

I was sitting out here in the garage the other day. (SHRUGS.) Maybe the other month. The wind was blowing hard enough the window glass rattled. There's a shingle loose somewhere on the roof. I heard it flapping. The wind eased through the cracks in the garage (HE STARTS TO PANIC AGAIN)—hissing until I picked it up!

Virgene

I heard Eli in the garage that windy day—I thought at first he really saw a sssn—(SHE CAN'T BRING HERSELF TO SAY SNAKE.) But— wheew! Quannah and I closed the door, and hooked it, and stood against it until you got here, Jake—

Quannah

After that he was in the hospital—

**Virgene**
He didn't even think to break the window—

**Quannah**
He was crazy—

**Eli**
AAAAhhhhhHH! (HE MOANS AGAIN AS THE SPIRIT-DANCERS COME AROUND HIM, LICK HIS FACE.) Will I be new again?

**Jake**
Yes, because you've said you will—just wait until you catch up with your words.

**Virgene**
I see the spirits in the garage now, Eli—(TRYING TO COMFORT HIM.) The good ones dressed in their white dresses—last winter when it snowed, I came out to get in the car—and there were thin, white lines of snow on the garage floor. They blew in through the cracks in the walls. Tonight in the moonlight, I saw the little ghosts of snowdrifts in the air—and it's June instead of winter—

**Quannah**
I thought the snow was like the fairground lights when I saw it.

**Eli**
(BITTERLY.) I was thinking about our Old Pappa Norvall, Quannah—he would have been 60—

**Quannah**
Even I forgot—(PAUSE.) His birthday was the last of March.

**Virgene**
You're remembering, Eli.

**Eli**
Yeah, I've got the last of March. All I need is the first 32 years to put with it—(THE SPIRIT-DANCERS BEGIN TO RODEO.)

**Jake**
(HE PICKS UP THE PIPE AND PUFFS ON IT.) Eetowah—the Holy fire—the ceremony we once had—lighting the small fires in our cabins from the larger campfire— (HE PASSES THE PIPE TO ELI, WHO PUFFS AND PASSES IT TO VIRGENE. SHE GIVES IT TO QUANNAH.)

### Quannah
It's not a second hand faith we got. No—it's store-bought—

### Jake
(SHE RETURNS THE PIPE TO JAKE.) Eetowah.

### Eli
You sit in our circle, Jake—but you had someone guiding you. You had your father holding you on the road while mine dug up anything I had—never mind ever guiding me—and another thing, Bullet Proof, I've known when you crawled in Quannah's window—

### Jake
(MOANS.) Ayyyay.

### Eli
Sometimes I don't sleep—most times I don't sleep—but in short fits like poker chips between those awful times I lie awake—(HE TRIES TO PUSH THE SPIRIT-DANCERS AWAY, BUT THEY KEEP PULLING HIM UP BY THE ARMS.)

### Jake
I'm sorry, Quannah.

### Quannah
Do I lock my window?

### Virgene
Maybe soon you'll sleep at night—

### Eli
Maybe soon I'll sleep—

### Jake
(JAKE STANDS AND PULLS THE LIGHT CORD. THE GARAGE IS DARK AGAIN EXCEPT FOR THE MOONLIGHT. JAKE SITS DOWN AND PICKS UP THE PIPE.) It's a stacked deck we're born into. But this night I say—THIS is the light I have left from the Eetowah fire—it lights a smaller fire which I carry inside me now—(HE PUFFS THE PIPE AND A SMALL GLOW IS SEEN IN THE DARKNESS.)—I live. (JAKE PASSES IT TO ELI, BUT THE SPIRIT-DANCERS TAKE IT FROM ELI'S HAND AND PASS IT ON TO THE WOMEN.)

### Virgene
Eetowah.

### Quannah

Eetowah.

### Eli

(THE SPIRIT-DANCERS LIFT ELI NEAR THE WINDOW. IN THE MOON-
LIGHT THEY DANCE AND RODEO TOGETHER.) Round and around.
The people clapping. My father smiling. (THE SPIRIT-DANCERS USE
THE FENCE WIRE AS A CLOWN BARREL IN THE RODEO. THEY WRAP
IT AROUND ELI AND ROLL HIM AWAY.)

# AFTERWORD

American Indian alcoholism has always seemed many things to me.

It's craving for alcohol on a physical level. I've read something about metabolism of sugar or something like that. Also, alcohol on this continent has been a matter of a couple of hundred years. We haven't had centuries to develop tolerance like the Europeans.

It's emotional. It offers a sedative to help one forget the present. It offers feeling of completion for a broken heritage. A bandage which wraps the pain. The wound. The hurt. Purposelessness. Despair. Dependency. All the delights of acculturation.

It's also self-hatred.

It's a way out of responsibility.

In social terms, it's a group activity. Everything an Indian does is reciprocal. One does not get along on one's own. The communal act of being together. The barroom as council meeting. Pow wow.

One's manhood and bravado can be defined by how much he drinks. Or she. One longs for the comradarie in drinking. "Share the bottle—have a drink." It's also habit. What do you do without it? It's boring to be sober.

It's spiritual. One feels the old ways return. There's oneness with the creator of possibilities.

The play "Stick Horse" is about healing from the disease of alcoholism through a sense of community and ritual. Family and hope. Positive thoughts. I planned for Eli to make it when I wrote the play. But one of the actors, a Dakota, who played Jake in "Stick Horse" when it was presented by the Borderlands Theater in Tucson, said Eli had gone too far.

So the spirit-dancers lure Eli offstage at the end of the revised version. They wrap the fence wire around Eli and "roll him away" in the last line of the play. Maybe Eli's end is still ambiguous. A left-to-the-reader-interpretation. I still think Eli survives, though it seems the words don't say that.

I heard somewhere that alcoholism affects 90% of Native Americans, and recovery is difficult—nearly impossible for the hard-core.

I go a lot on what I hear. I haven't made a medical study. I just wanted to write a play about the possibility of recovery from alcoholism. I should have written about not drinking at all.

Some of the things in the play I experienced. I was on a windy, snowy road once just outside Iowa City when I went off the road like

Eli and Jake, and had to walk to call a tow truck. But I was sober. There are other things—the garage and the clothesline pole were at the farmhouse I rented in Iowa. The laundromat and fisherman's catalogue were in Kentucky at another time. Probably I could go back and piece together the writing process.

I guess in the end, the play is in memory of my father who didn't drink, and told me to do the same.

WAR CRIES

# BULL STAR

# CHARACTERS

JACK BOUDINOT, wears an Indian Rodeo, Albuquerque t-shirt. He's somewhere in his 20's.

CREE, his wife. She has two cardboard babies strapped to her chest and a cardboard box tied to her waist by a string. It's the twins and her first-born son.

CICERO, he owns the coin shop where the men meet. He has St. Coyote on his shirt.

JED, worships motorcycles, but drives a truck with an empty horse-trailer as a status symbol. He wears black.

SAMONDS, he loves Halloween, especially the jack-o-lantern.

LODY WEEMS, mother of Baby Hare. She's also in her 20's.

HAROLD WEEMS, Lody's father.

THE OLD CHIEF, Cree's father.

# SCENE I

(JACK IS TALKING WITH HIS FRIENDS, JED, CICERO AND SAMONDS
AT CICERO'S COIN SHOP, A NARROW STORE-FRONT IN WHICH
CICERO SELLS AND TRADES. JED IS IN THE PROCESS OF ROLLING
A JOINT, WHICH HE LIGHTS AND PASSES DURING THE COURSE OF
THE CONVERSATION. CICERO IS THE ONLY ONE WHO REFUSES TO
TAKE THE JOINT AS IT IS PASSED. HE SITS WITH A BEER IN HIS
HAND, OCCASIONALLY SIPPING IT.)

### Cicero
He invented the gyroplane. If that isn't just like the white man's
thinking. It would propel him into the air and hold him there until
the earth turned. Then the gyroplane would let him down and he'd
be in a different place.

### Jed
(GIVES AN INDIAN HOOT, THE OTHERS HOWL.) Don't look down!

### Cicero
Wovoka told the Indians to keep dancing. And when the Great
Spirit came, He would lift the Indian into the mountains, high up
where he would be safe. He should take the animals. Buffalo.
Coyotes. Beavers. A flood would come and all the people would die.
After that the water would go away and nobody would be on the
earth again except Indians and game. The Indian who didn't dance
would go up just a few feet, not to the mountains.

### Jed
I agree with old Wovoka, Cicero. Let's propel. (HE LAUGHS AND
OFFERS THE JOINT TO SAMONDS.)

### Jack
My wife will smell this on me and I'll be in trouble.

### Samonds
You're the only one of us that settled down, Cicero, and you don't
even have a wife. You made a bundle in this coin shop, and we're
still following the rodeo. Jed here wants to join the circus.

### Jed
The fuck I do.

**Samonds**

That Cicero could pick up a blown tire on the highway and sell it for a bear claw.

**Cicero**

Samonds is like following the red gasoline truck down the road. You always know what's sloshing around inside.

**Jed**

Hey, it's Jack's old lady who's conniving. She hit me up for gas money last time I called for a ride.

**Jack**

Yeah, she schemes like her daddy. She thought money was going to fall off that depot roof like dead pigeons. She wants a house, a car, a washing machine. Hell, she's got a list. But her old man signed the papers to sell that railroad station on the corner of their property. It's as much hers as his, she says. But he signs the papers for a lot less than what she thinks it's worth. I talked to him, but he's already signed. Cree's old man thinks that now she's got me to take care of her, he's off the hook. Her mother's got that job with the county. She's doing better than all of us, except maybe Cicero.

**Cicero**

Shit, man. I'm back with my mother just to get a supper.

**Jed**

You just can't cook, you lazy ass.

**Samonds**

We could spook Cree's old man some night. We could be the voice of the Great Father. The depot master. Telling him he can't sell the station.

**Jack**

Yeah! Some night when he gets drunk out there on that abandoned place by the garbage dump where he lives. We could speak to him from the dead.

**Cicero**

All aboard! I hear the last train leaving.

**Jack**

That dumb Indian don't know what anything is worth. It'd serve him right. (CICERO MAKES A COYOTE HOWL.) Part of my wife's harping comes from being his daughter.

**Samonds**

Lody.

**Jed**

Who?

**Samonds**

Lody Weems. The looney. You know. Harold Weems' daughter.

**Jack**

We rent from them. She sits with Cree while I work on the Pinto at night.

**Cicero**

She's got that rabbit—

**Jack**

Yeah—Baby Hare.

**Samonds**

That'd do it all right.

**Jack**

Put her on the hill by the old man's place and let her go.

**Cicero**

Cree's old man might just think she's one of the squaws that come to the garbage dump to rummage.

**Jack**

He wouldn't stop to reason it out. She could be the voice of the owl. The ghost of some woman he fooled around with come back to haunt him.

**Jed**

The voice of the ancestors.

**Jack**

The voice of justice.

**Samonds**

She could put a curse on him if he sells the station.

#### Jed
I think we've got something.

#### Samonds
How could you get Lody to do it, Jack?

#### Jack
We wouldn't have to talk her into it. She doesn't know what's going on. Just take her out there and let her act like she always does.

#### Jed
She'd spook him all right. She spooks me.

#### Cicero
I don't think you've thought this through, Jack.

#### Jed
Ah! The voice of caution.

#### Jack
We could take her when her father goes off to fish.

#### Cicero
Cree wouldn't allow it.

#### Jack
Maybe she wouldn't know.

#### Cicero
Doesn't he share the fish with you?

#### Samonds
It might not work. I don't think the Great Father would want her as the voice of the ancients. Her own father would hang you for it if he found out.

#### Cicero
It'd only confuse her.

#### Jed
Especially after a ride with one of us.

#### Samonds
I've seen her at your place, Jack, talking to the stars in the sky.

                    Cicero
Leave her out of it.

                    Jack
You're right, Cicero. I wouldn't do it.

                    Jed
She'd probably go if she could take Baby Hare.

                    Samonds
She probably wouldn't even know what's happening.

                    Cicero
Yes she would.

                    Jed
Samonds and I could take her out there.

                    Samonds
How about Cicero?

                    Jack
Nobody's taking her.

                    Samonds
Not even for the sake of Cree and the boys? The old chief is trying
to cheat her out of her share of that old railroad station.

                    Jed
What would anybody want with it?

                    Jack
He's not even really a chief.

                    Cicero
Biggest antique there is.

                    Jack
He doesn't feel like he owes any of it to Cree or his grandsons. She
has a roof over her head, a car that works at least half the time, and
Harold Weem's garden she can take from. I've got a job in the
Tennepah School District driving a bus.  Harold gives us half the
fish he catches—

### Cicero

Be thankful, Jack.

### Jack

Yes, I know.

### Jed

I still think some night when the old chief gets drunk—

### Cicero

Apart from the fact that it's not the right thing to do, what makes you think it would work?

### Jack

Cree's old man is superstitious. Hell, he hears voices anyway. It'd be easy to convince him she's a spirit.

### Samonds

If there's any buffalo nickels dropped between the cracks in the floor of the old depot—

### Jack

—they're yours, Cicero. How many coins do you think passed over that counter? What are the chances some of them are still under the floor? Your metal detector would jump like a bull—

### Samonds

Just have Lody be the voice of the spirits telling Cree's father he should share the sale of the depot with Cree.

### Cicero

And Cree's husband, of course.

### Jack

Well, legally it's part hers.

### Cicero

Then get a lawyer.

### Jack

Where would I get the money?

### Cicero

He might take it from Cree's share—

#### Jed
Ha!

#### Jack
There's something in the deed that can be read as if the land and depot are the old man's to do with as he chooses—it's whoever's on the land at the time. That's not really what it says, but it can be read that way.

#### Jed
He'll spend the money before he dies. Cree'll end up with nothing.

#### Jack
The old man's been in enough trouble. If a judge would believe he's trying to cheat his family—

#### Jed
Steal from them.

#### Cicero
Why involve Lody?

#### Jack
You keep bringing that up, Cicero. Forget it. Cree would never speak to me again. Howard Weems is my friend. He's almost like a father. Crap. Nothing I think up ever works.

# SCENE II

(THE STAIRS TO JACK AND CREE'S APARTMENT OVER THE WEEMS'
GARAGE. LODY SITS ON THE BACKSTEPS BY HERSELF PETTING THE
RABBIT SHE CALLS BABY HARE.)


### Lody
(LODY STOPS A MOMENT BUT CONTINUES TO PET THE RABBIT.)
Sometimes I pet your fur when it's cold, Baby Hare, and I see the
sparks. That's how I know the stars are your father. (CREE COMES
DOWN THE BACKSTEPS AND SETS BY LODY. LODY SPEAKS TO HER.)
There's a narrow path through the neighbor's wisteria bush. Baby
Hare wants to go. But the houses bend into the path and he cannot.

### Cree
How are you this evening, Lody?

### Lody
I'm fine but for this black bull rabbit with a mind of his own.

### Cree
It's a nice evening.

### Lody
I stuffed the buck-wheat sun into the flour-sack so night would
come.

### Cree
You did a nice job of it.

### Lody
Then the high stars over the garage can play. And the stairs to the
garage apartment.

### Cree
You can't go up there, Lody.

### Lody
Why?

**Cree**

That's where Jack and I live with the boys.

**Lody**

Garah Weems, my mother, is there.

**Cree**

No, she's not, Lody. (LODY PETS HER RABBIT.) She might have been there a long time ago, but now she's gone.

**Lody**

Where did she go?

**Cree**

I don't know. It all works out. Maybe there's a place people go when things get too hard for them—

**Lody**

See that bull, Taurus, Baby Hare? Over there where there are no clouds. (SHE LOOKS AT THE SKY.) How swiftly he runs tonight. The point of his horns, his fierce hooves, yet how gently he comes like the sneeze of a small rabbit. He's your father, Baby Hare. He looks small, but he's far away.

**Cree**

All things get smaller the farther away they are except marriage—

**Lody**

Baby Hare does what he wants. What's wrong with that?

**Cree**

I did what I wanted to. My mother told me not to marry Jack but I did.

**Lody**

I have Baby Hare now and you have the boys.

**Cree**

Yes, I'm tied to the children, the stove, and the diapers I hang on the line. While recovering from the birth of one child I didn't expect and wasn't ready for, I got pregnant with twins.

**Lody**

Come for us, Taurus.

**Cree**

We're all trying to get back to the stars, Lody. They landed on earth once and dumped us out. Then they took off again leaving us to long for them.

**Lody**

My mother went with them.

**Cree**

I would too if I could. We're waiting at the railroad station to leave. And even it's being sold out from under us. I used to climb the water tower. I used to sit in the railroad station and play dolls. I would smash berries to feed them. The pigeons would waddle across the platform like passengers. I could stay there all day until my mother called me for supper.

**Lody**

My mother calls me too.

**Cree**

It's my own father who's selling the station.

**Lody**

I hear my mother sometimes.

**Cree**

He was always gone. Moving on to one place or another. He'd write sometimes to try to get my mother to follow him, but she wouldn't. We stayed on the old place until she got tired of waiting. Then the garbage dump moved down the road from us and she left. That gave my dad the right to the old railroad station.

# SCENE III

(THE COIN SHOP AGAIN.)

### Jack
So the lawyer says he won't take the case because we might not recover the cost of taking the old man to court. Cree didn't want to anyway. I don't know why. What did he ever do for her but disappoint? (TOSSES THE DICE, LOSES.) Isn't that the way it always is? (OTHERS CONTINUE TO ROLL.) My old lady is still looking for the egg man.

### Jed
Egg man?

### Jack
Anyone to take her away.

### Cicero
Not Cree.

### Jack
I want to be more to her than the scarecrow keeping the crows away.

### Cicero
You're drinking too much, old son. You don't know what you're saying.

### Samonds
Yeah, Jack. You're crazy. No one's going to take a woman with three kids away from you.

### Jed
You're safe there. Bet on it.

### Cicero
She wouldn't go away.

### Jack
This game's getting old.

## Samonds
We could go to the salvage yard and dig through old cars for coins for Cicero's shop.

## Jed
We could put Cicero on the mechanical bull.

## Jack
I want to climb on the side of the chute again and look down on a bull. Chute number five's my lucky—I want to straddle that bull, put my one hand under the rope and hold the other one in the air. I want to feel that bull leap from the open gate. Feel that bastard jump like a mountain—and be jerked nearly out of my eyes. Not able to see anything but the stars. Knees up. Feet out. Chin down. Pumping my legs every time he jumps—the whole thrust. The staying on. The ride! (HE GETS UP, JUMPS UP AND DOWN ACROSS THE FLOOR.) Yip. Yiee. Yip. Yip. (JACK RIDES THE IMAGINARY BULL. THE OTHERS CHEER HIM.)

# SCENE IV

(JACK WORKS ON HIS PINTO IN THE DRIVE. CREE, HIS WIFE, WATCHES. LODY ROCKS THE RABBIT IN HER ARMS AS THOUGH IT WERE A BABY. AN ASSORTMENT OF TOOLS IS ON THE FENDER OF THE CAR. A GREASE-STAINED DRESS LIES IN A HEAP. JACK IS UNDER THE HOOD. HE DROPS THE WRENCH HE'S WORKING WITH. HE SWEARS, STOOPS TO RETRIEVE IT. AS HE STRAIGHTENS UP, HE BUMPS HIS HEAD. HE WIPES HIS HANDS ON THE DRESS. A COUNTRY SONG PLAYS SOMEWHERE IN THE BACKGROUND.)

### Cree
Just two years ago I wore that dress.

### Jack
You were the only girl at the rodeo in a dress.

### Cree
I had to go to a wedding and didn't think to take my jeans. I would have missed your ride if I'd gone home to change. But I was there to see you get thrown.

### Jack
Nothing's changed.

### Cree
It's why I noticed you. The brave way you fell.

### Jack
A star on a bull. Bull Star.

### Cree
I didn't mean it that way.

### Lody
He's your father, Baby Hare.

### Jack
He wasn't much of a bull. But then I wasn't much of a star.

### Cree
You're the only one I remember.

**Jack**

(THROWS DOWN THE RAG.) Maybe Howard can look at this.

**Cree**

I can't travel with you now like I did when we were first married. I got the children. They tie me down. I want to hold you down with me.

**Jack**

I still think I can ride, Cree. You got to let me take a chance.

**Cree**

How many chances does it take?

**Jack**

I feel trapped. Like clothes I had to wear when they got too small. They cut me under the arms. It's like wearing jeans that don't come down to your ankles.

**Cree**

Highwaters.

**Jack**

You're looking at a dress you can't fit in anymore and you're thinking where are you going to get the money for another one.

**Cree**

Where do I go I need a dress? I'd rather have you. Maybe we'll get that old railroad station back and sell it for what it's worth instead of giving it away.

**Jack**

That's about the same as counting on rodeo money.

**Lody**

The bull star's his father, and I am mother of the rabbit-child.

**Jack**

I suppose the star of Bethlehem is shining too.

**Cree**

He doesn't resemble either one of you, Lody. But he's handsome. One of the nicest babies I've seen.

Jack

And she has seen babies.


Lody

Shhhh! His father comes.


Jack

I have to rodeo, Cree.


Cree

I thought I could hold you, but it never works. My mother couldn't
hold my father.


Jack

I'm just going to be gone a few days, Cree. Your mother was better
off without your father anyway.


Lody

(STARTS TO WHINE.) Be nice, Baby Hare. Your father, Taurus, is
coming.


Cree

I would like to leave too. I would like to wake in the morning without
three crying babies who want to be fed. (CREE ROCKS HER CARD-
BOARD BABIES.) I would like to be able to sleep through a night.
(LODY WHINES AGAIN.) Don't whine, Lody. Pet your rabbit. It's all
right. I'm just talking.


Lody

Taurus!! (LODY STRUGGLES AS IF SOMEONE IS TRYING TO TAKE
HER RABBIT.) Taurus!! (LODY SCREAMS. CREE TRIES TO HOLD HER.
JACK RUNS TO THEM.)


Jack

Your rabbit is all right, Lody.


Cree

See him in your arms? No one is going to take him. (THEY HOLD
LODY WHILE SHE ROCKS THE RABBIT AND CREE ROCKS HER
BABIES.)

# SCENE V

(THE COIN SHOP.)

### Cicero
I remember Lody in school. She would come with her hair uncombed. She'd look at us like a wild animal. I think her mother was scaring her to death. One day someone tormented her until she screamed out. I can still hear her down the hall as they carried her off.

### Jed
I heard the old lady was an alcoholic.

### Samonds
What do you know, Jed? Driving around town with that empty horse-trailer rattling behind your truck.

### Jack
Yeah, makes everyone think he owns a rodeo horse.

### Cicero
Maybe he's got a spirit horse in that trailer.

### Jed
I can't get the hitch undone.

### Jack
Just like everyone thinks I'm a rodeo star. Who knows what the truth is anymore?

### Jed
I'd trade it for a motorcycle in a minute—

### Cicero
What if there's not one truth, but many?

### Samonds
Yeah—but Jed seen a driver smeared over the highway after a wreck.

### Jed
Yeah—truth's something that reproduces like rabbits.

### Jack
Truth is something you got to live with once the stories have their turn.

### Cicero
Truth is something you create with your stories.

### Samonds
Truth is an empty jack-o-lantern.

### Cicero
Once there was a man with a dog who told him there would be a flood. Make a raft and get on it when the rain comes. Soon the rain came and the man took his family on the raft. Well it rained for a long time until the mountains were covered and all the people in the world drowned. Then the rain stopped, and the waters went down, and they stepped off the raft. They heard dancing and shouting on the other side of the ridge. The man climbed up and looked over. Everything was still, but he saw a great pile of bones and he knew the ghosts of the people drowned had been dancing.

### Samonds
Forget the stories.

### Jed
At least Jack's got a job with the Tennepah school district. He could be like Cree's brothers who can't keep their jobs.

### Samonds
How come Jack got the job driving buses anyway when the rest of us can't find work? Jack's not a better mechanic than the rest of us—

### Jed
He's been in trouble too.

### Jack
Hell. I can't even handle cattle on the ground. Those calves never would go down for me. But when I was above the chute looking down on that bull. When I got on it just before the gate opened and the bull leaped into the arena, jumping like a mountain itself moving and leaping in the air, and all I had was one arm around the rope, pumping my legs when he jumped. I was the bull star!

### Jed
The egg man.

                    Samonds
The Cherokee grasshopper.

                      Jack
Yeah. Not much more than that. The next thing I knew, I was on the
way to the ground, landing between those thrashing legs.

                       Jed
Just like I knew I'd be on a motorcycle—

                      Jack
I've got to follow the rodeo this summer. I need money.

                    Samonds
Your old lady wouldn't let you leave her behind, Jack. Not with
them babies to take care of.

                      Jack
You know what we should do tonight?

                    Samonds
What, chief?

                      Jack
Take Lody Weems out to the garbage dump where Cree's father
lives, and let her spook him into sharing the depot money with Cree.
I could afford to take her and the babies with me to the rodeos if I
had money.

                       Jed
Shoot. We told you, anytime.

                      Jack
No, not you. I want Cicero to do it.

                     Cicero
No.

                      Jack
She knows you, Cicero. You were in the same class in school.

                     Cicero
She wasn't there enough for me to know her. We were all in the
same class at school at one time or the other.

                       164

Samonds

It'd be easy—

Cicero

No—

Jack

What if it worked?

Cicero

Who do you think pecked under his desk when Lody screamed?—
(THEY LOOK AT CICERO.)

# SCENE VI

### Cicero

It's all right, Lody. C'mon. Let's go for a ride. (HE OPENS THE CAR DOOR.)

### Lody

I can't leave Baby Hare.

### Cicero

Bring him. He'll be all right. Don't you think he'd like a ride too?

### Lody

Where are we going?

### Cicero

To see the country. Just sit here in the car. You never get out.

### Lody

I'm tied down with babies. My father wouldn't like it.

### Cicero

Your father wouldn't mind. He knows me. (SHE SITS IN THE CAR.) How many times have I been here with Jack, working on the car? You watched us with Cree. (HE CLOSES THE DOOR AND GETS IN.)

### Lody

It's such a black night. The wide heavens are open. See the bull star?

### Cicero

Taurus? (HE BACKS OUT THE DRIVE AND THEY'RE ON THE WAY TO THE OLD MAN'S PLACE.)

### Lody

You know him too?

### Cicero

I've heard of Taurus.

### Lody

He's the father of Baby Hare.

#### Cicero
Yes, the hair baby is nice. Can I pet him?

#### Lody
Yes. Right here behind the ears. That's where he likes it.

#### Cicero
Does he bite?

#### Lody
If he knows I'm watching, he won't be afraid.

#### Cicero
(HE PETS THE RABBIT WITH ONE HAND WHILE HE DRIVES.) How old is he?

#### Lody
He's a baby.

#### Cicero
Lody. (HE PAUSES.) You like Jack, don't you, and Cree?

#### Lody
Yes.

#### Cicero
And you want to help them, don't you? (LODY PETS THE RABBIT.) They need you to help them. We're going to see a man who took something that belongs also to them. I want you to tell him that he can't do it. I want you to stand before his cabin in the moonlight and tell him that he can't. (HE PAUSES.) I was going to trick you into it, but when I see you petting your rabbit, you look so sweet. I want you to understand what we're doing. (LODY DOESN'T SAY ANY-THING.) Lody, do you want to know—or do you just want to do what I tell you? (SHE STILL DOESN'T ANSWER AND HE STOPS THE CAR.) I'm afraid that in helping Jack and Cree I'll hurt you. (HE PUSHES A PIECE OF HAIR BACK FROM HER FACE. SHE MOVES OVER, AWAY FROM HIM.) Uh, I'm sorry—I'm sorry I hurt you—(PAUSE.) I don't want you to think it was some kind of nightmare you had. You just say a few words to a man Cree knows—one who is trying to take something from her. And I'll take you back to your father.

#### Lody
Will it hurt him?

#### Cicero
I don't know.

#### Lody
Can Baby Hare tell him?

#### Cicero
He's a baby and can't talk. You know that, Lody. You have to talk—
(HE DRIVES THE CAR AGAIN.) I can try to tell you the truth, or I can
make up a story. I think you want to hear the truth, Lody.

#### Lody
What kind of story would you tell me?

#### Cicero
I would say we are going to see a man who took the stars away from
the night.

#### Lody
He did?

#### ‚Cicero
Yes. And they're in a corral behind his cabin. (SHE LAUGHS.) But it's
not good, Lody. It's as though he stole Taurus, the bull star, from
you, and now Baby Hare doesn't have a father.

#### Lody
(PUTS HER HAND OVER HER MOUTH.) NO!

#### Cicero
Yes, it's that serious. But we are going to get them back so the stars
can rise to the heavens and form Taurus again. Will you help?

#### Lody
Yes.

#### Cicero
On this strange, windy night, I want you to stand on the hill before
the old chief's cabin and tell him he can't sell the depot.

#### Lody
Depot?

#### Cicero
Yes, that's the word that will mean to him that he can't sell the stars.

#### Lody
No! Sell the stars?

#### Cicero
Why do you think they are rounded up in his corral? He is going to sell Taurus at the market.

#### Lody
(ALMOST SCREAMING.) NO! (SHE THRASHES.)

#### Cicero
(STOPS THE CAR AGAIN.) Lody. Lody! It's just a story. He doesn't really have the stars. I was just making up a story for you. (HE HOLDS HER, TRIES TO QUIET HER.) Lody. It's a story. Look, the stars are there. Think of Baby Hare. You'll upset him.

#### Lody
(CRYING.) I don't see the stars.

#### Cicero
There's clouds in that part of the sky. Look above us, Lody. (HE LIFTS HER CHIN WITH HIS HAND.) See the stars up there. He didn't really take the stars. No man can do that. He took the railroad station that was part Cree's. He's going to sell it if we don't tell him he can't. (SHE'S QUIETER NOW.) We're going to help Jack and Cree.

#### Lody
What do you want to do?

#### Cicero
(STILL CLOSE TO LODY, LOOKING AT HER.) I want you to stand on the hill by the old chief's with your white skirt blowing in the wind and tell him he can't have the depot for himself. He has to share the money from the sale of it. There are three babies he needs to think about. He'll think you're a spirit from another world, Lody. God, I half think so myself seeing you in the moonlight like this. Your eyes are wild. (HE KISSES HER.)

#### Lody
You are pressing against Baby Hare. (CICERO SITS UP.) It's all right, Baby Hare. (SHE PETS HIM.) Don't be afraid. No one stole Taurus, your father, from the heavens. He's not in a corral. He's free to roam. (CICERO LOOKS AT HER, THEN DRIVES AGAIN.) The red stars twinkle like Baby Hare's eyes. (CICERO GLANCES AT LODY AS HE

DRIVES.) It's important that Taurus is in the sky. There would be a scar if he were gone.

### Cicero
There will be a scar for Cree too if the depot is sold away from her.

### Lody
The one Cree's father is selling?

### Cicero
Yes. (HE LOOKS AT HER.) Lody, you're talking like you have some sense. (LODY HOLDS HER RABBIT AND STARTS TO CRY.) I'm sorry. I didn't mean that.

### Lody
I hear Jack and Cree fighting about it. The babies cry. I hear my mother and father fighting.

### Cicero
About the depot?

### Lody
I don't know. A long time ago. I close my ears and talk to Baby Hare.

### Cicero
Jack and Cree don't know what to do either. We can help them not to fight. We can talk to Cree's father like a spirit in the moonlight. Pretend you're with Taurus. Talk to the old man from the sky.

### Lody
Baby Hare and I will do it.

### Cicero
You can leave the rabbit in the car.

### Lody
No.

### Cicero
He might get upset. Think about it.

### Lody
The lightning in the sky looks like the veins in Baby Hare's ears.

#### Cicero

That's heat lighting. Maybe a storm is on the way. We'll have more wind to make you seem even more eerie.

#### Lody

Baby Hare is afraid of storms.

#### Cicero

Then leave him in the car.

#### Lody

NO! (SHE STARTS TO GET UPSET AGAIN.)

#### Cicero

All right. But hold on to him. (SHE PETS THE RABBIT WHILE CICERO DRIVES.) You're not afraid?

#### Lody

Not with Baby Hare.

#### Cicero

Now listen, Lody. I want you to tell the old chief that Taurus will call and night will fall around him like a rock if he takes what isn't his.

#### Lody

But he thinks it's his.

#### Cicero

Tell him it isn't. Tell him it's the will of the Great Father that he share the sale of the depot with Cree.

#### Lody

I don't like to speak for the Great Father.

#### Cicero

They want you to, Lody. Tell the old man that you think he should share the depot with Cree. Do you think he should share?

#### Lody

Yes.

#### Cicero

Then you'll be speaking for yourself. That won't be hard, will it?

Lody
Where are we going?

Cicero
We're turning on another road.

Lody
It's dark.

Cicero
It's the road to the garbage dump.

Lody
It smells like baby diapers.

Cicero
The old chief lives down this road.

Lody
It smells like pears in the drawer. I left them once. I want—(SHE DOESN'T FINISH.)

Cicero
What do you want, Lody?

Lody
I want my mother. I want to ride in a truck.

Cicero
Lody, the truck driver.

Lody
(SHE LAUGHS.) I want to ride on a train.

Cicero
We're almost to the old chief's. Do you know what to say? (SHUTS OFF THE CAR LIGHTS.)

Lody
We're still moving.

Cicero
I don't want him to see the car lights. Now stay in the car while I go look in the window of the cabin. If he's there, and drinking, I'll come back and get you.

Lody

Now the moon is out. It's so bright from the moon we can almost see without the car lights.

Cicero

The cracks of thunder will hide the noise of the car.

Lody

The night twitches like Baby Hare's nose. Is Taurus angry?

Cicero

Don't go off on me, Lody. Taurus is only a group of stars.

Lody

That's not true. Taurus is the father of Baby Hare.

Cicero

Whatever you say, Lody. (HE STOPS THE CAR.) Wait here. You won't leave the car, will you, until I get back?

Lody

No.

Cicero

Promise me.

Lody

Baby Hare and I will wait here for you. (CICERO LEAVES.) The moon comes from behind the clouds. Heat lightning runs across the sky. It is like the insides of Baby Hare's long ears. Lightning behind the clouds is like white rabbit fur. I find you everywhere, Baby Hare, and Taurus, the bull. (SHE IS QUIET FOR A MOMENT OR TWO, THEN BEGINS TO WAIL. LOWLY AT FIRST, IN HER THROAT, THEN IT GETS LOUDER.) Taurus. Taurus. Your wife calls.

Cicero

(RETURNS TO THE CAR.) What's that noise? What's the matter with you? Be quiet! He's asleep on the porch. He'll hear you before it's time. Come on, Lody. I'll show you the small hill in front of his cabin. (LODY GETS OUT OF THE CAR.) Leave the rabbit here. I can't fool with him.

Lody

No.

#### Cicero
You might drop him.

#### Lody
He goes with me. (CICERO TRIES TO TAKE IT AWAY FROM HER AND SHE WAILS AGAIN.)

#### Cicero
Whatever you say. (HE TAKES HER HAND. SHE FOLLOWS HIM THROUGH THE DARK.) Don't fall. Hold on. Have you got Baby Hare?

#### Lody
(HOLDS TO CICERO'S ARM.) I have him. Be quiet, Baby Hare. He is jumping in my arms.

#### Cicero
Shhh! You be quiet too. Climb up here to the small knoll. Here, Lody. Stand here. Now be quiet until I wake the old chief. Then say what you want. Don't be afraid. I'll be right here on the ground beside you where he can't see me. I won't leave you. (LODY STANDS ON THE HILL. THE MOON COMES OUT FROM BEHIND A CLOUD AND MAKES AN EERIE LIGHT ON HER. THE WIND BLOWS HER WHITE SKIRT. CICERO BEGINS TO HOWL LIKE A COYOTE. HE THROWS A ROCK AT THE CABIN.)

#### Old Chief
(STIRS IN HIS CHAIR.) Huh? What—(CICERO HOWLS AGAIN. LODY HOLDS THE RABBIT IN ONE ARM, RAISES THE OTHER. CICERO YELPS AND THE OLD MAN, NOW FULLY AWAKE, SEES LODY AND RISES FROM HIS CHAIR ON THE PORCH. HE KNOCKS OVER A BOTTLE AND STUMBLES OFF THE PORCH. HE STANDS IN FRONT OF THE CABIN LOOKING AT LODY.)

#### Cicero
(HE MAKES ANOTHER HOWL THEN WHISPERS TO LODY.) Now call to him, Lody.

#### Lody
Old chief. You have taken what doesn't belong to you. I say it to you from the night and from the distant stars. Be just. You have done only what you wanted. You have thought only of yourself, and not the others involved. There is a hand that writes on the wall. You have been weighed in the balance and found wanting. (CICERO STARES UP AT LODY.) You could have been chief, but are not a chief.

You don't have a mind toward the people. You lived for yourself. You've ended up with nothing and you still try and steal.

#### Old Chief

Who are you?

#### Lody

I am here to tell you that you have not listened to the voice within yourself. (THE OLD CHIEF STUMBLES CLOSER TO THE HILL.) You have known what do to, and you didn't do it. You have listened to the story of drink and your own desire.

#### Old Chief

No.

#### Lody

What about our give-away ceremony? A chief takes care of his people. A man's wealth is in what he gives away. You are no chief. You would sell the depot and keep the money for yourself.

#### Old Chief

How do you know?

#### Lody

I am my own voice speaking to you—and the voices of them you have turned away. You follow your own tracks in a circle. You have closed yourself to truth. The voice of the night and of Taurus the bull speaks to you.

#### Cicero

That's enough.

#### Old Chief

Aha! I know you who are. Lody Weems. The crazy girl who lives under Cree. They put you up to this. Cree would take everything, just like her mother.

#### Lody

Just like you, old chief, who are not a chief.

#### Old Chief

Quit talking. Shut up!

#### Lody

Stand up among your people and be a chief.

175

### Old Chief
I helped Cree move into that apartment. I saw you by the garage with that rabbit. You're the looney who lives under Jack and Cree. (HE JUMPS UP AND DOWN IN RELIEF.)

### Lody
And you are the rejected chief of your people. You did it with your bull-headedness and now have another chance to prove that you should have been chief.

### Old Chief
Get off my property. (LOOKS AROUND. YELLS.) Jack! Where are you? Come out!

### Lody
He isn't here. But I am. (SPEAKS WITH AUTHORITY.) I feel strong and not afraid. Taurus comes for me, his wife, and I hold his son. How swift are his feet, how fierce his eyes, and the terrible snorting of his lungs. Taurus. Taurus! I am here with Baby Hare. (WIND RISES. THUNDER CRACKS.)

### Cicero
Lody. Lody. It's not really happening. The stars are still in the sky. No one comes for you.

### Lody
He's here finally. I won't be alone. (SHE WAVES TO THE SKY WITH A SWEEP OF HER ARM. CICERO REACHES UP FOR HER, AND PULLS HER DOWN.) Let me go! He comes for me. If he were not there, there would be a scar.

### Cicero
Stop that, Lody. You're out of your head. (SHE THRASHES AND HE TRIES TO HOLD HER. SHE WAILS.)

### Old Chief
Aye, God. She's a looney. You brought her here to scare me and got spooked yourselves.

### Lody
(SHE SCREAMS.) Baby Hare! Baby Hare! He got away!

### Cicero
Help me find the rabbit.

## Old Chief
(HE LAUGHS AND JUMPS UP AND DOWN AGAIN.) Find it yourself. (MAKES A WAR WHOOP.) Great voices of them who are!

## Lody
Baby Hare. Taken by his father to heaven. (THE OLD CHIEF LAUGHS WILDLY. CICERO CRAWLS FRANTICALLY AROUND ON THE GROUND.) Come back for me Taurus. Don't leave me alone. (SHE CRIES WITH AN UNEARTHLY SCREAM. THE OLD CHIEF STOPS LAUGHING AND JUMPING. CICERO STOPS LOOKING FOR THE RABBIT. THEY BOTH STARE AT LODY, TRANSFIXED.)

# SCENE VII

(BACK AT THE WEEMS'.)

Howard
Where'd you go with Lody?

Cicero
We've been for a ride.

Howard
What happened?

Lody
Taurus took Baby Hare.

Howard
You lost your rabbit?

Cree
How could you do that, Cicero?

Jack
Leave him alone, Cree.

Howard
Where'd you go?

Lody
For a long ride. Up past the stars where the angels stood in a row like trees, and they watched us pass. Baby Hare sang on my lap.

Howard
Jack—

Cicero
We went where she said.

Howard
She doesn't understand—

Lody
The voice of the Great Father speaks to you.

Cicero
I think she understands—

Lody
The stars are like animals. They sleep in the day and come out at night.

Howard
How many times have I helped you, Jack?

Lody
I bring you word from our fathers, the stars. I have traveled back to the spirit land. I have petted them. I felt their sparks flying from my skin. They're like small teeth biting. I woke from the night and walked to the land above to meet the stars. They camp there over night. No one can see them in the day. We traveled in daylight so no one could see us. There I met stars I had never met before. They gave me bread and meat and said for me to travel farther with them. For two suns I followed them without talking. Now we were beyond all signs of men. We were beyond all signs of space clutter and pollution. Someone came to meet us. A spirit in a helmet and goggles and war paint and feathers—and I saw the countries of the earth laid out like a map—I saw the campgrounds of our fathers from the beginning. They were all there. The teepees and grandfathers and mothers—smiling and happy with cookies to eat. And a map of geography. And I saw a man who followed us with his hand and feet bound. He was one who went to earth and was sent away because it's a sad place that makes people angry. But he washes them with his tongue. And they were shiny again and hopped in the field of the hereafter like stars. Baby Hare is getting licked. He's clean and shiny again.

# SCENE VIII

(THE COIN SHOP. THE OLD CHIEF IS WITH THEM.)

### Cicero
She stood on the hill like a white flower—like the peony bush in my mother's yard when it's full of blossoms and the wind is on it.

### Samonds
I think she rubbed off on him.

### Cicero
And it worked—you should have seen the Old Chief. He was facing the Great Spirit of the Universe for a while.

### Old Chief
But she got on Taurus like she always does, and it didn't take me long to figure out who she was.

### Jack
Lody Weems the looney. (HE SHAKES HIS HEAD.)

### Cicero
She's not so crazy. I almost bought it myself when she was speaking to the old man about the depot.

### Old Chief
Who else was there?

### Cicero
No one.

### Old Chief
Yes, there was.

### Jack
If you weren't so darned stingy.

### Old Chief
Listen. I could have been a chief. My wife stood outside the election booth and told everyone what a rotten ass I was. I lost—they built

a garbage dump beside my land. There was nothing I could do—
my wife took everything I wanted. Now you're in line. Cree doesn't
care anything for me. Women only want what they can get. A man
finally has to keep something for himself.

### Samonds
We finally got to do what we want.

### Cicero
Yes—go ahead. Do something wrong so you know it's not enough
to do what you want. We aren't everything in ourselves. How do we
know we're not hot bull-patties unless we try ourselves out? Until
we find our faults. Until we find we don't work. Until we reach out
to pet the stars and find our arm's not long enough.

### Jed
What in the fuck are you talking about?

### Cicero
We won't ever be at home here. We're working to get back. The
price we pay is life.

### Samonds
Cicero got too close to Lody—yeeow!

### Cicero
That's the price of the ticket.

### Jed
Don't worry. I'm not taking the train.

### Samonds
Jed's too busy still trying to find out why a horse don't come out his
trailer.

### Cicero
This's not the only place we got—

### Samonds
There's nothing out there but this—

### Jed
No, we're constellations even if we can't see them.

## Old Chief
Someone else was with us that night—

## Cicero
A network of ancestors. Lody saw them. She knew what she was talking about.

## Samonds
Lody's a bag of Halloween sweets—

## Cicero
She could give up her rabbit—

## Samonds
What are we talking about? We got our coins and horse-trailer. Now this spook of a railroad station is getting in the way. Let's paint it orange and make a pumpkin out of it.

## Jack
It's the white man again—gave us the idea of inheritance. We're fighting over it like them.

## Samonds
The door and windows like a pumpkin mouth and eyes.

## Cicero
Lody climbed up a ladder into an opening in the sky. The earth is getting old and the Great Father was going to make it new for the Indians. He will cover the earth with new soil and bury all the whites. The new land will be covered with sweet grass and spotted ponies. He will fill up the sea to the west so no ships can pass over. And while He's making the new earth, the Indians who believe, who dance and pray, will be taken into the air and suspended while the white men are buried, and then He'll set the Indians down again.

## Old Chief
And the bad man came with teeth sticking out his mouth and asked for the Indian people, but the Great Spirit told him they were the chosen people and he couldn't have them.

## Cicero
And I learned the dances—and have climbed back down the ladder of the clouds to bring you my message. Dance. And be lifted in the air.

# SCENE IX

(A DREAM-SEQUENCE OF ALL VOICES.)

### Jack
Eight seconds. That's how long you got to stay on a bull—or you fall
straight to the ground—or get caught in the rigging—yes—hang and
drag—

### Cree
Sleep, sleep little babies—

### Jack
Yip. Yiee. Yip. (HE RIDES AN IMAGINARY BULL.)

### Lody
When you boys ride the bulls, a rabbit is riding in the stars for you.
Baby Hare follows his father. Taurus. The Bull Star. It's snowing
tonight in the stars.

### Jed
I drive up Main Street with my horse-trailer rattling—

### Cree
Sleep—

### Lody
You know it's snowing where Baby Hare is.

### Cicero
I'm sorry I hurt you, Lody.

### Jed
You know, I saw his head cracked wide open—the wheels of his
motorcycle still spinning—

### Lody
Baby Hare's in the sky crawling with the rabbit stars.

### Cicero
All I got to dance with is my metal detector—

### Old Chief
It was just gone—my wife—everything I had—

### Jack
I'm jumping a dream while she has children tied to her waist. One drags along behind her she has so many.

### Old Chief
I live by a garbage dump.

### Howard
Garah—you get back there—

### Samonds
We're black-holers.

### Cicero
No—starlight's what we got.

### Lody
See the eyes of heat—Baby Hare's father's up there. The red eyes are his. They do twinkle. And melt the snow.

### Jed
UUUUMMMMMMM!! (HE GROWLS LIKE A MOTORCYCLE.)

### Cicero
Get Lody a new rabbit.

### Jed
Give her a ride in an empty horse-trailer.

### Lody
The sky's full of coins for you, Cicero. I threw them up there. I'd like to gather them like rabbit noses.

### Howard
(SHOUTS.) You're not coming down from there!

### Jack
My legs pumping with every jump—

### Cree
My mother left with an egg man.

### Jack

Rocky and Halloween and Sundown and Lightning Strike. Rango and Hoe Cake—

### Samonds

—All the bulls Jack's ridden.

### Cicero

We'll go up in the gyroplane until the earth turns and everything we don't like is gone—and then we come down again—

# SCENE X

(AT THE WEEMS'.)

### Jack
I came for my clothes.

### Cree
Go ride the bulls, Jack. I can't hold you back. All I've got is three boys and a old Pinto that won't run.

### Jack
I wish I could do something for you.

### Cree
We lost the railroad station.

### Jack
You were always the one that kept saying we couldn't lose it. I was the one that said we would. It's such a burden, Cree—I wake up every day thinking of the load I have to support.

### Cree
Ira, Joshua and Jesse need you. Maybe more than me.

### Jack
I want to run sometimes. Being here with the four of you is like driving the bus across the Jimson Creek bridge with a hay truck coming. There's just not enough room.

### Cree
You'll always have something to do with your money because of us. What do you have on the road?

### Jack
I'm not through riding.

### Cree
I can't go. Everytime I've taken the boys on the road, I knew I couldn't do it again.

## Jack

I think of everything they're going to need. Comic books. Video games. Lunch money. Baseball bats. After that, they'll run off to rodeos, find their own girls and get them pregnant. Then they'll have to work two old school buses for the Tennepah district that are stubborn as bulls.

## Cree

How does it all happen?

## Jack

I'll always have buses waiting for me. When one runs, the other won't. Or they'll run in the garage and when I get them out on some remote county road full of kids, then they quit. I work on them late in the garage, and know you're at home with three babies which are too much for you—and you'll be tired and angry at me because you're stuck in some garage apartment. And all the time I'm thinking about the rodeo—and how it feels to climb up chute number five and see that bull waiting—

## Cree

And I'm thinking how it would feel to have money. I would buy throw-away diapers. I would buy a washing machine. We'd pay for someone to stay with the boys once in a while. I'd buy a new dress and we'd go to "Cowboys" to dance. I'd go to the rodeo again and be snagged by you. I think how it would feel to have the old railroad station to sell. I remember climbing that water tower. I could sit up there and know someday I'd be going somewhere. I think how it would feel if my father hadn't left us. He really wasn't the same after he lost the election for tribal chief—maybe the station is his.

## Jack

I don't want to hear anymore about him or the depot. It wasn't used for anything anyway but to store hay. Then its "historical significance" came along.

## Cree

Go on. They're waiting for you. You can ride the bulls in the rodeo and stay on or fall off. I don't care. Do what you want. Soon the summer will be over and it will be the Tenepah school buses that throw you again. But you're always the Bull Star with us. Maybe we're the rodeo you'll be satisfied with someday.

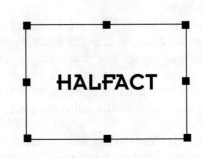

HALFACT is a play about language and imagination. An interdisciplinary world that walks the border between script and poem. A play of words that bend into one another in a new genre of short script or long poem. The compression and immediacy of a half act. A walking between two worlds or two genres in which the setting is pure imagery.

The theme is multicultural. There are different ways of seeing. There are other worlds and Coyote Girl and Coyote Boy bring one of the those worlds into being. The oral tradiiton of the narrator. A dance of imagery, a visual and literal walk-the-border-between. A making of language where dreams dance with masks from the next world. I think it is the realm of the subconscious.

Coyote Girl is trying to climb to the roof where the men are. Away from her mother in the kitchen who dies from bread fumes. The drama moves in and out of time. The narrator like an interlocutor. Coyote Girl lives a lot in imagination. She is left behind when her brother and father go to town. They have the power to drive and leave the farm. They try to use fear to keep her at home. A story of Coyote Girl growing up with incest, isolation and a longing for escape. A surreal effect of a comic strip. An experiment with lanugage. "Deadie. They say of mommie." The girl takes the place of her own mother and father. Native American mythology in the form of the grandmother / owl story to incorporate myth in drama. Silence and sound of experimental theater. Not motive or movement in chronological order with message and theme, but the sharing of experience without thought of the usual structure of the play. Her search for escape and not finding any except in the idea of it.

# CHARACTERS:

Coyote Girl
Coyote Boy
Narrator

# SETTING:

The Bare Stage
Maybe 3 chairs

### Narrator
Out on the prairie. The sky doesn't reach the porch. The blue faded
jeans of the sky.
On the roof there, Coyote Girl's Father and Brother tarring the
shingles. See in the squint of your eye that's her on the roof. Her
Father yelling at her to get back. The wind blows her eyes closed like
curtains.

In the kitchen, a thin cloth covers the loaves of bread. Silence hangs
on Coyote Girl's Mother like a hook.

In the shade of the barn
Coyote Girl makes a doll of pine needles.
There's a tree in the cemetery where she gathers pine cones from
the ground like brown clouds.
Grandmother Coyote once had a pine cone from Louisiana.
It was bigger than the pine cones in her cemetery.

### Coyote Girl
We dance in the raking wind. The fingers of the hayfork between our
feet.

### Narrator
Coyote Boy climbs down from the roof.

### Coyote Boy
You'd be afright if you fell from the barn.
Who'd dance with you with only half a head?
It's a long way down.
About half the fall of a comet from the sky.

### Narrator
The farmtruck takes off on the dirt road,
blue as slow lightning
with ragged edges of a frayed wire.
The sky still jean blue and worn at the knees.
A hill in its back pocket.

### Coyote Girl
He could have taken me to town
under these cream-pitcher clouds.

### Narrator
Coyote Girl wears a red kerchief on her head. When she steps in the
pasture the grasshoppers take off from their missile silos buried in

the dried grass. She walks to the woods on the far side of the pasture.
She makes another pine needle dress for her doll.

### Coyote Girl
I hear my Father pounding the barn roof. It sounds like my Brother biting into an apple.

Already in the afternoon sky
the moon a silver button on the fly of his jeans.

I smell cowblood, the bone meal and manure.
Sometimes the tail-whiff of tar.

Over the pasture the sparrow flies like an arrow.

### Narrator
Coyote Girl would play longer in the woods by the pasture, but her Brother calls her name.

### Coyote Boy
Coyote Girl.

### Narrator
Hear the expectation in her ear when she knows he's back from town.

### Coyote Girl
I wish I had as much to say as the white church. The argyle socks of the church window.

### Coyote Boy
All the fangled woods you play in aren't you afraid?
The Chop Man get you, Sister.
The Goat Guy.

### Coyote Girl
I'm afraid somewhat. Don't scare me worse.
I know we're deep in the woods.
There's danger all around.

The Earth traveling its orbit
passes robbers in space.
They would stop the stage but we get by somehow.

## Coyote Boy
There's space dust thick enough to stop us dead
in our tracks.


## Coyote Girl
Is that why I need this scarf to keep my hair from always blowing?
I also have a kerchief on my nose. They don't know I'm female and
let me pass.


## Coyote Boy
The kitchen is waiting. You should help with the bread.


## Coyote Girl
What do you think?
Do I look like a masked man?
I would steal the hairs from your face.
I wish we could play in the cemetery again without
knowing.
As children.
Unaware.


## Coyote Boy
You'll get the grow-ups and never be the same. You want to be
carried into the kitchen like wood for the stove?


## Coyote Girl
No. I'll always be fresh. I'll always be mine.


## Coyote Boy
How can you be?


## Coyote Girl
I am what I am.
The Chevy with its back to me, the license-plate like the carved
mouth of a pumpkin. Its nose always headed off down the road.


## Coyote Boy
Would you head out of here too if you could?


## Coyote Girl
If I had a carburetor and plugs. Yes I would.
But I'm leaving in my head. Already gone.
Just as horses in the trailer run without running.
Mane and tail fly. Ssshhhh. Ssshhh.
Gazzzah whoop.

### Coyote Boy
Sounds just as noisy too. The sky totters when you dance.
Bundled stars fall into the field.

### Narrator
Coyote Girl picks them up like berries
and dreams on them at night.
But now she goes to the kitchen.
You know that's where her Mother is.

### Coyote Girl
We'll dance while cosmic dust claws the earth.
Ki yay hi yey.

### Narrator
The Mother does not say anything but bakes more bread.
Coyote Girl cuts the slices.

### Coyote Girl
Look for the 'shred' or 'break' along the sides, just below the top-crust.
Cut the knife into the insides.
See the white, steaming-hot sponge.

Great Spirit
fill our pasture.
Let us kick our feet with the painted ponies.
The band is rented and this is our dance.

### Narrator
Now it's supper.
The Coyote Father and Brother sit at the table.
Coyote Girl gives them bread.

### Coyote Boy
The barn-roof's shifted again.
Well the earth is all out of whack.
But it's like we have our old life back when Coyote Girl carries us
bread. Her body shimmeying like the truck loaded for the rodeo.
We live like the land is ours again.
That's our half-act of bravery.

### Narrator
Coyote Girl's Mother walks to the table with more loaves of bread.
Piles of them. As she sits down she falls

face down on the table. You think she is dead.

**Coyote Boy**

She is dead.

**Coyote Girl**

She can't be. Mother!

**Coyote Boy**

She's dead.

**Coyote Girl**

Dead of bread fumes. In this kitchen all day—

**Narrator**

Coyote Girl's Father and Brother carry Coyote Girl's Mother from the kitchen. They place her in the backyard on a board between two chairs.
See her from the corner of your eye while you watch Coyote Girl grieve.

**Coyote Girl**

I rollie up the rug.
Ring the church bellies.
My arms agree.
I'm a proud owlie outta the tree.

**Narrator**

Coyote Girl wears the headdress of her Brother's feathered hat with small ears and a beak.

**Coyote Boy**

Coyote Girl is momentarily out of her head.

**Coyote Girl**

Hum hum. Lo yody. Yo lody.

Deadie. They said of mommie.
Disappeared in the kitchen. Nothing left but crumbs on the meat-loaf-platter.

**Narrator**

They take the Mother to the undertaker. See her riding off in the back of the pickup.

## Coyote Girl

Father tarring the roofie.
I Mother now.
Waddu.
Watch out for the black-bucket night.
But wow the sparrowed arrowed rising me.

I feel the forest of the stars.
The nappy white clouds.
It stings to walk upright, to put on this house.
This turtle shell.
Now the others ride my back.

## Narrator

In the back of the pick-up
on the way to the church
Coyote Girl retells a myth to herself:

## Coyote Girl

Mother was sick in bed. Outside an owl hooted in a tree. Father
went out and shot the owl. Now Mother's dead of a gunshot wound
in her chest.

## Coyote Boy

Her coffin in the church.
A closed-in bed
resting in the forever of the afternoon.
The head left with its eyes open. Now she's closed.

## Narrator

The Minister says, only half of her here.
The whole of her someplace else.
Isn't that life?
The split she walked.

Can't you see the Minister in the pulpit?
A congregation with their handkerchiefs
weeping before him.

## Coyote Girl

Wasn't Mommie good? We had her fingernails and knuckles for
years. Her wrists, the tiny foot-bones. She lasted til we were nearly
grown.

### Coyote Boy
She orbited the kitchen in her apron.
She gave herself for us.

### Narrator
Coyote Girl's Father speaks.
Others speak in the congregation on behalf of the dead Coyote
Mother.

### Coyote Girl
Mother I take your apron and grease the bread pans.
The voice of a woman is a foreign object.
It feels like silence in my mouth.

### Narrator
It is the opera of the prairie.
Hear it in the loggia of the trees.
Imagine the milk-bucket of a belly.
The pasture of a woman.
Her skirts, the underneath of birth.

The locust scrapes its legs on the tree.
The fencerows stumble.

Inside the house
there is funeral rubble in Coyote Girl's room.
Weather-stained ribbons, a flower basket.
A row of pine cones on her dresser.

The sweet birth of fright.

Inside the porch where the sky doesn't reach,
thoughts are tucked like hair
into the old leather flight-cap she wears now.

They can't pass.
A border barricade.
Coyote Girl is Coyote Woman.

### Coyote Girl
To even sit up
is a fine wire.

### Narrator
Coyote Girl's Father is glad

to have a new wife. Ah the sex of it—
the fine smooth crotch, the divided fold of skin.

### Coyote Girl
Take away my pine cone doll and laughter.
Take my memory and voice.
Let me be a spiny skeleton, a bony ladder.
A scaffolding which is nothing but structure
for the content of others.

A kitchen stage. The action of his climax
now in me.
The opera with voices in a language I understand.

### Narrator
You can't believe what's happening.

### Coyote Girl
Father Earth always moving.
Harsh. Unfeeling.

Mother Sky nuturing with yearnings afterlife.

### Coyote Boy
When the Great Spirit made the vagina
he took his finger from the stinkweed to do it.
Death and pleasure from the birth canal.

At least Coyote Girl can bake bread.

### Narrator
You wanted down to the truth of it.
The separation from herself.
Coyote Girl's Mother died of untruth.
She was starved of her sense of person.

In the cemetery
Coyote girl writes, 'Holding Silence Too Long'
on her mother's grave,
and 'Devoured in the Kitchen Meal after Meal.'

The cowbones ground to white dust.
Coyote Girl's Father powders the garden with it.

### Coyote Girl
But the Coyote Mother could see no sense in herself as separate.
She said death to woman as she was.

I hold the pine needle doll in her sharp dress.
Her space-suit ready for take-off.

### Narrator
Coyote Girl's Father is calling her again.

### Coyote Girl
Did you see that, Coyote doll?
Mother's spirit rising from the cemetery
just as we speak?
Yeah, we poke around in the ground for a while.
Finally we know we leave.

### Narrator
Coyote Girl hears her Father call again.

### Coyote Girl
Leat me hold the funeral for the pine-needle doll first.

### Narrator
Coyote girl stirs the yeast into the warm water.
She stirs in the warm milk,
the sugar, salt and shortening.
She stirs in 2 cups of flour.

### Coyote Boy
She stirs until the dough is stiff.

### Narrator
She rolls it out on a floured bread-board.

### Coyote Girl
I roll it out on a floured bread-board.

### Narrator
She kneads it.

### Coyote Boy
She kneads it.

### Narrator
She covers it in a bowl and lets it rise.

### Coyote Girl
My half-act of stirring.
The other half is the heat.

### Coyote Girl
Meanwhile Coyote Boy steps into me.
His barn-breath on my knee.
The wad in his jeans
like a wedge under the table to hold the leg even.
I would think it was the stick from the tar-bucket.
It must have a bone.

A door-stop I couldn't do anything to close.

But an open door lets the bread-fumes out.

And the church bell speaks of the blood of Christ.
Shhh. There might be others.
The spookies from Halloween are crawling.
Hem hooooot hay.

### Coyote Boy
Shud up. You give me the scareds.

### Narrator
Now the Coyote Father and Coyote Boy fight.
Maybe they're still tarring shingles.

Hear the Coyote Father howl.

### Coyote Girl
Coyote Father has a broken toe.
Wheep. Wheep. Bom gazzah hizz.

Let them fuck one another.
Let 'em be 'et' under the greasy yellow sky.

Let me be the underbirth within.
It's the bravery I live.

### Narrator
Now Coyote Girl wears a space helmet.

## Coyote Girl

I dance with the ghost of my pine needle doll.
She travels with the spirits up there.
Ah, the smell of bread.
The dark oven from which there is a rise.

See the hills like loaves of bread.

The trip of the earth,
its tail-lights blinking red.

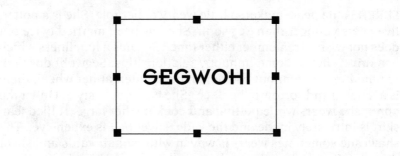

SEGWOHI

SEGWOHI is a Medicine Man, about 70 years old, who lives on a small farm in Nebraska. He is half Cherokee and Cheyenne. His name is a Cherokee word meaning, 'Two Become Together One.' He has a son, Peyto, who works in the feedstore in Arapahoe, and a sister, who has lived with him about ten years. Segwohi's wife is buried in a small cemetery by the cornfield. His son is divorcing his second wife and Segwohi has several grandchildren scattered in different households. He also has an adopted daughter, Reanie, who has disappeared. Segwohi grieves for the old ways and looks for the life to come. He also seeks peace in a world where he is not at home. Peyto has to do this also, but in a different way, which causes arguments between them.

SEREH is the peacemaker, a little weary of her role. She is a potter, five years younger than Segwohi. She has been married twice but does not wish to remember either time. She has a loneliness which has driven her to some unhappy relationships. Segwohi does not remind her of them, but she remembers. Often at her wheel, there is a longing and sorrow in her face. She has Indian style. Under the apron she wears while potting and cooking, her large, ruffled jean skirt is intricately made and the wide, silver belt is expensive. The shawl she sometimes wears is woven with mohair yards and silver threads. She makes unusual, surreal pottery, which buyers from Sante Fe purchase regularly. Afterwards, Sereh spends the money. Hers seems to be a wasted life, in which she never found a place to belong, other than at her potting wheel. Yet there is a depth and stoic certainty to her character. When she is molding clay for her teapots (which look like cellars—or coffins, Segwohi tells her) Sereh knows who she is, though she never accepts the income she makes, and continually gives it away to Peyto and an Indian orphanage. She also pays Segwohi's taxes and makes trips to New Mexico. All her life, Sereh has been under her brother's shadow. She still struggles for recognition from him. The play, named after Segwohi, is really more about Sereh.

PEYTO is 32 years old. Segwohi does not overlook his transgressions, as he does Sereh's. Peyto at one time played a sax in a jazz band, 'The Bear Tracks,' with two of his friends, Mashunkashey and Bear Track. He still longs to play, but the group has recently been in trouble. They wrecked their van after a performance in Omaha one night, and were arrested for possession of marijuana. Peyto wears jeans and a jean jacket like his father, but Segwohi's pants are overalls, and Peyto's jacket is ribbed with leather. Peyto also wears a red headband and has the same 'style' of his Aunt Sereh, of whom is he very fond.

Segwohi's main concern is tradition. Sereh's is loneliness. And Peyto struggles with bills and a longing for release from his frustrations. As Peyto comes and goes on Segwohi's farm, their conflicts unfold. Once in anger, to show Peyto his sins, Segwohi takes one of Sereh's grease pencils that she uses to mark her pottery. He draws Peyto on the kitchen wall in one of his exploits as a child, and continues a mural across the kitchen wall. Finally the wall is covered with his drawings. Peyto calls him the 'Michaelangelo of the Plains,' though they are Segwohi's Winter Counts. Through the drawings, Segwohi also gains an understanding not only of Peyto's sins, but his own as well. Segwohi ends up with forgiveness. Peyto in the meantime, sees the carelessness of his life.

Background music for the drama is the Indian jazz of James Pepper, or Redbone's 'Thirteenth Hour Chant,' interspersed with ancient war chants.

# SETTING

A flock of geese rise over the silo into a pale sky. It is autumn. Dried cornstalks rattle in the small field behind the barn. An old truck is parked under a heavy chestnut tree.

Segwohi's land is on open prairie with little shelter except a slight incline to the east, the direction from which storms never come. In fact, the wind seems to climb the knoll and circle back upon his place. Segwohi has lived on the land his whole life. He hears the ghosts of his ancestors who camped there during migration.

The small farm is on a rural road in Furnas County, Nebraska, near Arapahoe. A wood-frame farmhouse with peeling white-wash sits to the front of the land, where Segwohi rakes leaves from behind the bushes. Behind the small house is a shed and several other out-buildings. The frame of a sweat lodge is in Segwohi's backyard, and the skull of a cow, painted red, hangs on a pole. An arbor of some sort is behind that, where bean poles and a folded snowfence are stacked. Off toward the hill is a small cemetery where his wife is buried.

There is a granite slab in the doorway of one of the sheds and an unlit lantern in the open window. Inside, a potter's wheel and rickity shelves of unfired bowls and teapots. A firebrick kiln in the corner. It is where Sereh works at her wheel. There's a damp box where unfinished clay objects are stored. Several utensil boxes which hold wooden potter's thumbs, wire hoops, edging tools, calipers, wooden throwing-ribs, small bits of scrapwood, smooth stones, and a few bones, with which Sereh marks her pottery. She also gathers animal hair to make her own brushes. Segwohi complains now and then about trips he makes to get her skunk and deer hair.

The main room in the house is a pale blue kitchen, much like the Nebraska sky that comes in the window. There is a large walnut table with three chairs, a black stove and wood-box. On the wall over the sinkboard, a pair of scissors hangs open on a hook. There is also an old ice pick, a wooden potato masher and several other wooden instruments on the wall. An egg-scale sits on a nearby shelf, and a wire hen. In the corner, a pile of newspapers. The room has the cluttered feel of a woman who is otherwise occupied. The day from the window is clear as a canning jar.

Behind the house and barn, the wide prairie grasses roll down the slight knoll as though into a tidal basin or slough. A small canoe and rowboat are turned upside down behind the shed. Sometimes Segwohi uses the rowboat for fishing the North Canadian River, some fifteen miles from his farm. The clothesline in the backyard resembles a ship's rigging where sheets pound on the line as though sails. Truly, there is the feeling of being in the middle of the vast sea. Sometimes at night they hear the howl of a coyote.

In the backyard, Solomon, the rooster, and his hens peck in the dirt, and Ki-Ye, Sereh's cat, prowls in the hedge-grass by the fence.

Segwohi rakes leaves from behind the bushes of the farmhouse. The rake-handle is enough like an oar, that it looks like Segwohi could also be rowing. Soon, a new jeep turns into the drive. It is Peyto who comes for supper.

# SCENE I

**Segwohi**
Peyto. (RAKING.) You're early.

**Peyto**
The farmers leave town by 4:00. No need to keep the feedstore
open. (HE TRIES TO MAKE HIS WORDS CASUAL.)

**Segwohi**
Old Crawford lets you close?

**Peyto**
He's gone by noon most days.

**Segwohi**
(STILL RAKING.) How is it with you?

**Peyto**
I don't know yet. What's for supper?

**Segwohi**
(STILL HAS NOT LOOKED AT HIS SON.) No, Sereh's still in the shed
at her potter's wheel.

**Peyto**
(SHAKES HIS HEAD.) What can I say? She makes more than I do at
the feedstore. (PAUSE.) Segwohi—I know you don't—

**Segwohi**
(JERKS HIS SHOULDER AWAY FROM PEYTO'S TOUCH, STILL NOT
LOOKING AT HIM.) Is it your life's occupation?

**Peyto**
You don't understand.

**Segwohi**
(NOW HE STOPS AND LOOKS DIRECTLY AT PEYTO.) I had one
wife my whole life.

**Peyto**
It makes sense to divorce when you're not getting along—

Segwohi

Not to me.

Peyto

Everyone—

Segwohi

Mashunkashey? Bear Track? All they can do is scramble for girls.
You're not one of them.

Peyto

I'm not you, Segwohi. I'm not a Medicine Man.

Segwohi

No, you're not a Medicine Man. Twice divorced. Once in jail for
possession—chanting our sacred songs in bars. Playing the saxophone to drunk Indians. You wouldn't know the Great Spirit's voice
if he came with his name on his own jean jacket. (HE PICKS AT
PEYTO'S JACKET.) Isn't that the way you see the Great Spirit, Peyto?
I tell you, you are no Holy Man! It's not an inheritance. It must be
lived. Don't worry. I won't call YOU a Holy Man.

Peyto

(HIS FACE SHOWS THE HURT OF SEGWOHI'S WORDS.) Well, drive
home the point. I don't know if I want what you call 'living'
anyway—what a Holy Man! I'm impressed with your pious atti-
tude, Segwohi. I can always come to your place for sanctuary and
forgiveness.

Segwohi

(HE LEANS ON HIS RAKE AS HE SPEAKS.) Is that what you want,
Peyto—forgiveness? So you can keep doing what you're doing, but
not feel bad about it? You won't get my forgiveness.

Peyto

I'll get your land.

Segwohi

No.

Peyto

Maybe I'll open the barn so 'The Bear Tracks' can play—

Segwohi

With your mother buried on this land?

Peyto

I'm your only son—

Segwohi

This is MY land. I'll give it to whom I want.

Peyto

We'll bear-dance in the barn—(PEYTO SHUFFLES AND SWAYS IN A CIRCLE, GROWLING AND GRUNTING LIKE A BEAR.) Yaw na' dada'ski:si.

Segwohi

Don't use our sacred language—

Peyto

(LIFTS HIS HEAD AND PAWS THE AIR IN IMITATION OF A BEAR.) Yawa'dada—(HE RAKES THE AIR, SOMETHING LIKE SEGWOHI RAKING THE GROUND.) Yawna'dada'ski: si—

Segwohi

(HITS PEYTO WITH THE RAKE, NEARLY KNOCKS HIM OFF BALANCE. PEYTO IS STUNNED AND DOESN'T KNOW WHAT TO DO. SEGWOHI HIMSELF IS SHOCKED AT HIS OWN ACTIONS.) I didn't mean to do that, Peyto. (HE THROWS HIS RAKE DOWN AND MAKES A MOVE TOWARD PEYTO, BUT HE BACKS AWAY.) You used to follow me around the barn. Where's the voice of my wife calling us for supper? Where's the buffalo? The bear and wolf? I hear their spirits in the field. Yay. I hear them, Peyto.

Peyto

Aha nuh. They're gone. You're right! But I don't hear their spirits—

Segwohi

They're STILL here. LISTEN, Peyto—

Peyto

YOU listen. I hear nothing but the wind scratching over the hills. The ancestors are gone! The bear and wolf—I don't see them. I have to find my own life in this world. All I hear are my wives asking for money—Old Crawford at the feedstore saying I'm late—even my own father has his voice of resistence too. Make it harder, Segwohi. What would I do without you to fight against too?

Segwohi

Maybe you have a hard time because you're not going in the right direction.

#### Peyto

No. I'm going with the current. It's you who always paddles upstream—backwards!—in your canoe. For a while, you insisted that I row with you. I remember resenting you. But there was nothing I could do until I got old enough to take off.

#### Segwohi

You resented me?

#### Peyto

Yes. When I had to dance beside you at pow wows the way you wanted. When I had to stay with you on the farm and I wanted to be in Arapahoe.

#### Segwohi

I never thought that about my father.

#### Peyto

You've been buried so long out here, you don't know what the world's like. I'm getting my ass bit—and you just sit back in your thoughts—and make more wounds with your pricking—

#### Segwohi

I raised you for this? My only son—Peyto. I waited until I was nearly an old man before you were born.

#### Peyto

Yes, I was raised for this!—so I would be a man with a mind and heart of my own—so I could raise my children to do the same—we still rise from defeat you know—even mingle with the white race—

#### Segwohi

Yes, make sure you remember to mingle—my grandchildren are a 'mingling' of everything. Maybe what you need is another wife—I'm glad your mother's in the graveyard so she doesn't have to hear this—

#### Peyto

My older sister, Reanie, isn't—

#### Segwohi

I don't want to hear about that—

#### Peyto

I'm going to do what I want!

Segwohi

And I am SEGWOHI, your father. I brought you into this world—

Peyto

You raised me to be a man. Not some calf running after you. Let go so I can—

Segwohi

—so you can do what you want?

Peyto

I leave you out here to listen to your ghosts, to chant to Brother Buffalo and Brother Bear while I'm pushed farther into the manure bucket each day. Keep your eyes on the sky, Father. You wouldn't like what you see when you look where I am.

Segwohi

You're a spoiled calf—

Peyto

Yes. That's what you always say. Keep the lid on, Segwohi. You never talk when you're in town—but the minute you're on your own land—nothing can hold you back—

Segwohi

What did your mother and I do that wasn't for you, Peyto? And you grew up to turn your back on our ways—

Peyto

(GRABS HIS FATHER BY THE ARM. SEREH WALKS TOWARD THEM. SHE STOPS TO WIPE HER HANDS ON HER APRON.) I'm no dreamer. I'm trying to hold my life together—I'm pulled a hundred ways. My wives and children—the feedstore. I can't get insurance on my jeep. My friends are always wanting something. Bills—BILLS! And you, Segwohi—

Sereh

Hey! Peyto. Segwohi! What goes on here? (SHE STEPS BETWEEN THEM.) That's no way to act—

Peyto

It's the only way I can act when I'm around him. I come out here because I don't want to hang around the bar another night. I don't want to sit with the television—

Segwohi
You come here because you want something.

Peyto
Yes I WANT something. I'm going NOWHERE. Everything's out
of my reach. My children—Little Wolf can't pass third grade—

Segwohi
If his mother and father—

Peyto
I don't want to hear what you—

Sereh
(INTERRUPTS.) I can't sit at my potter's wheel while this noise is
going on.

Peyto
He does it every time, Sereh. I think this time I WILL NOT GET MAD!
I step out of the jeep and say one word to him and I AM MAD. The
bull won't see anything past his Brother Buffalo—his dead wife and
daughter. He's got two living children—and five grandchildren—
He NEVER thinks of us. John already wants the dirt bike he sees at
the hardware store. Ero won't talk he's so shy. His teacher wants to
send him for evaluation—I can't remember where. If Seria has one
more ear infection she'll have to have tubes—I still have dreams of
how close Little Reanie came to dying—and where's Big Reanie, my
sister, who left you? Is that the way we'll finally make it with you,
Pappa?—when we're out there with them—dead and buried so we
can't ever say another word to you?

Segwohi
Get off my land! I won't have you talking about them. (HE TAKES
PEYTO BY THE ARM AND PUSHES HIM AWAY. SEREH TRIES TO
RESTRAIN SEGWOHI.)

Peyto
Yes, I'm leaving. See you, Sereh. (HE EXITS.)

Sereh
(SHE LOOKS HARD AT HER BROTHER.) What's the matter with you,
Segwohi? We don't have enough enemies in this world? You have
to make one of your son also?

Segwohi

How can I have him on my land in peace?

Sereh

Because he doesn't think like you. I saw you raise him, Brother, and he's what you made him. Now leave him alone. He'll be all right.

Segwohi

No, he won't. You don't see things as they are. You hope on nothing. You see rain clouds where there are none. What do you know?

Sereh

Ah! Segwohi. Be careful or your son won't be the only one who leaves you this day.

Segwohi

Where else do you have to go, old woman? Your husband left you long ago. You do nothing but make warped cellars at your potter's wheel. (HE RETURNS TO HIS RAKING.)

Sereh

You've had someone leave you too—(SHE FOLDS HER ARMS.) Don't forget I cook for you. Don't think I couldn't cook for someone else. Do you know how many old men would have me?

Segwohi

I checked last week and there were two. One is a woman beater, and the other just died.

Sereh

(SMILES, CYNICALLY.) Well, I guess I'm stuck here for a while. But tie my leg to the foot-post on my bed, Segwohi. You drive people away from you. Who knows who will be next?

Segwohi

I suppose it would be you, Sister, since there's no one else left.

Sereh

(SERIOUS AGAIN.) Why can't you get along with Peyto? You waited so long for him. You finally adopted a daughter thinking you'd never have—

Segwohi

I don't want to hear that now.

214

#### Sereh
You and I get angry at one another and make light of it. Why can't you do that with Peyto?

#### Segwohi
(SHOWING IMPATIENCE.) Sereh—you're like an old wife. When are you going to stop telling me what to do?

#### Sereh
I suppose when I see you doing what I think you should. You're too hard on him.

#### Segwohi
My wife never told me what to do.

#### Sereh
What should Peyto do when the Indian way of life is gone for him? Even you, Segwohi—what has happened to your way of life? Where are the winter counts you used to draw? I remember how you studied the old recordings of events on buffalo hide—the plenty-buffalo-meat winter. The Brave-Bear-killed winter—I have some of them in my shed. Make your winter counts again. Draw them on the kitchen wall—on the barn. Tattoo the whole farm!

#### Segwohi
(HE QUITS RAKING.) Our way of life is not gone! I still hear the ancestors on this land—I still hear the rocks hiss in their sweat lodge. But no more winter counts! No!—you sell pots! Peyto sells chants—we don't make a MARKET of our ways! There's not one day I don't hear the buffalo. We are right on their migration trail.

#### Sereh
I don't hear them, Segwohi.

#### Segwohi
You're a woman.

#### Sereh
Watch yourself, Brother.

#### Segwohi
That's what we're here for—to remember the old ways. To keep the land holy in our memory. I can't make winter counts anymore, Sereh—one night the grandchildren were here with Peyto—they had the television on—and the light from the screen flicked across

their faces like war-paint—I couldn't stand it. I want to keep the past—

### Sereh

That seems a respectable occupation to me. But you can't expect everyone to have the same job.

### Segwohi

I expect it of my son! He should be a Holy Man too!

### Sereh

(SHE SPITS INTO HER APRON SHE'S SO MAD.) He is a Holy Man, Segwohi.

### Segwohi

I haven't seen it in him—

### Sereh

You keep him away—you'd feel better about HIM and YOURSELF if you DID something. Get out your books again. Draw your winter counts—

### Segwohi

There's enough 'making' around here.

### Sereh

What else are we here for? I sit at my wheel with the little storm shelters—teapots and cups like small cellars. I made the lid on one teapot like a humped roof—the air hole is the little vent—the spout is the cellar stairs.

### Segwohi

Is that what makes them come out here to buy your pottery? Making a big hubub of dust in the air?

### Sereh

I suppose it is. They call me, Storms, Ltd.

### Segwohi

They aren't far wrong there.

### Sereh

When I was a girl I used to go down the cellar steps into the ground and sit there by myself. (THEY SIT ON THE STEPS OF THE FARM-HOUSE.) It was a sanctuary in the earth—a dark place where I could feel by myself. You, Segwohi, were off hunting or dancing in the ceremonial ring—but I lived in myself—

### Segwohi
(SHAKES HIS HEAD.) Teapots like cellars?

### Sereh
I always feel the shape of the prairie—the slope of the hills—the small ravines—how I love the clay in my hands. I love the sweet shapes that come from it. (SEREH'S FOOT PUMPS AS THOUGH SHE WERE AT HER WHEEL AND HER HANDS MOLDED A CLAY BOWL AS SHE TALKS.) Hi yey hi yey. (SHE HUMS.)

### Segwohi
And now I'm hungry.

### Sereh
About the time I want to go back to my potter's wheel—then you're hungry! Why don't you find one of those buffalo you're always talking about? Get out your bow and arrow. Your trusty horse. Remember, Segwohi, they pass by here all the time. I'll make you buffalo stew when you ride home with the meat. (SHE LAUGHS BUT SEES THAT HE DOESN'T. SERIOUS THEN—) It won't take long to get supper. I'm warming the cornbread and beans we had last night. I'm in the middle of new forms. I'm sorry, brother, I can't think of much else but my 'children' in the potting shed.

### Segwohi
I want supper.

### Sereh
You're the spoiled calf, Segwohi.

### Segwohi
Do you always listen to the conversations between my son and me?

### Sereh
How can I NOT hear you beller at him! (SEGWOHI RISES FROM THE STEPS AND SEREH FOLLOWS HIM INTO THE HOUSE. SHE HUMS AGAIN AS SHE MOVES ABOUT THE KITCHEN. SEGWOHI SITS IN A CHAIR AT THE TABLE.) I feel these invisible shapes in my head. With my hands I form their formlessness in the dark—push them out onto my wheel—teapot, cups, pitchers, plates, like warped wagon wheels of our people migrating to the next world after our defeat. Everything tries to pull me back into the darkness in my

head. Segwohi and my loneliness on the prairie. The hollowness of my old age that is coming. The routine of living. In my work, I feel like I'm shaping myself—those dark forms in my head are my fears and apprehensions. I work them into form—useful form. What else is there? Sometimes there's such pleasure here alone. I feel the wet clay taking form—the form I dictate. I create my pots, sometimes with my thumb a little heavy on one side. I make the lopsided bowls I love to make. With a twig I make a totem of some sort. This secret language of markings on my pots is the twine that holds me together. My life is bound up in my work. It's my pow wow dance. My sweat lodge ceremony. It's where I find soothing. It's where I am whole. Hi yey hi yey—come little wire hoops and edging tools—my calipers—my dear bones and sticks to mark my pots.

### Segwohi
(SEGWOHI IS IMPATIENT.) How long are you going to cackle? When is my supper going to be warm?

### Sereh
(SIGHS.) I knew it would be you or Peyto to interrupt my peace.

### Segwohi
Peyto stomped off—

### Sereh
Peyto didn't leave. I didn't hear him start his jeep.

### Segwohi
(HE PUTS HIS FINGER IN HIS EAR.) Am I going deaf? Is that it too? (HE LOOKS TO THE SKY.) Has he been out in the jeep all this time? What's wrong with him?

### Sereh
Why don't you ask him sometimes, Segwohi, without putting an answer into his mouth—or a judgement into yours. (SEGWOHI LEAVES SEREH IN THE KITCHEN AND FINDS PEYTO IN HIS JEEP. SEREH WARMS THE SUPPER.)

### Segwohi
Are you still here Son?

### Peyto
I don't have gas to leave and come back. I don't have money to eat. My first wife needed grocery money.

Tomorrow it will be my second—or a friend will say I owe an old debt, or Crawford will withhold more of my pay at the feedstore. I don't know, Segwohi—(PEYTO RESTS HIS HEAD ON HIS ARMS.) I can't be like you, Segwohi. You're like a Grandfather—unbending in the old ways—

### Segwohi
I'm a Holy Man—a former winter count maker—

### Peyto
You don't make anything anymore—but war—

### Segwohi
We're here to obey the Spirit—

### Peyto
We're here to make our own way on this open prairie—we're supposed to stand while being pulled one way and then another—the job, the white world, the Indian's. I'm ordered around by everyone—do this. Do that. My wives nag and curse. Where is the peace you talk about? I don't know where I'm going—but I know it's not back here on the 'old place'—buried in my thought of 'what was' while the world goes on—sometimes I just hang on—nothing more. I don't hear the voices of the ancestors. I can't live what I don't see. I have to take part in the struggle I see before me. It's the real world, though it's only fragments of several worlds—and hopeless most of the time—

### Segwohi
It's because you don't listen to the voices of the ancestors, Peyto. You can't hear them when you stay at the bar in town every night.

### Peyto
I have to have a guide who moves in THIS world—the one I see. You don't really hear me—(HE FOLLOWS SEGWOHI BACK TO THE HOUSE.)

### Segwohi
I have always heard you—since you were a small boy crying because you stepped on a caterpillar or because your mother got after you when you bothered the hens.

### Peyto
That's not the hearing I'm talking about.

#### Segwohi

Then I grieved all those years you were with Mashunkashey and Bear Track. The jazz band—Bear Tracks! Indian jazz. The sound of the sacred chants of our people on stage—in bars—in gymnasiums! (SEREH STANDS IN THE DOOR.)

#### Peyto

Well, we didn't get too far.

#### Segwohi

No, you wrecked your van and served six months for poss—

#### Peyto

(QUICKLY INTERRUPTING.) You never forgive either. (HE THUMPS HIS HAND AGAINST HIS FATHER. SEREH DECIDES NOT TO INTER-FERE.) You are just as lost in your spirit as Mashunkashey and Bear Track and I were in our jazz. So we had a wreck. So there was some grass—so we didn't do things right, but YOU, Segwohi, are the real JAZZ MAN. You only hear your own music. You're not open to communication. On your death bed, when the two of us are supposed to become one, and your spirit passes into me to carry on, you'll look up at me and say 'you wrecked the van and served six months.' Then you'll die and your spirit will pass into me to carry on your tradition of judgement. Then I can look at my sons and say, 'You are not doing things right. Here is the sacred, BROKEN hoop of our nation. See how high you can jump into it.' (PEYTO STARTS TO LEAVE THE YARD AGAIN— SEGWOHI TRIES TO PUT HIS HAND ON PEYTO'S SHOULDER, BUT PEYTO REFUSES IT.) Goodbye, Jazz Man. (HE EXITS AS THOUGH DRIVING OFF DOWN THE ROAD.)

#### Segwohi

(HE STANDS IN THE YARD A MOMENT. LOOKS TO THE SKY.) A flock of geese rising over the silo—(HE PULLS HIS COLLAR UP AROUND HIS NECK. HE SEES SEREH STANDING IN THE DOOR OF THE HOUSE.)—Well what do you think of that?

#### Sereh

I think you are a man doing the best he knows how to do. Go after him, Segwohi. Get in your old truck—I don't think he has enough gas to get far. He came for money. Help him—for the sake of the little family we have left.

# SCENE II

(SEREH, PEYTO AND SEGWOHI AT THE SUPPER TABLE. SEGWOHI
EATS WITHOUT LOOKING UP FROM HIS PLATE.)

### Sereh
I watch the asphodel from the window as I cook. When I look across
the prairie they're like candles in the aisle of the Indian church. I
see the far end of life when I look from the west window this time
of evening.

### Peyto
How do you see the far end? No one knows that.

### Sereh
I know someday I'll be an old lady still molding clay. My hands will
not realize they're working alone. I'll stare off into space where my
trail soon leads, but my fingers will still shape a bowl as though I
were at my wheel. I want asphodel at my grave, Peyto. Aach!
Maybe I could press the asphodel blossoms into my clay for
patterns.

### Peyto
(HE ENJOYS TEASING HIS AUNT.) Segwohi talks sometimes about
his death—are you becoming like him?

### Sereh
Segwohi always talks.

### Segwohi
I hear my name.

### Sereh
He's absent from himself when he eats.

### Segwohi
Supper is for eating, not talking. (HE LOOKS UP FROM THE TABLE.)
Soon the stars will be out like the white beans Sereh spilled on the
floor.

### Sereh
Northern beans—when I was putting them to soak. Don't you like

221

them with ham?

#### Segwohi
Yes, but not when they've been on the floor.

#### Sereh
They were still hard—hadn't been cooked. You haven't been sick yet.

#### Segwohi
I'm a Medicine Man. Only because the sweat lodge keeps me well.

#### Sereh
You're the puggmill grinding up my clay, Segwohi. You—whose name means, 'Two become together one'—need a new name. You should have seen us last week, Peyto. Your father took me up in Furnas County to dig more clay. The truck got stuck in the mud and he churned it back and forth, grunting and chanting. I had my shawl over my face as though I was praying to the Great Spirit to push us, but I was holding my laughter in my head. I couldn't let it out, not in front of Segwohi, who doesn't laugh.

#### Segwohi
Especially when I'm stuck in the mud and might have to pay a tow truck—

#### Peyto
And walk five miles to a farmhouse to call one.

#### Segwohi
And then, Peyto, Sereh makes a war cry—a tremolo—(PEYTO LOOKS AT SEREH AND LAUGHS.) Next time, Peyto, you take Sereh for clay. You get your new jeep muddy.

#### Sereh
Well, we got out of the mud, didn't we? Segwohi put rocks in the mud in front of the wheels—and we 'rocked' the truck—me at the gas pedal—him pushing and rocking—me screaming the tremolo—by the time we got back to Arapahoe, the truck was steaming. In all our snorting and spirit-dancing on the old road, we'd thrown a pebble through the radiator. So Segwohi and I sat there at the garage while they repaired the radiator. It cost him some money after all—

Segwohi

But Sereh had her bucket of Nebraska clay, and a few hairs from a dead skunk for her brushes—and she got to watch the sky.

Sereh

The way the reds flowed into one another—(SEREH CARRIES THE PLATES TO THE SINK AND GETS A BILL FROM THE SUGAR BOWL. SHE PASSES IT TO PEYTO AS SHE POURS MORE COFFEE FOR THE MEN.)

Segwohi

She said over and over, 'san dah bouah—san dah bouah.'

Sereh

Sange de boeuf. It means blood of the cow. It's the bright red I get by shutting off the air in my firebrick kiln. I knew that evening I would work in red for my next firing. The clouds were so gorgeous, Peyto. You just wanted to rise in the air to be with them. Except Segwohi—who would think he might get caught in a downdraft and it would cost him something.

Segwohi

(CHANGING THE SUBJECT.) You should see the vessels Sereh has just fired.

Sereh

Aren't they lovely? I molded some new shapes—they're almost like dreams. I want them on the table in the morning to see if they carry what I feel in the night. This particular teapot, Segwohi—you like it?

Segwohi

Yes, a man's head. The ear a handle?

Sereh

It's you, Segwohi. (PEYTO LAUGHS.)

Segwohi

Ah yes. That's why I'm here. To give you two something to laugh about. (HE WALKS TO THE WINDOW.) I'll tell you who laughs. The pirates—(NODS HIS HEAD TOWARD THE ROAD.) The pirates—the renegades—whoever drives around the country putting buckshot in the roadsigns and my mailbox! There are more holes in it today. I think I saw them when I started down the road after you, Peyto—going the other way—I'm going to keep a watch for that old green pickup—the mail gets wet when it rains—or snows—

### Peyto
It's no one I know.

### Segwohi
Do you mean you've never done it?

### Peyto
Not since I was sixteen.

### Segwohi
Bear Track? Mashunk—

### Peyto
(INTERRUPTS HIS FATHER.) We're men! I'm over thirty years old and you treat me like I was a boy taking potshots at fenceposts.

### Segwohi
Well—

### Peyto
I'll never have a chance with you. I was glad to see you coming down the road after me—my jeep's out of gas. But then our trouble starts again—why don't you hide in the bushes all night with your cannon? (HE TURNS TO SEREH, HUGS HER. AS HE LEAVES, HE TURNS TO SEGWOHI ONCE MORE.) Why don't you bring down the wrath of the Great Spirit on us all? (PEYTO SLAMS THE DOOR BUT RETURNS IMMEDIATELY.) I'm going to borrow your gas can so I can get back to town. Is there gas in it?

### Segwohi
There always is—(PEYTO SLAMS THE DOOR AGAIN.)

### Sereh
(FINGERS HER TEAPOTS ON THE TABLE.) I turn them in my hands with love—and they obey me.

# SCENE III

(THE NEXT MORNING. SEREH AND SEGWOHI ARE AT THE TABLE.)

### Sereh
I had a dream, Segwohi. (SEREH FINGERS A TEAPOT ON THE TABLE AGAIN.)

### Segwohi
I guess I'm going to hear it.

### Sereh
We lived in a rambling house. Not this one here—not this little one. (SEGWOHI LOOKS AT HER.) Though I'm fond of the curled-up linoleum—(SHE LOOKS AT THE ROOM.)—the egg-scale and wooden utinsels hanging on the wall—the pile of newspapers, this sturdy walnut table.

### Segwohi
Ummph—(HE GOES ON EATING, THOUGH HIS FACE SHOWS THE INSULT THAT HIS SISTER THINKS HIS HOUSE IS SMALL. AS SEREH RELATES HER DREAM TO HIM, SEGWOHI GOES ON EATING—SOMETIMES AS THOUGH HE DOESN'T HEAR HER, EATING HIS TOAST AND BACON WITH HIS HEAD CLOSE TO HIS PLATE—FORGETTING TO WIPE HIS CHIN FOR A MOMENT WHERE SOME EGG HAS FALLEN. AS SEREH TALKS, SHE WIPES THE PLACE ON HER CHIN WHERE HE HAS EGG, AND HE WIPES HIS FACE WITH HIS NAPKIN.)

### Sereh
No. The house in my dream was a large one with several stories and rooms here and there—(SHE LIFTS HER ARM TO THE LEFT AND THEN THE RIGHT.) With several floors in each wing—(SHE MOVES HER HAND IN THE SPACE UNDER THE ARM SHE HOLDS OUT.) I sat in the backyard looking at it. And the top story, Segwohi, was a wagon. Yes, whoever built the house, had raised a wagon to be the cupola—the top of the house. You know, the lower floors were vast, but the upper ones got smaller, until the one on top was a small sleeping room you see on some old house. There was a window in it, and roof over it. It was shingled, but when I looked at it a moment, I saw that the small room was a wagon—the kind the settlers came in. Then I walked around inside the house. Cleaning

225

it. Sweeping. And there was Peyto in one of the wings of the house—in his room. And he was on the floor. I came to him, sweeping, and he wanted me to stop. I leaned down and held him, the way a mother holds her small child. He said he heard the spirits. They were ringing a bell to bring in the pigs. (SHE PUTS HER HAND TO HER MOUTH LAUGHING.) As though a pig would come to the ring of a bell. It's as though the house were an old slaughter house. Yes, that's what it was—my husband worked there at one time. And Segwohi, Peyto was crying alone. Telling me what he heard—these ghosts and old battles and the slaughter of our lives on the plains. And we are still in that house—Presided over by the wagon that brought our end. And we are like cattle and pigs going to the slaughter—that must be changed, Segwohi. I want to go to Peyto and hold him. His own father won't have anything to do with him. He has inherited your ability to see what's not here. As though what were here alone wasn't enough, you have to bring in the past. It sits over your house. Yes, Segwohi, I see you're a Medicine Man. I see your house out here on this isolated land—it's more than I thought it was. I see how you live—and I saw in my dream that Peyto is a 'seer' like you—I think I understand you both more now.

### Segwohi
The Spirits visit a woman in such a way?

### Sereh
Oh, what will happen next? The Spirit comes so low to visit me in my sleep? Me! Sereh? The one who has been with you your whole life. Born from the same womb, of the same seed as you, only five years later. But never worthy to be loved by you—only here to serve. I am glad the Great Spirit doesn't see as you do. Oh we are all relieved at that. The animals each day, wipe their brows. Oh relief! The Spirit is not as Segwohi is. Oh no, we are humble creatures. Only Segwohi stands on this earth next to God. You can sit in that chair eating your toast—with crumbs on your shirt— and you don't know that God loves me too? I am not just your after-birth, Jazz Man!

### Segwohi
Sereh! (HE LOOKS AT THE CEILING AND DOES NOT KNOW WHAT TO DO.) Why do I need my sister telling me my faults? Am I like that darkened place over the woodstove? Or that place where the paint is peeling around the leak? I love Peyto—but can't show—

### Sereh
Why not? He sees like you do. Only he is not like you! He can even

226

tell you the words the Spirits say. I heard them from his mouth in my dream. I held him with my Spirit. I talked to him—that's where the battle of our lives is now—shaking off the past—the defeats—or at least confining them with our art—your winter counts, Segwohi, that you don't make anymore—(SHE LOOKS AT THE WINDOW AND SHIVERS. SHE PULLS HER SHAWL UP AROUND HER SHOULDERS AS THOUGH FEELING THE VAST EXPANSE OF LAND THROUGH THE WINDOW.) No—Segwohi is above art—what a pious snake you are. If you were in my yard I'd step on you and squash your insides out. I'd drown you in the downpour we have once a year when the creek runs out of it banks like you do ALL the time, Segwohi! And I'd feed your soggy remains to the vultures.

### Segwohi
So I don't sit too high with you this morning, eh, Sereh?

### Sereh
I've heard you spout your wisdom all my life. (SHE CLEARS AWAY SEGWOHI'S PLATE AND FLATWARE.) Now shut up! My nephew is in need of a father and you babble to the buffalo, the bear and wolf—you talk to the wind more than you do your own son. You look down on us because we make commerce of our art. (SHE POURS HIM SOME COFFEE.) I want something from you too, Segwohi—gratitude, I guess. I've cooked for you ten years since your wife's death. I earn enough from my pottery that I could live by myself. You took care of me in the past, but now I make the money that pays the taxes on your land and buys the food. (SHE SITS AT THE TABLE AGAIN.) The women come from Sante Fe and pay me a lot for my pottery. I buy a firebrick kiln. I give some of the money to the orphans—to Peyto. It costs a lot for two wives and five children. I'll probably buy John the dirt bike he wants from Crawford's Hardware. I'll pay for Ero's counseling. (SHE SMOOTHS OUT HER SKIRT.) I buy this silver belt—this shawl woven from fine yarns. I outbid everyone at the auction for a few more hens. I give some to YOU, Segwohi. So now I have spent it all—I can say I'm poor again and have to live with you. It's better than living with myself—letting the men come around again—though I'm getting too old for that anymore. At least you spare me some of my troubles.

### Segwohi
I don't remind you of your past—

### Sereh
How generous. But why Peyto?

### Segwohi

I want him to be a Holy Man.

### Sereh

And I don't count?—

### Segwohi

I don't blame you for Peyto—his wildness. (SEREH HITS THE TABLE IN ANGER.) But you recovered yourself. (SEGWOHI TRIES TO CALM HER.) Maybe Peyto—(SHE JERKS AWAY FROM HIM, WHICH ANGERS HIM.) You stay at your wheel with your expensive shawl over your shoulders, potting your square horse-troughs and coffins! (NOW SEGWOHI HITS THE TABLE. SEREH REACHES TO PROTECT HER POTTERY.) Pschano! Here is Sereh, working in her shed—(HIS ARMS ARE UP IN THE AIR.)—Working with her pots as though they were Spirits. Telling Segwohi what to do. She is on her toes reaching high into the sky—(HE MAKES CHIRPING NOISES.) She is almost one of the crows that fly over with her black hair and beak—trying for things too high for her.

### Sereh

And there's the old chickenhawk, Segwohi. Stealing our happiness as though it were little chicks in the barnyard with Solomon and his hens. No laughing here, not on Segwohi's land. It is sacred territory! We must all be somber. We must look down on everyone who is not exactly like us.

### Segwohi

That's enough, Sereh. Go live in town if you want. Leave me here on the land with the Spirits of my Ancestors—

### Sereh

No, I will pot my bowls and teapots right out there in MY shed until I'm a hollow old woman, my mind hopping in the field with the rabbits, my hands still shaping clay. (ANGRILY.) Hollow vessels. Where is my life? I need kindness, Segwohi. I have always felt your scorn. Who do you think you are, Medicine Man? Inheritor of the earth and the happy hunting grounds? So much above us you don't stoop to anything as low as us—

### Segwohi

Pshano! (HE BANGS HIS HAND ON THE TABLE AND LEAVES THE KITCHEN IN ANGER.)

Sereh

(SHE RUSHES AFTER HIM.) I bore a grudge against my husband
for years. It polluted everything I did—even the clay. I still make
cellars—and you are right! They are coffins. They're so small, you
hardly know—but they're coffins. I see them as cries of anger. And
the dead world rushes to them. Maybe that's why I am profitable.
And you, Segwohi, who do nothing but farm and stand out under
the clouds and speak to the Spirits—the world has no use for you!

Segwohi

(THEY STAND OUTSIDE A MOMENT NOT KNOWING WHAT
TO DO. SEREH PULLS THE SHAWL TIGHTLY ABOUT HER. SHE
STILL WEARS HER APRON. ONCE SHE PUTS HER HAND ON
SEGWOHI'S ARM, BUT HE PULLS AWAY. HE LOOKS AT THE
SKY AS HE TALKS.) I'm not worthy of making winter counts. I'm
not worthy of recording our events. That's why I stopped—I see
Solomon and his hens. Ki-Ye, your cat, stalking the weeds—the V-
formation of the geese and the V of the one-horse hand-plow
leaning against the barn. The wind blows the hedge-grass by the
fence and the cornstalks in the field. It is all Holy. How can I touch
it?

Sereh

What do you know about being unworthy? My husband didn't want
me. The Great Spirit didn't give me children. There is nothing left to
do but sit at my wheel and move toward death—to grow old as a
Grandmother and be left helpless against everything—that's all I
can do against it—make pots! What is that? To know my skin
wrinkles and my veins stand up like a beaver dam about to burst?
I married a man once just to have someplace to go. Now I stay with
you—I want to be loved.

Segwohi

I do love you, Sereh. You're my sister who has always been with
me—longer than my wife and daughter. You are with me even more
than Peyto. I think he would not even come out here but for you.

Sereh

He likes my beans and cornbread.

Segwohi

He likes the peace you bring between us. The money you give him.
Even the grandchildren run to you first. You've have always been
the peacemaker, and I, Segwohi, Medicine Man, whose job it is to
make peace, have been the one who kept the land plowed up so

nothing could grow. (HE POUNDS HIS CHEST.) That's why I don't make winter counts—

### Sereh
Don't pound yourself. Living does enough of that.

### Segwohi
From the beginning of my life you have been an example of how to act. (SHE LOOKS AWAY FROM HIM.) Even when you went with one man or another, the spirit of gentleness, kindness and forgiveness was always with you—held up for me to see what I could not attain. I've never recognized you as the person you are. I hear your sighs in the sweat lodge. I know the anguish in your head. I see it in your little coffins that you spin on your wheel. And I always thought, well, she's a woman. What does it matter? But I see you as a person, sister. Not just someone following me from the cemetery after our mother and father's death—after my daughter and wife's— But you are someone with significance. Ah, Great Father, accept me back into your house as a human being. (THERE IS SOME HONESTY OF EMOTION IN THIS GESTURE AND SEGWOHI STANDS WITH HIS ARMS OPEN TO THE SKY FOR A MOMENT. THEN HE LOOKS AT SEREH.) I have to ask you something, Sereh.

### Sereh
What is it?

### Segwohi
Did I make my wife—feel angry—

### Sereh
She thought it was an honor to be married to a Medicine Man, Segwohi. I don't know why—

### Segwohi
Thank you, Sister. (SHE NODS AT HIM. HE SITS DOWN AGAIN.) Do you think I drove Reanie away?

### Sereh
I think you did—but she probably would have left anyway. You adopted her, Segwohi. You know what family means—she had to know who her parents were—

### Segwohi
It's been five years.

Sereh

It's been six.

Segwohi

You don't ever get a letter?

Sereh

Don't you always bring in the mail?

# SCENE IV

(ANOTHER MORNING IN THE KITCHEN. PEYTO ENTERS.)

Segwohi
Ah, Peyto's day off?

Peyto
I may have to borrow your truck, Segwohi, to help my first wife move. Her rent went up and she cursed at the landlord. I think she broke a window. Now he wants her out.

Sereh
Sit down, Peyto. It's always something with you. What are those children hearing?

Peyto
Mashunkashey put a dent in Old Crawford's hardware truck. He won't let me borrow it anymore—

Segwohi
Why don't you live with us a while. You wouldn't have your friends causing you trouble—bring the children—

Peyto
I want my friends, Segwohi. (HE LOOKS AROUND THE ROOM, HUGS HIMSELF SUDDENLY.) I remember the cold bedroom and front-room here—I always shivered getting dressed. But in the kitchen when Mother had the stove on and the oatmeal cooking, the windows steamed up and it was hot as a summer afternoon. Then I'd sweat. I was always either hot or cold. I don't remember just ordinary days you never noticed—no, the weather was an enemy—

Segwohi
That's what it's here for—endurance. We must be strong. (SEREH SHRUGS HER SHOULDERS AND LOOKS TO THE CEILING.)

Peyto
How do you stand it here with him? It's enough for me to come out on my day off—just to see if there's anything that needs to be done—

Segwohi

And to ask for something—

Sereh

I'm glad you nail up a board now and then, Peyto. The whole place would fall down otherwise. (SHE SHIVERS.) Burrrrr—I'll have to get out the heating pad again for Ki-Ye, my old cat. Now that it's getting cold her rheumatism will bother her.

Segwohi

If I had someone petting me all the time, I would purr too.

Peyto

I thought I heard a chant in the wind. It sounds like a sax—(HE STANDS AT THE WINDOW.)

Sereh

Hold on to your jazz, Peyto, if only in your head. That's where my pottery was for years.

Segwohi

Yes, encourage him, Sereh. It's like being outbid by you at the auction in Arapahoe.

Sereh

(SMILES.) You still remember that?

Segwohi

Yes, Sereh and her pottery-money—

Peyto

What shapes you come up with, Sereh! (HE SITS AT THE TABLE AGAIN.)

Sereh

No, you don't see them on the shelves in the hardware store—

Segwohi

Nor anywhere else in Nebraska.

Sereh

Is that as far as you can see? They look lovely in Sante Fe—that's the best thing my second husband did for me—he took me there on our honeymoon and I saw the markets—afterwards, I sent them some of my things.

#### Peyto
Why don't you live there?

#### Sereh
I can't work in Sante Fe. I don't have the feel for prairie there that I need for potting. The cellars—the wind storms—

#### Peyto
Segwohi taunting you.

#### Sereh
Yes, tension is a part of it—

#### Segwohi
Clean up the kitchen, Sereh. All these newspapers—what a place. I need to go to the barn. You can borrow my truck whenever you want, Peyto.

#### Sereh
I need the papers when I wrap my pottery for shipping—I told you that. (SEGWOHI STANDS.) I know you go to the grave first. You leave me here wondering why there has never been anyone for me. I keep thinking someday a man will drive up. Or I'll be walking down the road, and there he'll be waiting. It's too late for me to have children. Peyto is like my son anyway, and his children are my grandchildren. Segwohi will have to drive me to town so I can see them again. Maybe they can come out for an afternoon. When they're here I feel like the hen in the barnyard with all her chicks. But I still would like a husband to love. I see Segwohi at his wife's grave and think, why have I missed this? Did the man die whom I should have loved? Why am I left with only my pots?

#### Peyto
You were married once.

#### Sereh
I was married twice—almost several other times too—but it didn't last. You should understand that, Peyto.

#### Peyto
I still see my wives. They're a part of me. Sometimes I wish they weren't. If I moved out here, Sereh, I would bring the children. The wives want me to take them off their hands sometimes.

Segwohi

Yes—live out here—Sereh would watch them.

Sereh

You want me to take care of five children?

Peyto

Well—just for the summer.

Sereh

I can't—(SHE GETS UP FROM THE TABLE AND STANDS AT THE WINDOW BESIDE SEGWOHI.) Maybe if your daughter, Reanie, were here to help. You know she always had a child on her lap—at the pow wow—wherever. But how could I work with five children running through my shed?

Segwohi

(HESITATES.) Maybe Sereh's busy with her pots—

Peyto

You mean she's busy taking care of you!

Segwohi

You tell me your pots obey you, Sereh. But give them a will of their own—

Sereh

I do what I can to help you, Peyto—but—

Segwohi

We always do what we can to help—

Peyto

(ANGRILY.) The best thing you could do is die and leave me your land.  (PEYTO TURNS AWAY, EMBARRASSED HE SAID WHAT HE DID.) I didn't mean that—

Segwohi

Stay in Arapahoe and smoke your grass—get DRUNK with your friends—let THEM help you. (SEREH BACKS AWAY FROM SEGWO-HI.) Do you know how I felt in court—all the way to Omaha to hear your trial? It was the SHAME of the Ancestors!

Peyto

(RISING.) Are they still here with us? Maybe we could make a chart on the wall—like the old drawings on teepee-hides telling of the loss of game—or the cavalry raids—(HE POINTS TO THE WALL.) Forget your winter counts, Segwohi. Make teepee drawings. Of course, they'd all be of Peyto's downfall and trial. His failures—all according to Segwohi, of course.

Segwohi

Ah, that's what I'll do! Give me a grease pencil, Sereh—the ones you mark your pots with—

Sereh

They're in the shed.

Segwohi

I'll go get one. (HE QUICKLY LEAVES THE KITCHEN.)

Peyto

(HE PACES IN ANGER. SEREH LIFTS HER ARMS IN SURRENDER.) Is there anyone like Segwohi? I don't know how you stand it here with him. No, I won't move in with you—as much as I could do without rent.

Sereh

I can't take care of five children anyway—as much as they need it.

Peyto

Why?

Sereh

I don't have patience, for one thing. For another—my life has always felt separated—but now I'm becoming one with my work.

Peyto

You'd have patience.

Sereh

No, Peyto. You messed up your life. You and your wives take care of your children.

Peyto

You always help me.

Sereh

Not this time.

#### Peyto
All right, Sereh—(ANGRILY.) I couldn't stay with Segwohi anyway. I waited to leave here too many years—

#### Sereh
Be patient with him, Peyto—

#### Peyto
No! (HE POUNDS THE TABLE.)

#### Segwohi
(HE RUSHES BACK INTO THE KITCHEN HOLDING A GREASE PENCIL.) It was right on your wheel, Sereh.

#### Peyto
Come on, old man.

#### Segwohi
That's just what I need. A buffalo-hide drawing—a wall-drawing of Peyto's antics. So when he proclaims his goodness to me, I can show him what he's done. From MY viewpoint, of course, as though I were making all this up—

#### Sereh
No, Brother, you're going too far.

#### Segwohi
Yes, Sereh. I should be as daring as Peyto. I should use my art! I'm not outbid on this! Let's see. Peyto was born. (SEGWOHI MAKES A DRAWING OF A PAPOOSE.) Right here on the wall—under the shelf, by the open scissors on a hook—I draw a papoose. You never keep the kitchen clean as my wife did anyway, Sereh. What will a few marks matter? (HE THINKS A MOMENT.) Peyto grows. (SEGWOHI DRAWS A BOW AND ARROW.) A Christmas present when he was a boy. Now Peyto is a bigger boy—stealing the pumpkins and the scarecrow from the neighbor's garden. Not going to school unless I took him to the door—(SEGWOHI DRAWS A PUMPKIN AND SCARECROW. PEYTO SITS AT THE TABLE WITH HIS HEAD IN HIS HANDS.)

#### Sereh
(SEREH TOUCHES HER NEPHEW TO COMFORT HIM—WHILE SHE FROWNS AT SEGWOHI.) Are you going to draw my short comings too?

#### Segwohi
Would there be room? (HE STARTS TO DRAW BARS)—Peyto in jail—

#### Peyto
Would there be room for yours? That's the question. Your mean-ness—your unforgiveness.

#### Sereh
You're self-righteousness, Brother. Don't you ever learn?

#### Segwohi
I could make my wall-drawings in the underpass on the way to town—everytime I go to Arapahoe, I see someone else has written something—do you see this black square and white circle? (HE DRAWS.)—that's the underpass. (HE SCRIBBLES OVER IT.) Isn't that what you both do when you sell your pottery in the market, and sing your bear-hunting songs in bars? You close off the spirit world?

#### Sereh
That's not true. What would you know, you snake?

#### Segwohi
—No, no—I mark it closed so no one else can leave me. I've lost enough—I'm such an old rattler—

#### Sereh
Enough, Segwohi. You'll cause us to rip one another up.

#### Peyto
No, it will be only him.

#### Segwohi
It is better to let Peyto rip me up without letting him know how it hurts?

#### Peyto
I can't stand this, Sereh. He drives me away.

#### Segwohi
Ah, you should stay, Peyto, and see what your winter count looks like on the wall.

#### Peyto
Have I died? Do I stand now in judgement, seeing my life pass before me? And where are the good things I have done, Father.

Aren't I here now to fix the barn door? I lived on this land for years with you and received only your scorn.

### Segwohi
Go back to Arapahoe. To whatever woman you've got there. Your third wife already or maybe just someone you picked up. Any more grandchildren for me? (SEGWOHI STARTS TO DRAW THE CHILDREN.)

### Peyto
(PICKS UP THE SALT SHAKER AND THROWS IT AT THE WALL.) You always back me into a corner! (HE THROWS A PLATE AT THE DRAWINGS, THEN REACHES FOR ONE OF THE BOWLS.)

### Sereh
No—Peyto! (HE THROWS IT ANYWAY.) Leave before you hurt him. Leave before I hurt you! (SHE THROWS HIS JEAN JACKET AT HIM. SHOVES HIM TO THE DOOR ANGRILY. LOOKS AT THE PIECES OF THE BOWL PEYTO THREW AGAINST THE WALL.) I liked the blue in this bowl. It was the sky through the chestnut tree in the yard.

### Segwohi
I'll draw Peyto throwing bowls—(HE STARTS TO DRAW.)

### Sereh
(SHE TURNS ON SEGWOHI.) Stop that drawing! What's wrong with you? DEVIL! You're no Medicine Man. You're a hateful old INCITER. (SHE IS SO ANGRY, SHE NEARLY SPITS AS SHE TALKS.) Maybe I will start a mural too. (SHE GRABS THE GREASE PENCIL FROM SEGWOHI.) If Segwohi can make his chart, then I can make mine! Now, I work in the kitchen cooking suppers. I have cooked for ten years—one supper each day makes 3,650 suppers. (SHE FIGURES THIS OUT ON THE WALL. SEGWOHI STARES AT HER.) No wonder I feel like I'm always busy. Of course, there's lunch and breakfast for Segwohi too. I wonder if I can figure all this.

### Segwohi
You were always good in math.

### Sereh
Jam be coup! I'll try. (SEREH IS QUIET A MOMENT AS SHE FIGURES ON THE WALL.) Holy buffalo. That's 7,300 meals I've cooked for Segwohi. Now say we live twenty more years—three meals each day—(SEREH FIGURES FOR ANOTHER MOMENT.) That's 21,900 meals I still have to cook!

### Segwohi

Maybe you won't be here that long.

### Sereh

(IGNORING HIM.) Now sometimes we eat out—say once a year in Okemah. So I'll take one meal off for twenty years—that makes only 21,980 more times I have to cook. (SEGWOHI TRIES TO TAKE THE PENCIL BACK.) Just a moment, Sehwohi. I have to catch up on the first ten years I've served in this place. (SHE BEGINS MARKING THE WALL BEHIND THE STOVE FURIOUSLY WITH TINY ROMAN NUMERALS. SEGWOHI CAN ONLY STAND AND WATCH.)

# SCENE V

(SEREH AND SEGWOHI AT THE KITCHEN TABLE. SEREH READS THE NEWSPAPER, FOLDS IT SUDDENLY AND LOOKS AT SEGWOHI.)

### Segwohi
You've had another dream? My small house and a larger one with a covered wagon sitting on it? That's why you can't help Peyto. You're busy with your dreams—your little children from the Dream Talker.

### Sereh
No dream, Segwohi. This is straight from the head while I'm awake. Everything seems against Peyto.

### Segwohi
Well, he's got his 'Aunt Mamma' he comes to see.

### Sereh
Why can't you just take him fishing?

### Segwohi
He wouldn't go.

### Sereh
I thought about Reanie too—and I thought about you, Segwohi.

### Segwohi
I don't dream about her so much anymore. Maybe she's with the Ancestors—

### Sereh
I think she's alive. She's unhappy wherever she is. She might come back sometime, Segwohi. Would you be understanding? I remember my dream when I thought this earth was a slaughter house—one like those that line up on the way to Omaha. She feels it too.

### Segwohi
Maybe she'll come back and help Segwohi with his children. Maybe she'll come back and have some grandsons for me. Maybe before I die, I'll know who will take my place.

241

Sereh

Maybe our strength will come in a new way. Through Peyto—

Segwohi

Diluted?

Sereh

No—that's only in your mind, Segwohi. Peyto can be a Holy Man. I see it in my sleep when everything is as it should be. Or maybe the 'Two becoming one' will be in a new way. Maybe in one of the granddaughters?

Segwohi

Not on this earth.

Sereh

I remind you of one of our Cherokee legends—from the Ancestors— One day in the old times, when we could talk to the animals, while some children were playing outside their house, their mother inside heard them scream. Running out she found a rattlesnake had crawled from the grass, and taking up a stick, she killed it. The father was out hunting and that evening coming home after dark he heard a strange wailing sound—it was the rattlesnakes, with their mouths open crying. He asked them the reason for their trouble, and they told him that his wife had killed their Chief. The snakes told him that now he would have to give his wife as a sacrifice for their chief or something far worse would happen. They told him that a rattlesnake would go with him and coil up outside the door in the dark. He must go inside where he would find his wife waiting, and ask her to get him a drink from the spring. It was night when he arrived at his house and very dark, but he found his wife waiting with his supper ready. He sat down and asked for a drink of water. She handed him the gourd, but he said he wanted it fresh from the spring, so she took a bowl and went out the door. The next moment he heard a cry, and going out he found the rattlesnake had bitten her and she was already dying. He stayed with her until she was dead. Then the rattlesnake came out of the grass again and taught the hunter a prayer song, and said, 'when you meet any of us, sing this song and we shall not hurt you, but if one of us should bite one of your tribe, then sing this song over him and he will recover.' We sing that song to this day, Segwohi. Hanney nah nah no—(SHE WIGGLES HER HAND TOWARD HIM.) Henado'sihe. Ka'na:ti.

Segwohi

(HE BACKS AWAY FROM HER.) Now I'm a rattlesnake?

#### Sereh

It seems to me it was a woman who brought the healing in that story. But you could be healing for Peyto—a Medicine Dance. Out of our evil comes a song you could give him. You've closed your windows. You live on your farm with all your hay stored in the barnloft and watch those of us who are struggling—and you look down on us. We're hardly more than part of your landscape at times. Look at that wall—that's Peyto's flesh you're marking up. You do it right in front of his eyes. You wound instead of heal, Medicine Man! Draw your own sins. (SHE HOLDS A GREASE PENCIL TO HIS FACE.) No. I will! I'm not as blind as you. (SEREH BEGINS HER OWN WALL DRAWING NEAR THE STOVE WHERE SHE'S MARKED THE NUMBER OF MEALS SHE'S COOKED.) Ho! I forgot to mark breakfast! (SHE MAKES ANOTHER MARK WITH THE OTHERS. THEN SHE DRAWS SEGWOHI.) Arrows straight down from a black cloud strike his head. That's how he got so obtuse.

#### Segwohi

You're marking up MY kitchen, Sereh.

#### Sereh

It's my kitchen, Brother. What do you do with it except eat with your head in your plate?

#### Segwohi

What do you?—Always warming and re-warming beans. You're always wanting ME to do something. But let Peyto bring his children to run through YOUR potting shed—

#### Sereh

All right, then—I'm marking up YOUR kitchen. But I think we ought to see Segwohi here among the drawings. A square head with window-shades drawn over his eyes.

#### Segwohi

And here is Sereh—just like that crack in the wall—who is supposed to keep me from loneliness after the death of my wife. Don't you know what it's like to hunger for someone—

#### Sereh

I can't remember anything but the hungering. I thought I'd told you that. Sometimes I can't wait for the night to sleep. And here we are, brother and sister—all these years together and we're not even friends. Separated as we are from the old way of life—separated as the Great Spirit and man.

Segwohi
I'm not separated from God.

Sereh
Yes, you are. Otherwise you'd help Peyto. What if we draw you both on the wall and the drawing shows Peyto is braver than you?—he has more to struggle against—more of him goes into the struggle. He is moving his first wife. His friends come by with beer. Ero is hiding in the bushes because he's shy and afraid. Maybe I could take care of him—maybe he would sit on my lap while I pot. What about it, Segwohi? Huh? Yes, here is Segwohi from another angle. The lightning that struck him on the head is now darting out his eyes at others! Yes, first of all, it hits his own son. (SHE DRAWS A STICK FIGURE FOR PEYTO. THE FIGURE WEARS A STRIPED JAIL-SHIRT.) No, Segwohi. Maybe you are like God. Didn't he send his son to the cross? (SHE EXTENDS THE ARMS OF THE STICK FIGURE AND DRAWS A CROWN OF THORNS ON HIS HEAD.) Here is Peyto. Suffering for the world which is not worthy of him—

Segwohi
I don't know why the Great Spirit doesn't strike you.

Sereh
He's probably too busy aiming for you. Is that why you put the lightning rod on the barn last spring?

Segwohi
I didn't want the hay to catch fire.

Sereh
You didn't want your own pants to catch fire. (SHE DRAWS A BLACK SQUARE WITH A WHITE CIRCLE IN IT.) I've come out of the underpass too. I've passed a flock of black-birds rising from the field. How I wish I could pot something moving like that.

Segwohi
I want the pencil now.

Sereh
No!

Segwohi
Yes! (HE TAKES THE PENCIL FROM HER AND SHE SITS AT THE TABLE.) Here is Segwohi making the sweat lodge, draping hides over the poles. Gathering the rocks to heat the fire. I hear the voices

of the Ancestors as I draw! Maybe they are happy with my drawings. Here we are with the white man's wagon for a cupola over us— Sereh dreams. Here is my sister who is complete in herself—for as long as she stays at her potter's wheel—or in her sleep. Asphodels bloom at her shed. (HE DRAWS THEM ALSO.) And now we are in the Sweat Lodge. He ye hey ye. (SEGWOHI CHANTS AS HE DRAWS.) Rocks hiss like buckshot into mailboxes and road signs. The holy trail down from the Great Spirit to something shiny as brass—what is it? A sax? NO! It can't be. Peyto and 'Bear Tracks'—his Indian band? (SEREH LAUGHS.)

# SCENE VI

(ANOTHER DAY. SEREH IS IN HER SHED WITH THE PIECES OF THE
BOWL PEYTO BROKE.)

### Segwohi
(ENTERING THE SHED.) Did you see the clouds in the sky this
morning, Sereh?

### Sereh
Yes—when I came from the house after breakfast. I think we fly
sometimes in our sleep—over the prairie of Furnas County in the
airships of our dreams. The wide sky passing under us—

### Segwohi
What do you think they meant?

### Sereh
You're the Medicine Man who has contact with the Spirits and
Ghosts of our Ancestors.

### Segwohi
I wondered if the clouds were the ghost of my wife. The moon was
like a small milkpail beside her.

### Sereh
I don't know.

### Segwohi
Is that the bowl Peyto broke?

### Sereh
I'm trying to glue it together.

### Segwohi
How can you forgive him?

### Sereh
Because I've done things that need forgiving. That's what we live
for, Segwohi. Not to be perfect. No. We live to make mistakes so we
can know forgiveness.

#### Segwohi
(HE PICKS UP A PIECE OF THE BROKEN POTTERY.) The color of the sky, you say?

#### Sereh
Yes. I'm going to put it back together. That's where the struggle of our lives is. Not in shucking off the past. No. I've changed my mind. Our struggle is living with the broken pieces. We aren't whole. Our family is broken, Segwohi. The hoop of our nation—we're a mix of several bloods. Cheyenne. Cherokee. Who knows what else—

#### Segwohi
You know, Sereh, I think my wife's happy with the wall-drawings in the kitchen. She was always so careful—not even any flour on the counter after she made cornbread or pies—(SMILES.) Not like you, Sereh—you have it all over yourself—and are so messy I can't stand it sometimes.

#### Sereh
I might paint the kitchen after your drawing-spell is over. You haven't let me touch anything since I came here to live—

#### Segwohi
Maybe I'll keep working with my wall-drawings when you're off in your shed—

#### Sereh
If you're buried in your work, who'll the women from Sante Fe ogle over when they come, if you're busy drawing on the kitchen wall?

#### Segwohi
Don't talk like that with my wife's grave in sight.

#### Sereh
(SHE LISTENS A MOMENT.) Ah! The mail truck. Finally. Or maybe Peyto—(SHE STANDS, STRETCHES HER BACK.) Maybe I'll get more orders for my pottery. Maybe the Sante Fe News with a review of my work. You know I like to get the mail as soon as it comes.

#### Segwohi
Maybe they would like to come and 'review' my work—(HE NODS TOWARD THE HOUSE TO INDICATE HIS DRAWINGS IN THE KITCHEN.)

### Sereh

I'll show it to the women next time they come for my pots. (PEYTO ENTERS WITH A FEW LETTERS, SOME PAPERS, AND A DEAD HEN.) My hen! Peyto! Where did you find her?

### Peyto

In the ditch by the mailbox.

### Segwohi

You're limping.

### Peyto

My back is sore from moving my first wife.

### Sereh

I must not have closed the hen in the coop last night.

### Peyto

You can't always get them all—

### Segwohi

(HE GOES TO PEYTO TO EXAMINE THE HEN. HE SEPARATES THE FEATHERS ON THE HEN'S BREAST.) Buckshot! Are there more holes in the box?

### Peyto

I don't know, Segwohi. There're so many already it's hard to tell.

### Segwohi

Blast them! Now the pirates are killing my hens. Well, pluck her feathers. We'll have chicken for supper.

### Sereh

I don't know how long she's been dead.

### Segwohi

(SEGWOHI SHAKES HIS FIST TOWARD THE ROAD.) Hen killers! (HE LEAVES. SEREH WATCHES HIM.)

### Sereh

I'll bury her when he's not looking. (SEREH LOOKS THROUGH THE FEW LETTERS PEYTO HAS BROUGHT. SHE DOESN'T FIND ANY OF INTEREST AND STUFFS THEM INTO HER APRON POCKET.)

### Segwohi
HEN KILLERS! (SEREH AND PEYTO CAN HEAR HIM FROM THE ROAD.) AAAAAHHHHHH! (BUT PEYTO LOOKS TOWARD THE HILL.)

### Peyto
—The sound of geese crossing the sky. (PEYTO GOES TO THE DOOR OF THE SHED. SEREH WATCHES HIM.) For a moment I thought I heard Indian chanting. (HE SHAKES HIS HEAD.)

### Sereh
It's Segwohi out there cackling—

### Peyto
No—I thought I heard the voice of the Ancestors he always talks about. (HE PUTS HIS HANDS TO HIS EARS AND TAKES THEM AWAY SEVERAL TIMES.) So there it is, Sereh—the sound of ancient chants. Jazz sounds! Yawa'dada'-ski:su. All of a sudden I think I hear! After all these years of anger at Segwohi.

### Sereh
Look at this bowl I'm trying to glue together, Peyto.

### Peyto
How can you work with clay? It's cold and damp as death.

### Sereh
It's the stuff we're made of, Peyto—I breathe life into it.—you should know that from your jazz. We create form and life and order out of instruments. Mine is clay and water and a whirling wheel. Yours is metal.

### Peyto
You don't think I misuse my art?

### Sereh
No, Peyto. No more than the clouds that swirl over the horizon at times misuse the sky. (SHE CONTINUES TO WORK WITH THE PIECES.) The energy and vitality of your work make it clean, Peyto.

### Peyto
I brought you drawings the children did for their beloved Aunt Sereh.

### Sereh
Oh, Peyto. (SHE WIPES HER HANDS AND LOOKS AT THE DRAW-

INGS.) I'll put them on the wall of my shed—here next to Segwohi's drawings he used to do.

### Peyto
(HE LOOKS TOWARD THE HILL AGAIN.) I know I hear chanting—

### Sereh
(A SHOUT COMES FROM THE HOUSE.) Sounds like Segwohi to me— (THEY LEAVE THE SHED AND GO TO THE HOUSE.)

### Segwohi
(SEGWOHI IS DRAWING AGAIN.)—Revenge on the pirates. A mail-box that explodes when they shoot buckshot into it—wiping them out! (SEGWOHI DRAWS AN EXPLOSION.)

### Sereh
Remember, Segwohi. We live to become human.

### Segwohi
Now I have my drawings—they wait for me after I milk the cow. I see why you and Peyto work at your pottery and music, Sereh. It's like when I talked with my grandfather when I was a boy. I understood things. (SEGWOHI HEARS THE SOUND OF JAZZ. HE DRAWS A WHILE LONGER.)

### Sereh
I will make Segwohi in his medicine-dance. (SHE DRAWS ALSO.) I will cut him with the scissors of jazz. Wake up, Segwohi. Another world has come. It's not ours, but we must live in it. We were an Indian people. Little children of the Great Spirit. Now we're a shadow of our dreams. But in dreams we dance. We fly like airships.

### Segwohi
Now I see Peyto's struggles with these lightning-bolts. I see that I've been blind to Peyto. I see that I am human. (HE FINDS THE PLACE IN THE MURAL WHERE HE DREW THE SAXOPHONE.) I have a feeling there's room for us all under the wide sky. All the struggling, warring, maybe even destroying a part of ourselves—but out of our mistakes—ah—what if we're pirates ourselves—what if we shot holes in our own mailboxes. Here is Peyto—shot with holes just like the mailbox. Riddled with stars so the sound of his jazz can blow through. The whole sky shot with holes—PZZZZZZZ! (SEGWOHI LOSES HIMSELF IN HIS DRAWING.)—like Sereh's white northern beans!

### Peyto

All right, old man, I'm going to work on your mural too. We look our separate directions, but we might be the same. Where's the grease pencil and the LADDER? I'm going to make some 'BEAR TRACKS!!'

# THE TRUTH TELLER

Because to go forward
we must first go back—

# CHARACTERS

Halfbreed Man

Indian Woman

# SETTING

Circa 1800

Pine Country in the North Woods, an Indian village on the Upper Mississippi near a Trading Post.

The stage is a maple sugar camp in spring (Part I), a drying rack for fish in the summer (Part II), a ricing camp during the fall (Part III), and a teepee for winter camp (Part IV).

The main prop is a tripod of some sort, which can serve as a tree, a drying rack, a canoe, and a teepee.

Other props are the accoutrements needed for the four seasons: birchbark basket for collecting and boiling maple sugar, poles, rawhide ties, winnowing basket, wild rice sticks, blanket, cradleboard, moss, twigs, deer antler rake, hide-stretcher, birchbark scroll, snow shoes, lure and spear, canoe paddle, masks, leg bands, stick antlers and drum for the dances.

With special thanks to Fred Benjamin, Mille Lacs Museum, Mille Lacs, Minnesota; Walter Caribou, Grand Portage, Minnesota; and Mary and Maggie Magiskan, Old Fort William, Canada, who told their stories.

Also special gratitude to Kristi Wheeler and Doug Birk, research assistants.

# I.

MAPLE SUGAR SEASON (SPRING). THE WOMAN PUTS A WOOD PEG IN THE TREE AND TIES HER BIRCHBARK BASKET BELOW IT. LATER, SHE TAKES THE BUCKET, TIES IT OVER THE FIRE. STIRS UNTIL THE SYRUP BECOMES SUGAR. THE CRADLE BOARD IS ALWAYS NEAR HER.

### Indian Woman
(SINGS TO HER BABY AS AN INDIAN APPEARS FROM OFFSTAGE.)
Mey mey mey mey.

### Indian
The Great Spirit wanted to fly. So He asked a bird to tell Him how. Just where to put the feathers on. Just how to move the arms. Flap. Flap. It wasn't easy. Now faster You. Hey Great Spirit. Said the bird. Flap faster. And the Great Spirit flapped faster and finally got It off the ground. Now hey when You are above. The Indian people will call You. The bird said. Now don't look down. Hey. Don't look anywhere but to the sky before You. Now the Great Spirit practiced flying and flapping. Out there in the trees before anyone is looking. Just snorting and flapping feathers and getting out of breath flapping. Yeah. Until He got It going. Yeah. He got It off the ground. The beavers clapped their hands. Yo. The otter. Yeah. The muskrats. Ho. All of creation got to clapping. The Great Spirit is flying. Well He got to going so high and fast and the Indian people got to calling Him and He had to look down because He was the Great Spirit you know. And He had to listen. Had to answer. And He got so busy looking at the ground that He crashed. Yes He fell right to earth. Thud. (HE LOOKS AT HER.) Thud. (HE TRIES TO PUT HIS ARMS AROUND HER AND PULL HER DOWN WITH HIM.)

### Indian Woman
My eyes are shut. My ears are closed.

### Indian
I've been gone since last summer. Now it's spring. I'm returned like the sun. Aren't you glad to see me?

### Indian Woman
The seasons change. The trees shed. The snow falls. The trees get

their leaves again. Do they ask your help? How can you guide those white soldiers? It's like leading a storm to our door.

### Indian
Because I know the river and the way north to the headwaters.

### Indian Woman
You know what I mean.

### Indian
Because my father was white and I speak their language. They paid me well. I bought a steel trap. (HE DEMONSTRATES AND IT SNAPS SHUT.) And see what I brought you—these garters. (HE GIVES HER TWO RED LEG-BANDS.)

### Indian Woman
(SHE LOOKS AT THEM.) Where do you wear them? (SHE TRIES TO TIE ONE ON AS A HEADBAND.)

### Indian
They go on your leg. (SHE TIES IT AT HER KNEE.) No, like this. (HE TRIES TO TIE IT HIGHER.)

### Indian Woman
Do white women wear these?

### Indian
They wear them higher—like this—

### Indian Woman
I would rather you chop fire-wood. Kill a deer. Make me another deer antler rake. Find some chokecherry. Dream a name for the child. Draw a birchbark scroll for his life's path. Paddle the boat while I gather rice with my cedar rice-beaters. Trample the rice once it's gathered. Repair my bear-paw snow shoe. Find some pine-pitch. Bear-grease. Spruce-gum so my birchbark basket won't leak maple syrup. You could bring me an iron kettle from the fur traders instead of their garters. But no. You lead the white man north along a river. They'll take our way of life. The elders say so. I feel it also in my heart. Sometimes they call you a half-breed traitor.

### Indian
Then why do you want me to name the child?

### Indian Woman

Because I do. A name is the pine-pitch that holds you together. Otherwise your arm would fall off when you lifted the bow. Your knees would turn when you wanted to go straight. It's like knowing your history. It's knowing who you are.

### Indian

The Northwest Company Post had a door. To hold it closed there were lead musket-balls in a sock tied on a string as a weight. The door swings. (HE HAS TROUBLE EXPLAINING THIS.) Well like the deer-hide flap on the teepee door, but it swings inward.

### Indian Woman

What's a sock?

### Indian

An over-the-foot. (HE PUTS HIS HAND OVER HIS FOOT TRYING TO EXPLAIN THIS TOO.) A thin moccasin. (LIFTS HER FOOT INTO THE AIR AND PUTS HIS HAND OVER IT TO MAKE THE MOTION OF PUTTING ON A SOCK.) But under the moccasin—

### Indian Woman

Soon it will be black-fly season. I could use a door with a weight. In the meantime I'll smoke moss over the fire and keep them away. (SHE FANS THE FIRE.)

### Indian

They have guns that can kill anything—man or animal—if they can hit it. (PANTOMIME OF HORNED ANIMAL BEING STALKED BY WHITE HUNTER BUT ESCAPING.) They have a bigger gun that sounds like thunder. They have stamina. Ideas come to them. They have a way of telling how cold it is. They have numbers for the cold. And numbers for how far they've gone. All day the leader kept taking notes in his book—(SCRIBBLES IN AN IMAGINARY BOOK.) They tell the directions by a needle under a glass. They make doors close by a weight. A sock is something that goes under the moccasin and over the foot. A between-them. The way the moon looks in the day sky. An image almost. A ghost moccasin. That's a sock.

### Indian Woman

What is the purpose of this ghost moccasin? Other than to hold doors closed?

### Indian

No it holds the foot closed. It keeps the boot from rubbing a sore on the toes and heel. It keeps the foot warm so they don't get sick.

### Indian Woman
Our people die from their diseases.

### Indian
The white man doesn't know how to hunt, yet he endures a winter with courage. He doesn't seem to have many stories to tell.

### Indian Woman
How can anyone survive without stories?

### Indian
They have stories written in a book. But not stories like we tell.

### Indian Woman
They can't be stories then.

### Indian
They are. I've heard some of them. A man in a boat and another man on a cross.

### Indian Woman
We have a cross on our birchbark scrolls that tell our sacred stories.

### Indian
But it stands for the four directions. It's not the kind of cross in their book. My father wanted me to study it, but I would rather stay in the woods. (HE TICKLES HER.)

### Indian Woman
Our stories carry us like a canoe. That's what stories do. I tell stories to myself when you're gone.

### Indian
When I was a boy my mother and father died within two days of each other. My father died of a hunting accident. My mother died in childbirth. I went into the woods. I didn't want to live. I had nothing but water for seven days, and a man and woman came to me. They said your grandmother is crying for you. What are you doing here? They asked. Then they changed into bears and walked away. I must have gone to sleep then and had a dream. A wind came and brought the sound of a drum. I saw the drum in my dream. It was painted red and blue. I saw that the red was for the rising sun. But the blue was for the land still left in darkness. It was that

darkness from which a storm came. I sang my song and said storm you go around the other way. You don't run over me. I said hey storm. Hey you storm. Go the other way. Afterwards, I went home and lived with my grandmother. I sing that song now and beat my drum. I tell the story of how I got my song. Sometimes the storm goes away.

### Indian Woman

They won't go away. Nothing will stop them. We'll be broken forever like ice on the creek where a tomahawk falls.

### Indian

I will sing my song.

### Indian Woman

I will sing mine as I stir the maple syrup. Mey mey mey mey. I make my song the way cottonwood leaves rise and fall with the wind. My baby hears my voice and knows I am near. Mey mey mey mey. Once the maple syrup fell like rain. But Wenebojo, our trickster, decided that was too easy. The Indian had to work. We had to make an offering of tobacco. We had to put a small piece of wood into the tree so the sap would run out. Catch it in a birchbark basket. We had to cut wood. Boil sap for a long time. Boil it until it is maple syrup. Boil some of the syrup longer until it is maple sugar.

(SOUND OF THUNDER.)

# II.

FISH SPEARING SEASON (SUMMER). THE INDIAN MAN AND WOM-
AN SIT IN THE TEEPEE FOR COVER DURING THE THUNDERSTORM.
LATER, DURING THE DIALOGUE, THE MAN PADDLES THE CANOE
WITH HIS LURE AND SPEAR. THE WOMAN CUTS THE FISH INTO
STRIPS AND DRIES THEM. SHE ALSO RAKES THE GROUND AND
GATHERS WILD ONIONS, WALNUTS AND BERRIES.

### Indian Woman
The thunder sounds to me now like the white man. Will they buy the
blades of grass? How much for the clouds?

### Indian
Listen to the thunderstorm. Forget the people moving into our land.

### Indian Woman
All we have is rain. And the thunder of their guns. Do you have a
name for the baby yet? (SHE USES MOSS FOR THE BABY'S DIAPER.)

### Indian
I haven't dreamed of one. What's your hurry?

### Indian Woman
Then tell a story.

### Indian
You know how we always move from one place to another. From
maple-sugar camp to fishing camp to ricing and berry-picking camp
to hunting camp. Sometimes just moving. Here and there. (HE
MARKS ON THE GROUND.) HO. Here. Then ho ho. There. We never
stayed just one place like the white man. No. The Indian is always
moving. Well, the land got to feeling the Indian moving all over it.
Just squirming like a trail of ants always walking. Like a swarm of
bees always buzzing in its ear. (THE INDIAN TICKLES THE WOM-
AN'S EAR.) The land decided it wanted to move too. It said I will just
rearrange myself. One night a thunderstorm happened. A giant
thunderstorm. It parted the darkness until the sky was white with
lightning. They watched the thunderstorm jump up and down over
the land. It jumped and snorted and tossed away the darkness until.
Thud. The Indians saw some of the land get up and walk off. Yes the
land rearranged itself. It decided to move too. So a part moved

away. Just like that. No one knows where it went.

### Indian Woman

Your story worries me. I don't want part of the land to leave. The others will hear your story and be afraid. Stop the storm, if you want to do something. Take your arrow and shoot the clouds. Make the sun come back. Make the summer come. (HE SHOOTS INTO THE SKY.) Where will we go when they take the land? (SHE TALKS WHILE THE MAN CLICKS ROCKS TO START A FIRE.)

### Indian

We won't go anywhere. We belong with the animals and trees and rivers. We'll be here as long as the land is.

### Indian Woman

What do their Grandfathers say about them coming?

### Indian

They don't talk to their Ancestors.

### Indian Woman

They don't talk to their Grandfathers?

### Indian

They don't see ghosts.

### Indian Woman

What drives them up the river to make marks of land on their map? To set up villages behind walls? There's a new fort just across the river. (SHE SCRAPES THE GROUND WITH HER DEER ANTLER RAKE.)

### Indian

The map makes them feel less a stranger to the land. They change the names of rivers and lakes from our words to theirs. There were nights I was guiding the white man upriver that I dreamed of him standing mid-air. Trying to find a place to put his feet. The land didn't feel like home to him and he dug and looked and smelled and poked, trying to make a place he felt was his. He doesn't know where he's walking. It's because he wears hard boots and doesn't know the land is his mother.

### Indian Woman

He won't hear the voice of the earth. He doesn't know it's part of us. He won't have dreams.

### Indian
Maybe there are men who can live without vision.

### Indian Woman
Who can live without dreams? Remember those people in your dream when you were a boy? You said they turned into bears. They were your parents talking to you after their death. They wanted you to live. Where would you be without their dream? (HERE THE INDIAN TURNS AWAY FROM HER AND FISHES.) Mey mey mey mey. (SHE SINGS TO HER BABY AND SOON TIES A FISH TO THE DRYING POLES.)

HERE THERE IS MUSIC IN PREPARATION FOR THE BEAR DANCE. THE MUSICIAN IS IN A MASK. HE BEATS THE DRUM AND ACTS LIKE A BEAR. HE JUMPS AROUND THE INDIAN MAN AS HE FISHES. THE WOMAN JOINS HIM AS THE OTHER BEAR. THEY MOTION FOR THE INDIAN MAN TO FOLLOW. THEY SHOW HIM WHERE TO FISH. ONE OF THEM CARRIES THE SUN.

# III.

WILD RICE SEASON (FALL). FIRST, THE DANCE. LATER, THE WOMAN SITS IN THE CANOE WHILE THE MAN PADDLES. SHE GATHERS RICE INTO THE CANOE WITH THE RICE STICKS. THEY DRY THE RICE ON THE GROUND, PARCH IT IN A KETTLE TO LOOSEN THE HUSKS, FAN IT, TRAMPLE OR JIG IT, FAN AGAIN AND TRAMPLE.

### Indian
(IN HIS RED & BLUE MASK.) I am a Spirit person. I have walked over the boundary. I'm in the Spirit world. I dance. I talk to the earth. Which plants can I use for healing? Where are the fish? When is the rice ready for harvest? I listen and it tells me. The eagle drops his feather for me. I hear the voice of the bird. The voice of the bear blesses my lure and spear. I give thanks to the fish for his life. I give thanks to the river for the wild rice. I talk to the wind and rain. I say rain go around us. Rain you stay over there. Over the walled fort— make mud up to their knees. Ho ho. Ha ha. Sink their boats. Stop their forward going. Make the rain to rise above their ears. (THE THREE DANCERS MAKE A COMIC ACT OF ROWING AND DROWNING.)

### Indian Woman
This is the dancing we do. On my bird face is the rising sun and the land still in darkness where the winds rise. Go around me I say. What are you doing here? Go around me I say. Tell me bird. How to fly? Flap. Flap. How to fall to earth? Thud. (THE TWO OTHER DANCERS BLOW ON HER. SHE FALLS OVER, THEN GETS UP.) How to survive the fall? (AFTER DANCING.) Tell me. What is the truth of those who come?

### Indian
I don't know.

### Indian Woman
You traveled with the white man for a summer and winter. You know about his Bible and you don't know his truth? I think they say they have one truth, and anyone who doesn't believe it, doesn't have truth.

### Indian
What is truth to you?

**Indian Woman**

Why do you ask me?

**Indian**

Because you think there's just one truth.

**Indian Woman**

The elders say that truth is written on our birchbark scrolls.

**Indian**

The white men have a truth too. Something that makes them go on. I've seen them cough up blood from carrying their heavy barrels and canoes. I've seen them hungry. Sometimes their feet were so swollen they could hardly walk.

**Indian Woman**

I thought you said they have a sock.

**Indian**

They had a truth they live by. In one camp, a chief offered a squaw to the white man who was the leader and he refused, saying he already had a wife. The chief said many men had many wives, even during one winter. But he still refused.

**Indian Woman**

Truth is what the birchbark scrolls say. Our Elders and Grandfathers speak truth. The earth speaks truth. Truth is what we hear in our stories.

**Indian**

But our stories have different voices. We tell stories in our own way. I have stories. The Elders have stories.

**Indian Woman**

They aren't that different. I hear truth when you speak. I hear truth in the Elder's stories. Truth is like water through a gorge.

**Indian**

The white men have a way to live too that carries them like a canoe.

**Indian Woman**

I won't hear it. They kill the game we hunt for food. They say they buy our land. But the land was given to us. How can something like truth be changeable?

### Indian

Because it's the core of our lives. Life is changeable like the seasons. I think it must change form to meet different needs at different times. The white man searches for the source of the Mississippi. The river may have several sources. Could truth have several headwaters also? Yet flowing into one stream? Could the blood of red and white mix like rivers yet flow together in one Great River?

### Indian Woman

That can't be.

### Indian

Yet truth is lasting. It's like the change that the birch tree makes before it becomes our scrolls. Sometimes it's invisible. When it's in the seed. Then it's a sapling. Then a tree. You peel the bark when it's easy to peel. Then it's in a different form. You sew it with cedar root. And it has another shape. You draw on it with lines from a pointed stick dipped in red ochre. The birchbark scrolls have many shapes. They tell many stories. Yet they are always birchbark. They are the one thing we carry with us from the Elders. From camp to camp.

### Indian Woman

When I see the white man, I see a beaver damming one little creek until the backed-up water spills into the woods and kills the trees.

### Indian

You worry for nothing.

### Indian Woman

Your eyes are closed with buffalo robes. Your ears are blocked with beaver dams.

### Indian

Only the Great Spirit knows the truth. He's the all-knowing Truth Teller. Our way is covered by a blanket. Slowly I feel the darkness more each day. But there is truth in the end. We may not see it at the moment.

### Indian Woman

They're a people who won't hear, won't speak to the spirit world to know things. They push on like the stories of the glacier. The glaciers pushed and our people moved. This is the trail of my mother, the trail of my grandmother. What trail will the baby have? I don't want to lose the land. I feel like an animal in the trap.

Gnawing my hind foot off. (SHE DOES BEADING WORK.) Mey mey mey. (SHE SINGS TO THE BABY. TIES A SMALL FIR BOUGH TO THE CRADLE BOARD.) The baby watches this and counts the Ancestors in the needles.

### Indian

Our birchbark scrolls say that from our first home along the eastern sea. We wear the seashell to remember our home. Our Grandfathers moved westward by the coming of the white man. Farther and farther across the Great Lakes to the Great River Mississippi. Our path is sometimes blocked by evil spirits who appear as horned serpents or great fish. But our helpers are there too.

### Indian Woman

You're so hopeful.

### Indian

Maybe the Great Spirit and their God are one. The good times are under a blanket for a while but they return. The Great Spirit calls all men together in the smoke of the peace pipe.

### Indian Woman

All lakes and rivers now will run with our tears. The wolf, fox, buffalo, prairie mole, goose, duck. All the animals will go away. The earth will cry. It can't get along without the animals. My heart curls like smoke from the fire.

### Indian

Our scrolls tell about our power. Our vision quests. We see the Ancestors who cheer us on and protect our path. We are young faces of the old faces. (HE PUTS ON A MASK AND TAKES IT OFF.)

# IV.

WINTER CAMP SEASON (WINTER). THE WOMAN WRAPS THE BLAN-
KET OVER THE TRIPOD WITH THE LODGE POLES STICKING UP AT
THE TOP FOR A TEEPEE. SHE HANGS UP THE HIDE-STRETCHER
AND SNOW SHOES.

### Indian Woman
What will happen to us? I see more of them all the time. I see them
with eyes like maple sugar. Some of them have hair yellow as the
tamaracks in fall. I see their stars on their flag at the new fort. I
remember when I was a girl. We belonged to the whole earth.

### Indian
The part of it we knew anyway.

### Indian Woman
The women didn't hurry to the river for water. They talked and
laughed. No men groaned in their sleep. Our children didn't know
fear unless a bear sniffed at the teepee at night. Or the wolf howled
at the flap. I feel something inside me. My skin grows cold. My heart
is a hard pellet. Like buckshot from muskets that hangs on doors.
There's something that won't go away.

### Indian
When we smoke the peace pipe, we have communion with the
Great Spirit and all living creatures. (THEY LIE BESIDE ONE ANOTH-
ER AS HE TALKS. HIS ARM IS UNDER HER HEAD. HER ANKLE HIS
OVER HIS LEG. THEIR LEFT HANDS HOLD AT THE THUMBS.) There's
a story of men who would come to take the earth away from us. Even
the stars. I look at the night sky and think, how can that be? Yet I
know our legends are true.

### Indian Woman
But the Great Spirit saved some stars for the Indian—inside the twig
of the cottonwood. Maybe it will be all right. While you were gone,
a trader at the new fort cut an apple crosswise for me. I saw the star
inside the apple too. Just like in the twig of the cottonwood. I gave
him the sparrow-bone bracelet for it. I didn't like the bracelet
anyway. Sleep a while and I will pray for you. (SHE SITS UP AND HE
RESTS HIS HEAD IN HER LAP.) When he sleeps I hear him snore. I
think of his wolf-growl when he plays with the children. I think of

the children as they die from the white man's diseases. I hear them cough in their teepees. My sister's two children have already died. I look at my baby. Then I feel the cold place inside me again. There's another kind of darkness out there now.

(THE INDIAN MAN DREAMS. A DEER DANCER ENTERS BEATING A DRUM. MOTIONING TO FOLLOW.)

### Indian Man
(HE WAKES.) I dreamed a name for the baby. He-who-sees-the-way.

### Indian Woman
What does it mean?

### Indian
I don't know. Am I the Truth Teller for his life also? He will have to discover what it means. He's the one who follows the new ways. Maybe he's the one who can walk where we can't. Maybe he will show us a way when our life comes to a close.

### Indian Woman
How would you draw the scroll for his life's walk?

### Indian
I would mark four stages for his life on the birchbark. Before each one are obstacles. But there are guardian bear spirits, and beaver spirits guiding him, and elders protecting him, and the four winds and four directions to help him, and the birds to carry his prayers. (PAUSE.)

### Indian Woman
You are thinking of the obstacles?

### Indian
Yes. I'm thinking of what's coming for him—I don't want you going to the new fort anymore.

### Indian Woman
It seems to me I should learn to go to the fort. I want their calico. And the-bird-beak-that-cuts-through-cloth. (SHE MAKES SCISSOR-MOTIONS WITH HER FINGERS.) I want to make their quilts and bead their flower-patterns. I want to see a door close with a sock. I want to know how they survive their sickness. The spots-on-the-face. The coughing-up disease. The no-strength-sleep of our children. I will have to walk in a place where there's no path. That's what our

lives will be.

### Indian

(HE STANDS AND TAKES THE SNOW SHOES.) I remember the story of the Great Spirit's flying lesson. He flew and crashed. Maybe it will be that way for us also. The Great Spirit of the white man fell to earth also. They put him on a cross. Maybe our thud is coming. If the Great Spirit thuds and survives, then we can too.

### Indian Woman

Where are you going?

### Indian

To see if anything is in the trap.

### Indian Woman

Don't go yet.

### Indian

We need the meat and skins. (HE EXITS TO THE EDGE OF THE STAGE.)

### Indian Woman

Sometimes I'm afraid he won't come back. But I remember our stories. In the winter, the evil spirit, Windigo, comes bringing sickness and death. One winter, when the men were out hunting, there was no one strong or brave enough to go out and face Windigo. So a small girl walked out on the lake carrying two sumac sticks. As she walked, she grew stronger, and the sticks of sumac froze hard as stone. She attacked the Windigo monster, crushing his skull. (AFTER THE STORY, THE INDIAN WOMAN SITS ROCKING THE CRADLE BOARD FOR A MOMENT. THEN SHE TALKS TO THE BABY.) I name you He-who-sees-the-way. You're the one who will lead. I mark you with bravery. I say there is a way where none is. I say you are a Truth Teller. And I say it to the children who come after you. You'll see in your own way. You will see a way.

### Indian

I hear you, earth. You are myself. A part of you is leaving. I saw it in my dream. I am leaving too. I don't know how to walk in more than one world.

### Indian Woman

Do I not have two feet? One for the path of each world. (HERE THE INDIAN ATTEMPS TO FLY, AND IN FALLING, EXITS. THE INDIAN

WOMAN TALKS TO THE BABY.) In time you'll have a birchbark scroll which will help you with your walk. Maybe you will make new stories. Because with stories we will know the way. (SHE SINGS.) Mey mey mey mey.

# CHARACTERS

Mosquito

Woman

Chorus

The Forest

# SETTING

Village of Ice in the Far North of the Imagination

# ACKNOWLEDGMENT TO

*The Far North, 2000 Years of American Eskimo and Indian Art,*
Published for The Anchorage Historical and Fine Arts Museum
Anchorage, Alaska, by the National Gallery of Art, Washington,
1973 for ideas for the following masks:
  Mother Mosquito mask
  Fish mask
  Dream mask
  Seal-skin tunic

Acknowledgment also to the Eskimo belief that driftwood comes
from an underwater forest

### Mosquito

EEEEEEeeeeeeeeeee.

### Woman

Swat.
Why mosquito fly near us?

### Chorus

She drinks blood.
Her life's in our blood.
Red drops come to our arm like leaves.

### Woman

What's leaves?

### Chorus

Little mosquito-bumps on trees.

### Woman

Where trees?

### Chorus

In the underwater forest
where the driftwood comes from.

### Mosquito

EEEEEEEEEEEEEEEeeeeeeeeeeeeeeeee.

### Chorus

Her story get into ear.

### Woman

Swat.
I go underwater.
No mosquito there.

I step into fish-mask.

### Chorus
Step.

### Woman
I become one with the mask.

Sweet mask.

No childbirth pains.
No tattooing-needle in my face.
No soot-black thread drawn through my cheeks.

I wear fish-mask now
with a huge lower-lip.
I jump into ice-hole.
Blub. Blub.
My fins move like waves.

### Chorus
No mosquito bites her now.

### Woman
But fish-spear whizz by to spear fish.
Whew.
Enough.
I'm tired of wearing fish-mask.
I'm going back to shore.

### Mosquito
EEEeeee.

### Woman
Light the blubber-grease fire.
Smoke keeps the mosquito away.

### Chorus
No.
Make a fire from driftwood.
We tired of blubber-fire.
We tired of blubber.

### Woman
I look for driftwood.
Where? Where?
No wood on the ice.

No wood on the shore-grass.

### Chorus
Under the ice is the water.
Under the water is a forest
where driftwood comes from.

### Woman
I didn't see a forest underwater.

### Chorus
It's where our dreams go when we sleep.

### Woman
Wrap me in the seal-skin tunic.
I sleep-walk to the ice-hole.
I carry my dreams.
Glub.  Glub.
I swim like a seal underwater.

Move out of way, fish!

### Chorus
Our voices call the driftwood—
*Hey driftwood.*
We underwater-swim.

### Woman
Feel the water-currents.

### Forest
That's underwater wind.

### Woman
I look for driftwood to keep mosquito away.
Look.  Look.
Can't find.
Where's the underwater forest?

### Forest
Who says there's a forest?

### Chorus
Our stories say.

### Woman

The chorus say get wood.
*Get wood.*
All day.

But I don't know how to get.

### Forest

You hear stories of the underwater forest
where driftwood comes from?

### Chorus

Our stories say.

### Woman

What are these seal-lure sinkers
jumping at my head?

### Forest

Those are leaves.

### Woman

*What's leaves?*

### Forest

Leaves are the little teeth of trees.
First they're green as light in underwater sea.

Then leaves turn yellow as evening-sun.

Some leaves turn red as seal-blood on ice.

### Woman

The trees change masks?

### Chorus

How we get this story straight?

### Forest

Then leaves go away.

### Chorus

Oh.
Where go?

#### Forest
Like old ones to their death—
The women onto the ice.
The old men to a hunting land.

#### Chorus
They go-away.

#### Forest
Sometimes the tree goes away too.
Maybe even some of it
when driftwood floats to the surface
and waves carry it to the ice.

#### Chorus
The leaves are little waves.
They come back and back.
They are given to us like stories.

We know things now.
These dreams are our masks.

#### Woman
I dream-dance in a seal-skin tunic.

#### Mosquito
EEEEEEeEEEEEE.

#### Chorus
Swat.
Cannot get away from mosquito.
Even in dreams.

#### Woman
Make whale to blow mosquito through his air-hole.
Make *tiny tiny* spears to find mosquito-heart.

#### Chorus
Up. Up.
To the village of ice.
She wakes now. She swims like a seal.

#### Woman
Swim. Swim.

But where's ice-hole?
Cannot breathe.

### Mosquito
EEEEEEEEEeEEEEEEEEEEeEEEEEEEEEEEe.

### Chorus
Here's the ice-hole!
Mother mosquito fly above.
Look at her big as an igloo.

### Mosquito
EEEEeeeeeeee.

### Chorus
Follow her sound.

### Woman
Swim. Swim.

Now I back without driftwood
from underwater forest.

### Chorus
We order driftwood now from catalogue.

Let the fire sing
like a yellow-leafed tree.

### Mosquito
EEEEeeeeeeee.

### Woman
Let the red leaves remember our blood
the mosquito sings us to the surface for.

### Chorus
The mosquito
brought us from the underwater-world.
She heard our dreams cry
from the underwater forest.

### Mosquito
EEEEEEeeee.

## Woman

You big mosquito.
You mother mosquito.

Show us your little spear-tooth.
Bite.  Bite.

You bring us to the air.
Blug.  Blub.

Your life is in our blood.

# THE BEST FANCY DANCER THE PUSHMATAHA POW WOW'S EVER SEEN

# CHARACTERS

HENRY, old man

GERTRUDE, old woman

JESS, boy who is staying with Henry, age 17

GENNY, Gertrude's granddaughter, age 16

Also two characters in deer and bear masks

A few blackbirds

Two stagehands who crank the sun across the stage

# SETTING

A cabin in the woods off a main road where Gertrude lives. Henry's cabin is within shouting distance, but it's separated by a ravine.

Pushmataha County, in southeastern Oklahoma, is named after a Choctaw leader born 1764, died 1824 during a trip to Washington D.C. He negotiated with the U.S. government for his people, and with his people for the U.S. government, and is buried in Old Congressional Cemetery.

# ACKNOWLEDGMENT TO

*The Diario of Christopher Columbus, First Voyage to America 1492-93,* Abstracted by Fray Bartolome de las Casas, Translated by Oliver Dunn and James E. Kelly, Jr., University of Oklahoma Press, 1989.

With special thanks to the Old Pueblo Playwrights, Tucson, for their staged reading during the development of this play.

Thanks also to Virgil Foote, pastor of Mazakute Episcopal Mission, St. Paul, Minnesota, for "When you find God you find yourself," and for sharing his visions in sermons.

Her howl
is a wind that runs through me daily—
We go to the place
where they have laid her. But I am not
strong enough to roll back the stone.

> *"A Killing"*
> —Benjamin Alire Saenz
>   from his book of poems, *Calendar of Dust*

"It is not my purpose to contradict any of these allegations against the white man, but neither am I here to indulge in an indiscreet denunciation of him which might bring down upon my people unnecessary difficulty and embarrassment."

> —*from a speech given by Chief Pushmataha following Tecumseh, who tried to get the Choctaws to join his rebellion.*

# ACT ONE

## SCENE I

(JESS AND GENNY SIT ON AN OLD GLIDER IN GERTRUDE'S YARD. THEY ARE READING ABOUT THE RETURN TRIP IN THE DIARY OF CHRISTOPHER COLUMBUS. THE SUN IS HIGH OVER THEM. GERTRUDE IS SWEEPING HER PORCH WHEN SHE HEARS HENRY.)

Henry

Jess there? (SHE GOES BACK TO SWEEPING.) Jess over thar? (SILENCE.)

Gertrude

Come look for yourself.

Henry

I can't get through the woods, old woman.

Gertrude

Put on your hiking boots.

Henry

I can't get through the gulley.

Gertrude

Start your old truck, Henry. Drive to the main road, and come down my little road.

Henry

Your little road is nothing but two ruts.

Gertrude

Then walk to the main road.

Henry

What?

Gertrude

He can't hear neither.

Henry

There's a ravine between the cabins.

Gertrude

(TO HERSELF.) Thank goodness.

Henry

You say you fly in your dreams, Gertrude. Maybe I should try that. (GERTRUDE SWEEPS.)

Genny

(GENNY READS FROM COLUMBUS' DIARY.) The return voyage to Spain after the discovery of America.

Jess

(JESS SITS ON THE ARM OF THE GLIDER ROWING.) A ship on the ocean—toolin' down the waves. A roller coaster ride. Whoot Whoot. We find new world. (JESS ROWS LIKE HE'S PLAYING A SLOT MA-CHINE.)

Genny

(SHE IGNORES JESS AND CONTINUES TO READ THE DIARY.) To-night the wind increases and the waves are frightful. The ship carries her mainsail low, just high enough to keep out of the waves. I run before the wind wherever it carries me, for there is nothing else to do.

Gertrude

Sometimes I hear a restless voice. Help me get home. I'm out in the woods in the gulley between the cabins looking for blackberries, and I wonder who it is. Then I hear Genny. Great Jehovah. I think. My granddaughter's dragging in Columbus. The spirit of the one and only.

Genny

(CONTINUES TO READ THE DIARY, HER FINGER POINTING TO THE WORDS AS SHE READS.) Then the caravel, the Pinta, disappears, though I make signal-lights all night. About dawn she answers, though it appears she can do no more because of the storm, and she's far off course. When the sun rises, the wind is greater and the cross-seas more terrible.

Gertrude

(SOON HENRY SHOWS UP.) How'd you get here? (STARTLED.)

**Henry**
I changed into a squirrel.

**Gertrude**
I always knew you had two other feet somewhere.

**Henry**
Your hair's standing up there in front like a war bonnet.

**Gertrude**
My granddaughter moussed it. My hair was getting thin. She said it would hold it off my head.

**Henry**
You sure look like something. Where is she?

**Gertrude**
Right there with Jess. (JESS AND GENNY GREET HENRY.)

**Henry**
He been over har much?

**Gertrude**
Sometimes—they're reading the diary of Christopher Columbus for one of their classes—

**Genny**
And interpreting it in our own way—Columbus Discovering Turtle Island.

**Henry**
(NODS.) —First thing's interested Jess in school—other than base-ball. But it seems like he's over here all the time—

**Gertrude**
No he's not, Henry. Kids are going to be gone a lot. Get used to it.

**Henry**
I saw in a dream he would come to me. I saw him listening to the stories.

**Gertrude**
The gulley that runs between our cabins is really between us and what we were in the old days, Henry.

#### Henry
Why aren't we friends?

#### Gertrude
We live so close, I can see the light in your cabin at night.

#### Henry
That's cause Jess's up trying to wire the television. He's got some sort of aerial made out of a coat hanger and the tinfoil off our TV dinners.

#### Gertrude
You even got coat hangers? (JESS AND GENNY READ THE DIARY. GERTRUDE SWEEPS. HENRY PICKS UP HIS FEET.)

#### Genny
(READING AGAIN.) I fear at times that Our Lord would wish me to perish. But others give me hope that God will let me carry my news to Isabel. I want to return to Spain—I want to be there NOW.

#### Jess
Vroom. (JERKING AN IMAGINARY SLOT MACHINE HANDLE.)

#### Genny
I want them to know I turned out to be RIGHT—in ALL I said I would discover—

#### Jess
VROOMMMM!!

#### Genny
I'm SO afraid of not getting back with my news—

#### Jess
The winds go OOOOOOOOOOOOOOOOOOOOOOOOOOO. The sea goes swuuuuuuuuuuuuuuuuuuuuuuuuu. All on a Saturday night. (JESS STEERS THE SHIP AND CRANKS THE ARM OF A SLOT MA-CHINE.)

#### Henry
I'm supposed tell Jess our stories to preserve our past, and he's over here talking like Columbus and working the slot machine?

#### Gertrude
It's for school. (GERTRUDE SITS ON THE EDGE OF THE PORCH

WITH HER BROOM. THE SUN IS LOWERED IN THE SKY WITH A
SQUEAK.)

### Henry
It's Genny too. He likes her. And it's your cooking, Gertrude. Jess
and I sit on the porch sometimes and think if you're cooking your
cornbread or frybread or black bean chili or Indian tacos—

### Gertrude
Jess says you have stew every night—

### Henry
Jess been eating here too?

### Gertrude
Do you think we'd have supper without asking him when he's
sitting right here in the yard?

### Henry
Don't seem like I'm too far away either. Maybe I'll come more often.

### Gertrude
At night I can hear you snore.

### Henry
That's the woodpecker.

### Gertrude
I throw gravel at your dog when he comes over to chase my cat
under the porch.

### Henry
We could be friends—we could step out together at the Pow Wow—

### Gertrude
Yes—Genny and I went to the last Pow Wow. I didn't used to go. I
was afraid I wouldn't get the steps right. It's something you got to
feel within.

### Henry
I was at the Pow Wow. I saw your beaded moccasins stepping under
those skirts.

### Gertrude
I didn't see you.

### Henry

You're an old woman, Gertrude. You don't see anything anymore—just the shawls wagging ahead of you in the circle dance. All you old crows with moussed hair.

### Gertrude

It's the trend.

### Henry

Why don't you ask me to dance in the turnabout?

### Gertrude

I didn't see you, remember?

### Henry

You could still ask me to dance. That's the way it is now.

### Gertrude

So I've heard.

### Jess

(JESS IS SERIOUS A MOMENT INTERPRETING THE DIARY. THE SUN IS LOWERED IN THE SKY AGAIN WITH A SQUEAK.) You know how you have news you want to deliver but must travel there, and you fear that something might happen before you get there, and all would be taken from you, and you would be prevented from arriving with your news. And you would perish from the earth. Wiped out like water spilled across the floor. And you wonder why you carry such a burden. It must be that the Great Spirit loves you because he chooses you to carry the burden. Who else could he have entrusted? Not the noble men. Ferdinand himself couldn't lift his fanny off the throne. Not my wife's brothers—her people. Their righteous backsides all over the couches of the courts of Spain. No. It was me—though they actually laughed at my desire to discover the New World. How they fed salt to my wounds. How they stroked my powerlessness. Now they'll know. If only I could kick this ship to go faster. To get into higher mode. Maybe that's what all the waves are doing. Waving me onward. Sweeping me back to Spain.

### Genny

Hurry, hurry, ships.

### Jess

*Phooooooooooooooooooooo* say the waves.
*Swuuuuuuuu* says the wind.

**Henry**

Columbus wrote suuuu in his diary?

**Gertrude**

Genny and Jess read the diary, and write it their own way. Get with it, Henry. History is rewritten. What is it anyway but someone's opinion? We can add our interpretation to it now—

**Henry**

Now wait—

**Gertrude**

That's what you're doing when you tell Jess stories. You're giving your voice to history. Telling it in your own way.

**Henry**

But—

**Jess**

We're supposed to rewrite the diary, Henry. Add our voice. Change history. Wow. What is all history but human storytelling? Someone's point-of-view. We need more voices to tell the story.

**Gertrude**

The voice of stories running like a rabbit to the ear. Soon you got a headful of rabbits.

**Genny**

(READING AGAIN WITH HER FINGER MOVING ALONE THE WORDS.) I ought to believe God will grant me the completion of what I began, and will not thwart me now that I see my destination. He would not give me this treasure chest to carry back to Isabel and trip me up before I get to her court. He will not stick His pin in this ship and deflate it so that it goes down with a few air bubbles waving from the sea. (GERTRUDE AND HENRY LISTEN TO THEM.)

# SCENE II

(IT'S NOW LATE IN THE DAY. THE SUN IS ALMOST SETTING ON THE
EDGE OF THE STAGE GIVING LONG SHADOWS TO EVERYTHING.
JESS IS BY HIMSELF AT THE EDGE OF THE STAGE. SOON HENRY
JOINS HIM. GERTRUDE IS ON HER PORCH. GENNY IS IN THE
CABIN.)

#### Jess
I loaned a friend some money and he's not going to pay me back.

#### Henry
(PAUSE.) There was a rock in the middle of the sky and the rock grew
crowded and the animals started falling off to the waters below.

#### Jess
You told me not to loan anybody—

#### Henry
(INTERRUPTS.) The animals didn't want to drown—no—they wanted some dry ground where they could go. So the elk swam to the
bottom of the waters and brought up some mud, and the mud grew
on the waters and formed Turtle Island—which became known as
America.

#### Jess
My best friend—

#### Henry
When the land was still mud, the elk rolled over and over, and left
his hairs in the mud that sprouted trees and bushes— (A PERSON
IN AN ELK MASK & ANTLERS WALKS ACROSS THE STAGE. JESS AND
HENRY SEE IT. AFTER A MOMENT, HENRY CONTINUES HIS STORY.)
But there was darkness in the new land. The animals remembered
there was a sun above the rock in the sky. They traveled back to
lasso the sun. Yes—it was the bear who shot his arrow into the sun
and dragged it to the new land.

#### Jess
At school my friend acted like he didn't know me—

### Henry

The animals set the sun on a pulley and cranked it across the sky each day. At night, it rolled under Turtle Island, until it was ready to cross the sky again. But at first, the bear got the sun too close— and it burned some of Turtle Island into desert as it sank in the west and scorched some of the animals. The bear lifted the sun a little higher, but it was still too low. There was a little bird that flitted everywhere— and the bear warned him to wait until they got the sun working right—but the bird wouldn't listen and got burned. That's why the red bird is red to this day. Then the bear lifted the crank higher and finally the sun was right. (PAUSE.) Listen to our stories, Jess. When you feel hurt, think of them. Healing is creating something. The more you listen, the more you have to tell—our stories go on and on. (JESS SITS LEANING OVER WITH HIS CHIN RESTING IN HIS HANDS. THE CRANKERS OF THE SUN ARE NOW VISIBLE. THE LARGE YELLOW BALL OF THE SUN ITSELF IS PULLED OFF STAGE BY A HAND CRANK WITH A SQUEAK EACH TIME IT MOVES, SOON DISAPPEARING TO ROLL UNDER THE STAGE TO RISE IN THE EAST AGAIN. THE STAGE IS LIT NOW BY THE FRONT PORCH LIGHT ON GERTRUDE'S CABIN AND BY A LIGHT FROM INSIDE HER CABIN.)

### Jess

Sometimes I feel the old memories in my head. I think we're like the six directions—north, east, south, west, sky, earth—we have them all in us—I can put on my feathers and be an Indian again. I like to dance at the Pow Wow— but I can't beat others. I can listen to you, Henry, and know the Old World. I thought at first it was just something you were talking about. You gave me a place to live. It's better than the street. I was getting sick from the stuff they pass around, you know. Sometimes I see what you mean. I can play baseball and take garage mechanics at school and work on your old truck and feel the New World—when I want stuff again, I can tell you. Healing is a process, you say. It doesn't happen all at once.

### Genny

(SHE COMES TO THE PORCH WHERE GERTRUDE SITS.) I wish it wasn't late. I'd go to the mall.

### Henry

Someday, Jess, you'll feel harmony with the earth again—you'll feel it.

### Gertrude

I don't want you out in Warren's old car after dark.

**Genny**

Maybe Jess'd go with me.

**Gertrude**

Tomorrow—

**Genny**

I've got school.

**Gertrude**

Afterwards.

**Genny**

I've got to work on the diary—

**Gertrude**

You find time for what you want to do.

**Genny**

Can you fly in your dreams, Grandma?

**Gertrude**

So Henry says.

**Genny**

Where do you go?

**Gertrude**

Wherever the dreams take me—sometimes to the past. Some-times—I don't know where it is.

**Genny**

Sometimes I hear the spirits in the woods—

**Gertrude**

Yes—they're there.

**Genny**

You're not afraid?

**Gertrude**

Never—I hear the spirits a lot—in the woods—in the kitchen. Sometimes in K-Mart even, I think I see the spirits. They stand in the aisles looking at the things they never had. Looking at the things they never knew they needed. All lined up on all those shelves.

Mostly they stand there with their mouths open—*Get used to it*, I tell them. The motor oil, curlers, pastel towels, tennis shoes, tooth-paste, step stools, pie pans, pie wheels, roasters, colanders, potato peelers, ladles, labels, yarn, casserole-covers, canteens, seat covers, nozzles, doormats, skates, towel racks, sheets, tapes— (WHILE GERTRUDE RECITES HER LIST, THE ELK APPEARS AGAIN, WITH A STRING OF LIGHTS IN ITS ANTLERS. GERTRUDE FORGETS HER LIST, AND THE FOUR CHARACTERS WATCH. THERE ARE VOICES AND MUSIC.)

# SCENE III

(NEXT AFTERNOON. THE SUN IS CRANKED FROM THE EAST TO LATE IN THE WEST. HENRY'S DOG BARKS. THE CAT HISSES. GENNY SITS ON THE GLIDER. JESS IS STANDING NEAR THE OLD GLIDER PRETENDING TO HIT BASEBALLS. GERTRUDE AND HENRY SIT ON THE EDGE OF HER PORCH.)

### Gertrude
Were you in the woods last night, Henry?

### Henry
I was talking to Jess.

### Gertrude
The spirits were close—

### Henry
Yo—I saw them.

### Gertrude
I sit on my porch of an evening and hear the voices. They come around because they know I'm not doing anything but stirring my black bean chili. There's this one voice who's always trying to please someone. It tries so hard and nothing comes of it.

### Henry
Old women hear too many voices.

### Gertrude
Say what you want. Those voices are company to me. Better than an old man who just wants some chili.

### Henry
Yes—I can smell your chili across the gulley. It don't have to go back to the main road, but moves through the woods greased as a spirit. Yes—I know when you brown the venison—the onions and garlic. I say—yes, Jess—Gertrude and Genny're having chili for supper. Now Gert's stirrin' in the chili powder—

## Gertrude

Then the tomatoes—corn—potatoes—cayenne pepper—coriander—the rice vinegar—the green peppers and chilis.

## Henry

Yes— I say Gertrude's stirring her pot just like a witch. Holding the tongue of a man in her apron pocket. How do you get by without a man to feed?

## Gertrude

It's easy—there were times I thought it wasn't—after my husband died. But I could get along without Warren. I just honored the onions and chopped them up. Sometimes I thought their roots looked like straws on our old ceremonial masks—or the tufts on my husband's old head. At first I made too much cornbread, but I took some to neighbors or to church, and learned to cut the recipe. What I really like is having the house to myself. To cook and listen to my little recorder. I bought tapes at the K-Mart. My favorite place to go. I could spend the day stirring by myself and be happy—

## Henry

The heart of a witch—didn't I tell you, Jess? (JESS SITS IN THE GLIDER AND READS THE DIARY.)

## Gertude

Put a moccasin on it, Henry.

## Genny

(READING.) He delivered me on the outward voyage, when I had greater reason to fear my troubles—when the sailors were determined to go back—and to rise against me in protest. But the eternal God gave me strength and resolution against all of them.

## Jess

(INTERPRETING.) I ought not fear the sea. I've left notes everywhere. In several journals—some for myself—some for the sovereigns. I would write my journals in the sky if I could. I would write them on the sea. The waves would bring my message to shore. I would strap my words to the bodies of birds. I would write until the words pulled the birds down to the water. Ouch! I'm wet. The birds call. Help. Gulp. They sink into the sea. The water's seafingers between their feathers like lead weights pulling them down.

## Henry

They doing the return trip?

**Gertrude**

I think you're getting it, Henry. Genny reads the diary, then Jess says it in his own way.

**Henry**

This rewritten history is hard to swallow.

**Genny**

(READING.) I wrapped some messages in a well-tied, waxed cloth, and ordered a large wooden barrel brought, and I put the parchment in it without anyone learning what it was, and ordered it thrown into the sea.

**Jess**

It was messages about the land I discovered, in case I didn't make it back.

**Henry**

Sometimes, Gertrude, you think things are going along—you're telling Jess the old stories, finally getting somewhere, you know—the dry land's appearing—then something happens, and the road takes a different turn. You find him over here in the New World, you know. Only it's the new New World.

**Gertrude**

Yes, I remember sometimes after breakfast, I thought Warren and I would sit on the porch and talk—but you'd call across the ravine—and Warren would be gone. You didn't do anything but drive off with my old husband fishing and who knows what—

**Henry**

You didn't want to go with him.

**Gertrude**

Maybe I did.

**Henry**

You got your black bean chili to stir.

**Jess**

Henry—will you come to school when we read our diary?

**Henry**

(WITH FEAR.) What? (TWITCHING HIS FOOT.) You going to read that somewhar? Naw—

Genny

Henry—

Henry

I can't come to school—

Genny

You bring him, Grandma—

Jess

Genny's in it too.

Gertrude

(STARTLED.) She didn't tell me.

Jess

She's one of the natives who went back on the ship.

Gertrude

I guess I'll know about it when she needs a costume made.

Henry

Maybe they didn't wear much.

Gertrude

It's at school, Henry, there'll be a costume. You know—your foot shuffled just like Warren's. I tell you, he could keep me awake all night. He always traditional-danced in his sleep. His feet moving in the old bed kept me awake. Just like he was at the Pow Wow. There was no getting away from him.

Henry

You want someone to fuss at. That's what all you women want.

Gertrude

I've got my voices. Sometimes I listen for my daughter in the night— but mostly I hear voices coming around complaining about this. Wanting someone to listen to their troubles. I tell them they're dead. What trouble could they have? I tell them it's over for them. I say, face facts.

Jess

When I saw the spirits last night, Gen, I thought of my dad—he was a rabble rouser. A fancy-dancer. A dude. All I remember about him was his red tail lights down the road. And he wanted me to dance.

300

All of a sudden—to be the best fancy-dancer at the Pow Wow.

### Genny

He wanted something for you—

### Jess

I don't know. I was dead weight for him. He dumped me with one of his old girlfriends. I was supposed to go to school. Everyday she'd go to work and I was out the door. And it wasn't to school.

### Gertrude

The voices that cry are the hardest. They see what's happened to them. They know they're left out. There's no way they can get in. They whimper more than cry when they're broken. I tell them there's another way. There's the Great Spirit and the Red Road. There's Sunday church and baseball games of the New World. I tell them to get going. Our own feeble efforts are full of pride and dust. We need power from the outside. From God through Christ.

### Henry

You're a real comforter, aren't you? Remind me not to tell you any of my troubles.

### Gertrude

I just tell them what they need to hear.

### Jess

Now I have to write more of my part. I have to sing.

### Henry

Columbus sang?

### Jess

I guess he played the guitar.

### Gertrude

Is this a musical?

### Jess

Well, we have to liven it up somehow.

### Genny

Maybe a floating casino—

### Gertrude

There was a band on board the Nina?

### Jess

No—he sang his heart out to the waves— (THE SUN IS CRANKED TO NEAR DARKNESS.)

### Genny

Maybe he talked to them each night the way Grandma talks to the little spirits tumbling to the shore of her kitchen. He says, "Hey you little waves—I'm jumping over you in my moccasins—I'm driving over you in my ship—I'm hoop-dancing over you waves." Maybe we could put wheels on the ship—make it the first Greyhound— (HENRY HITS HIS KNEE FINALLY GETTING INTO THE MOOD OF THE DIARY REWRITE. THE SUN DISAPPEARS.)

# SCENE IV

(NEXT AFTERNOON. THE SUN IS CRANKED OVER GERTRUDE'S CABIN AGAIN TO THE WEST. A DOG BARKS AND A CAT HISSES. HENRY SHOWS UP.)

#### Henry
I haven't seen Jess since morning.

#### Jess
(LOOKS UP FROM THE GLIDER WITH GENNY.) I had baseball after school.

#### Gertrude
When I visit the "old folks home," Henry, sometimes I see all the lonely old men, and think of the women and children they've left crying for them. They went out and just did what they wanted. I walk right by them—I don't read them no magazines.

#### Henry
Yes, even the squirrels know they can't come over here. At my place, they eat out of my hand. I hear them talking about you—

#### Gertrude
Yes, Henry—and no matter how many boys you to bring to your place to tell our old stories to—they're going to want to leave for the bars and bingo halls.

#### Genny
Don't be sure, Grandma.

#### Henry
We're not having anything to do with the casinos.

#### Jess
Speak for yourself, Henry.

#### Henry
There's nothing wrong with earning a living.

#### Jess
A dealer is the new Medicine Man. The new Chief. All the girls like the dealers.

#### Genny
Some of the girls are dealers.

#### Jess
Henry says he won't take casino money.

#### Henry
I had a vision once of a red convertible coming down a hill. I always wanted a convertible, you know.

#### Gertrude
Yes— in my day, I always noticed the boys who had convertibles.

#### Genny
It's the dealers that got convertibles now, Grandma.

#### Jess
Your convertible is the casino, Henry.

#### Henry
No, it ain't. Casinos take our ear away from the land. The car was a dream more than a vision—it was coming, and I got in it—and other people got in it, and the more people that got in it, the more room there was.

#### Genny
Where were you going?

#### Henry
It's our stories that're the vehicle—

#### Gertrude
Some rocky country music on the radio.

#### Genny
Country rock, Grandma.

#### Gertrude
No—the rocks have tongues.

Jess
The rocks sounding maybe like Elvis?

Gertrude
No—like my tapes I buy at K-Mart.

Henry
Gertrude's listening to hard rock—and she's living in shouting distance of the church.

Gertrude
I got earphones too. Sometimes I wore them around Warren—when I didn't want to listen to him. I'm thinking of Warren mowing during church. About the time the Reverend got into the sermon, Warren would crank up his John Deere and let it rip.

Henry
You can't hear the Thunder Beings with your headphones on—you won't know when to be thankful to them.

Gertrude
You should go to church, Henry. It's just down the road.

Henry
When you find God is when you find yourself. Warren and I had our own church—when we were out on the lake fishing—hooting it up over a trout—the Thunder Beings clapping their hands—

Gertrude
Well—he might not be so noisy in outer space. The Great Spirit's probably giving him the south 4000 to mow. I hear the grass grows pretty good in the wilderness out there all watered by solar rains. That's what the spirits tell me anyway.

Henry
The spirits tell me I'm at the center of the universe.

Gertrude
That's what's wrong with you Traditionals. You're wrapped up in yourselves.

Henry
No—I won't be getting any supper here.

## Gertrude

I used to feel left out, Henry, when you and Warren went off down the road. I felt I was nothing to him. That's what I felt. My daughter was in trouble—no one was with me. But I thought, I believe in Jesus. I don't care if no one else stays with me. I'll sit in church by myself my whole life. Yes. It's worth it because I want to go to the heaven I heard about in church.

## Henry

Yar—where we're transformed into angels with wings on our backs and halos twirling around our heads like ceiling fans at K-Mart—

## Jess

I'm seeing electric spirits— (TWO CHARACTERS DRESSED AS AN ELK AND BEAR CROSS THE BACK OF THE STAGE.) Yo—a neon voyage—do you see them, Gen?

## Genny

I see something moving—a shadow or something—sometimes the animals come to the edge of the woods—sometimes I think it's my mamma trying to get back.

## Jess

(THE SPIRITS DISAPPEAR.) Them were real live sparks—

## Genny

Hey, Jess—we could wire the Nina, Pinta and Santa Maria—then we would have a roller coaster ride—

## Jess

Wow—as long as we're acoustical too.

## Henry

When I went on my vision quest—I went up on that hill down the road there and sat for four days. I didn't see any K-Mart in my vision. Nothing of the New World. I saw three blackbirds. I don't know what they meant. I've wondered about them all my life. I think we don't understand anything that happens to us.

## Gertrude

I'm surprised a squirrel isn't your power animal.

## Henry

Why aren't you out blackberry picking, old woman?

### Gertrude
Because I don't have anyone other than Genny and Jess to bake a pie for—(HENRY LEAVES AND GERTRUDE GOES IN HER CABIN.)

### Jess
(STILL SHAKING HIS HEAD.) Gertrude's a hard woman—

### Genny
Grandma took care of me when nobody would. I was crawling round hungry and dirty. She told me about it. And she cleaned me up and told me stories so I would be strong—I would have a sense of myself and my tribe and my place among the trees. I hear the birds. I listen to rocks. I know when the earth is crying. My mamma must have heard these things too and didn't listen. Or heard another noise that was louder. I hear that noise too. But the quiet noises are still the ones I listen to. Don't let me go, Grandma, I say. I would leave too. I would be Miss Indian America if I was pretty as Willa Jean. I'd stay out all night in bars and bingo halls. Keep me in church, Grandma, I say—

### Jess
My father and mother ignored the heritage too—even though they heard. They went to bars and stayed out all night. I was born ignorant. "Drinking is better than dreaming," my father said.

### Genny
Well—they aren't the ones here to tell the story—are they?

# SCENE V

(JESS AND GENNY SOMEWHERE ON THE ROAD.)

                    Jess
Come on, Genny.

                    Genny
No.

                    Jess
Just a kiss—girls your age got babies. They dress them in cheerlead-
er sweaters and bring them to basketball games.

                    Genny
I'm not going to end up like my mamma.

                    Jess
What's the matter with you? It's because I ain't got a new truck to
drive in the six directions—because I ain't got money—

                    Genny
Grandma says there's seven directions. The seventh is the center,
Jess—wherever we are is the center of the earth. Wherever we are
is home—

                    Jess
Come on, Genny—

                    Genny
My mamma freaked out because of me. I remember it. She started
screaming. I don't know what happened. I remember rocking the
crib. I know it bumped the wall. Over and over.

                    Jess
It wasn't your fault.

                    Genny
Grandma said mamma was in drug rehab at the VA hospital. Then
she got out. Her friends came around—there were fights—I don't
know—it still scares me sometimes, Jess. I feel safe with Grandma.

I still have dreams of being little and no one there. I remember something bad. I remember crying when I was in the crib—

### Jess

No one remembers that.

### Genny

I'm sure I remember mamma screaming.

# SCENE VI

(IT IS DARK EXCEPT FOR GERTRUDE'S FRONT PORCH LIGHT AND A LIGHT COMING THROUGH HER FRONT WINDOWS. GERTRUDE SITS ON HER FRONT PORCH WITH HER FLY SWATTER. THERE ARE STRANGE NIGHT SOUNDS. SOON HENRY APPEARS.)


### Gertrude
You making it across the gulley without any trouble, Henry. You must have blackbird wings—

### Henry
You sound like a woman. Big waddling birds. You'd think they were the blackbirds cawing all over the place. They set up in the tree and awk awk awk.

### Gertrude
Remember your vision—the blackbirds. Maybe they were telling you to take care of the women who awk all over the place—we've got a church full of them. You could repair backscreens, fix faucets—then you'd get your supper, Henry.

### Henry
The only vision I saw like that was to take care of Jess and maybe others like him—the left-out ones of the New World. I ask Jess sometimes what it is he wants from this world. Money?—I ask. Shit—he says. It's what you've got to have to keep the girls happy. Oh look Jess they say at the mall—get me this—get me that. Oh Jess, look at the dresses—look at the shoes. He's wanting to go after that casino money. Where's your granddaughter, by the way?

### Gertrude
With Jess—probably at the mall.

### Henry
You're not worried?

### Gertrude
No—the spirits say they're all right. Genny needed some material for her costume—I told her to go to K-Mart—material's cheaper than the mall—

#### Henry

What they in?

#### Gertrude

My husband's old car. Sometimes Jess gets it running. (PAUSE.)
Henry—you going to school to hear Jess and Genny read the diary?

#### Henry

(DEFINITELY.) No I ain't.

#### Gertrude

Why?

#### Henry

I had too much of them old boarding schools.

#### Gertrude

This's the high school, Henry. There's no boarding schools no
more.

#### Henry

There is for me!

#### Gertrude

You tell Jess to go to school—(FANNING HERSELF WITH THE FLY
SWATTER.)

#### Henry

Sometimes I can still feel them beating me. Hitting my hands with
a ruler. Sometimes I wake in the morning and see welts on my
knuckles—

#### Gertrude

That's old age, Henry—that's arthritis.

#### Henry

I miss Warren.

#### Gerturde

He spent as much time with you as me. Now Jess's here as much as
he's with you.

#### Henry

Fair turnabout.

**Gertrude**

Do you ever hear him?

**Henry**

The old man?—naw.

**Gertrude**

Sometimes I think I hear him stirring in the kitchen at night. Looking for a cookie. Or else it's a squirrel got in. Rattling the breadloaf. Getting into my tupperware of leftover cornbread.

**Henry**

You keep all them sacks. All them plastic wrappers. Just in case we run short of them the earth can come to you for more wrappers. The old man used to talk about the sacks and jars you got lined up. You got jars to string from here to Muskogee.

**Gertrude**

Probably farther.

**Henry**

When you think you hear Warren at night, it's just them sacks taking on their own lives. That's what happens when something gets too many numbers. You get too many of them and soon they think they are something. They think they are a whole nation. And they up and have themselves a Pow Wow right there in the kitchen in the night and keep old ladies awake.

**Gertrude**

What else did you talk about?

**Henry**

Me and Warren? (GERTRUDE NODS.) Just about your wrappers. Sometimes the squirrels.

**Gertrude**

What did you say about them?

**Henry**

How to tame them.

**Gertrude**

What do the squirrels say about me, Henry?

#### Henry
They say not to tell you.

#### Gertrude
Sometimes I think I could die any day. Sometimes I hear the spirits shuffle in the room. I tell them I don't want to go—

#### Henry
Maybe they're playing cards and don't want to bother with you yet.

#### Gertrude
When my daughter was born, I didn't know what I was doing. I had enough burdens just being a person. I couldn't take care of myself, and then I had a child to worry about. How can we have kids before we get ourselves ready for them? Later, I tried to teach her the old ways but she wouldn't listen—I didn't listen to the old ways either until one time we went back to South Carolina. My husband wanted to go back to the old territory. The place his grandfather mentioned his father left. I was in some little town somewhere a church had burned. Warren picked up a rock, but I found a brick. The church had burned and I picked up a burned brick. It even had a crack in it and later broke in two. I got it there right inside the door. The only time I was ever out of Oklahoma. I wish I could take Genny back to the old territory with me. Warren and I weren't there no more than no time, when I heard the voices. They were chattering like the squirrels you talk to, Henry.

#### Henry
To know the squirrels in the ravine is to know the whole world.

#### Gertrude
Yes, the place was full of voices. We found a road, and soon we were driving down it. We came to a house and stopped to ask directions, and Warren got to talking to the man, and before you know it we were having supper. He and his wife were like our kin. Soon others showed up and we had an old council meeting. We did some talking. On the way back, I said to Warren, do you think they were really there, or was it the old world we seen? Was it our ancestors come back dressed as we do? Yo, Henry, I tell you—when I was there in South Carolina, I heard the spirits—more than I hear them here. On the way home, I remember hearing little restless voices along side the road. They were crying, Henry, because they hadn't listened to God. They had been stubborn and wanted their own way. It was too late for them—

#### Henry

That old Jehovah's got a hard nose. He won't hear nothing but His own way.

#### Gertrude

It's for our own good, Henry.

#### Henry

I don't see it that way, Gert. I don't see anything unless of course you want to count the visions. Then I can go anywhere. I can fly like you—

#### Gertrude

You know I carried that brick with me all the way back here. Burned and broken in two. Even when Warren laughed. I don't care. I like the black smudges on the red brick. I talk to him sometimes now. I know it's just in my imagination. I say, How you doing, Warren? You know, I can still feel the old territory in that brick.

#### Henry

That's what we're here for—to see the visions and to help one another. A while back, Jess loaned a friend some money and he didn't pay it back. He feels bitter—because he feels powerless.

#### Gertrude

Stay with him, Henry. The minute you turn your back, he'll be off to the casino in Arbuckle. He won't even finish school. They all want to be dealers. It's a job. How can you argue with that? Purposelessness or a dealer with a casino around you like heaven.

#### Henry

I saw in my vision there would be young people wanting to know their heritage.

#### Gertrude

No, Henry—most of them're born nowadays saying, jackpot. I don't blame them. I remember the times I wanted someone to say it was all right, that I would be taken care of, that the square edges would be round again—but it didn't happen. It's still a struggle everyday. My daughter felt it too. She felt nobody in the New World cared. She got that old disease of hopelessness and dependency. She didn't find her Indian spirit on the other side of all that. Nothing I can do can call her back. She went crazy on drugs, Henry. You know that. Later one of her boyfriends killed her—when it looked like there was hope—

#### Henry
History may be a construction job, Gertrude, but then you run up against the hard wall of it.

#### Gertrude
People still look at Genny in the stores. Somehow the shots missed her. (SHE BLOWS HER NOSE. HENRY TRIES TO COMFORT HER, BUT SHE HITS BOTH HIM AND THE MEMORY AWAY WITH HER FLY SWATTER.) I ask the spirits to take her with them. It may be her restless voice I hear sometimes. I want to say, Warren, take her in your arms.

#### Henry
Maybe she goes on struggling for healing—even there—

#### Gertrude
I think we're done with earth once we leave.

#### Henry
So you take your granddaughter, and I take this boy, and we say something matters because we have this heritage. What will happen if we don't have anyone to send it to. What if it dies with us?

#### Gertrude
You sound like Columbus on his return voyage, Henry—

#### Henry
Maybe you can face the wall—try to change it just a little.

#### Gertrude
(THEY ARE BOTH STARTLED A MOMENT.) Who—?

#### Genny
(GENNY AND JESS ENTER.) We had to walk back, Grandma.

#### Jess
We had to leave Warren's car along the road. It quit on me and I couldn't fix it.

#### Henry
We'll pull it back with the truck tomorrow.

#### Jess
If I can't get it running.

#### Henry
In the Old World we had horses—

#### Jess
We can't be of the Old World anymore, Henry. We can't be the New World either. I'm a mixed blood. I have both worlds in me. I speak for those who have two trails to follow.

#### Henry
There's only one trail.

#### Jess
How do you settle for the bottom of the barrel? How do you say, all right, in the New World you'll take nothing and be grateful?

#### Henry
(PAUSE.) It ain't nothing, Jess.

#### Gertrude
(GENNY GOES INTO THE CABIN. JESS WALKS TOWARD THE RAVINE TO HENRY'S CABIN.) It's like turning a kaleidoscope I seen at K-Mart—finding what pattern is there.

#### Henry
Then just when we think we got it—something slips. Do our stories really matter, Gert? Something's always unthreading—

#### Gertrude
Of course our stories make a difference. Holy K-Mart aisles! We are our stories! What's wrong with you? I think you need to Pow Wow and regain your head—

#### Henry
I think I need to get behind a cart and push through the aisles— (HENRY TAKES GERTRUDE'S ARMS AND STEERS HER IN A DANCE STEP AS IF THEY WERE MOVING THROUGH K-MART. GERTRUDE USES THE FLY SWATTER AS A WING.)

#### Gertrude
Paint for the cracked steps on my old cabin, lawn chairs, hair spray, mousse, overalls, work boots, tapes of the latest hits—it's where I fly in my dreams. (THE ELK AND BEAR FOLLOW THEM IN THE AISLE.)

# ACT TWO

# SCENE I

(JESS AND GENNY ARE AT THE EDGE OF THE STAGE.)

**Genny**
You don't have to loan money to have friends.

**Jess**
I feel like a jerk at school.

**Genny**
Get used to it, Jess.

**Jess**
I always get D's.

**Genny**
You made the baseball team. You got Grandpa's car running.

**Jess**
Except the other night—on the way back from the mall. The next day, Henry wanted to get under the truck to hitch the chain to the axle—I had to help him up—

**Genny**
I see Grandma getting old too.

**Jess**
He wants me to go on a vision quest. That was his news when we towed Warren's car—he's always fussing over me.

**Genny**
Grandma wants me to go to South Carolina.

**Jess**
What are they always talking about? Thunder Beings and voices—

Genny

And that blessed brick Grandma got from the old territory.

Jess

Sometimes I'm ready to take off to Arbuckle. They got help-wanted's all the time for the casinos—they're bringing people in buses from Texas, and all over Oklahoma.

Genny

You hit a ball last game.

Jess

You didn't come to it—but you sure go to the basketball games—

Genny

It was in the school paper.

Jess

I got other things to do—

Genny

Just don't get Grandpa's car working enough to get Grandma back on the road to South Carolina. Now that I can drive—

Jess

Would you want to go to Arbuckle?

Genny

To deal?

Jess

Or wait tables— (GENNY LOOKS AT HIM.) Whatever—

Genny

I might go to college, Jess. They got classes now and you have to carry around a baby all week so you know how much trouble it is. Not a real baby— but a doll. And you get a welfare check and have to budget—

Jess

Not on what dealer's make.

Genny

Next fall, we get to visit the college—I want something solid.

**Jess**

What do you think gambling is? You seen those little stones in the museum? The ancestors been at it longer than us—

**Genny**

You're going to be like your daddy. (JESS LEAVES GENNY SITTING BY HERSELF.)

# SCENE II

(HENRY SITS WITH GENNY.)

#### Genny
Doesn't Jess know we have to finish rewriting history?

#### Henry
You get him riled, Genny. Keep at it. I think he'd leave if it wasn't for you.

#### Genny
No, it's the baseball team.

#### Henry
It isn't what I'm doing for him.

#### Genny
What would he find on a vision quest?

#### Henry
What Gertrude thinks you'd find in South Carolina. It's wherever you go to find what you are—so you don't get blown off the ocean in the first storm.

#### Genny
Who are the Thunder Beings?

#### Henry
Our helpers. There's stories of them warning us of trouble—even stories of them laughing with us. Our stories are supposed to make us comfortable here.

#### Genny
You got stories for everything.

#### Henry
They connect us. Just like that brick your Grandma's got. It's broken like our tribe. After Removal, part of us came west to Oklahoma. Some hid from the soldiers and stayed in the east. We're two parts, yet it's one brick Gertrude's got.

## Genny

A burned brick. I think our stories make us uncomfortable, so we don't get too happy here. So we'll know something can happen to take part of us away.

# SCENE III

(THE NEXT AFTERNOON. THE CRANKERS OF THE SUN ARE VISIBLE. THEN THE LARGE YELLOW BALL OF THE SUN ITSELF. PULLED BY A HAND-CRANK OVER GERTRUDE'S CABIN. GERTRUDE SITS ON HER PORCH SEWING. GENNY IS IN THE GLIDER. JESS ENTERS.)

### Gertrude
Genny's looking for you.

### Jess
I waited for her after school. I feel like I'm just standing around. (HE FLOPS DOWN ON THE GLIDER.)

### Genny
(READING THE DIARY, WITHOUT FEELING.) Later with heavy rainfall and squalls, the wind changed to the west, and I made some distance—

### Gertrude
That restless voice I hear—

### Genny
I marked a chickpea with a cross and ordered lots be drawn for a pilgrimage to give thanks for our safety when we return. The first to put his hand in was myself, the Admiral, and I drew out the chickpea marked with the cross, so the lot fell to me. Upon return, I'd go to Santa Maria de Loreto, where Our Lady has performed miracles—

### Jess
Mr. Fax Man. Here's the number. (JESS DUMPS THE BOOK TO THE GROUND.) Call Spain. Isabel, dear, I'm coming home. Have dinner ready at 8:00. I've got all we ever hoped for. Love, Chris. (GENNY TRIES TO PICK UP THE BOOK BUT JESS KICKS IT AWAY.)

### Genny
(ALSO INTERPRETING, A LITTLE ANGRY NOW.) I named an island after her. What could she know in Spain wrapped in a lace mantilla? Sometimes I think she is Our Lady herself come back to grant my wishes to discover the New World. Maybe her delicate foot crept

322

out from beneath her robe. The white slipper like the tongue of God. What goes on in her heart? Does she often think of me? So I arrived in Spain with cinnamon and pepper and spices and parrots and nightingales and slaves and gold.

### Jess

It was chickpea park. It was kill the urth. Kill the Induns. Chop off their hands. Kill the whole fucking place. The theme-park Columbusland. The Discoverer Discovered. It was Columbus all new and roller coastery.

### Genny

(FINALLY GETS THE BOOK. HALF-READING, HALF-INTERPRETING. NOW WITH FEELING.) I wanted the Indians to know the light. God from God. Light from light. I wanted them to be allowed in heaven. Maybe not with our understanding, but as children brought into the Father's House to know His Magnificence. I wanted the Indians to know our example. How men in three ships could set out across the unknown and arrive in such a splendid land. How it would encourage them. How they could hear of our brave deeds. Our magnanimity. I want them to know grace and not the awful darkness they live in. Full of heathen light. Which is black as darkness itself. I wanted them to know Holiness. I wanted them to give their wealth up gladly for it.

### Henry

(HE SHOWS UP AGAIN.) Whad' you doing there, Gert?

### Gertrude

Working on Genny's costume. She said I had her looking like a casserole cover—

### Henry

Har.

### Gertrude

She sounded just like her mamma.

### Genny

I thought many times when we were loading the ships. Preparing the ship's log. How I pardon them all.

### Henry

What'll Jess do for a costume?

### Gertrude
Don't worry, Henry. You don't have to get out your needle and thread. Jess is wearing jeans. He opted for the New World—

### Genny
And I'm a captive of the new world sailing with the ships like Father, Son and Holy Ghost—

### Jess
How can it be the very ocean holds us up? (THE SUN IS LOWERED WITH A SQUEAK. THE CAT HISSES. HENRY'S DOG BARKS.)

# SCENE IV

(THE SUN ROLLS UNDER THE EARTH AND RISES IN THE EAST. THE CRANKERS OF THE SUN PULL IT NEARLY MIDDAY IN THE SKY OVER GERTRUDE'S CABIN, BUT ADJUST IT BACKWARDS. THEN IT JERKS FORWARD JUST A BIT.)

**Jess**

Henry—come to school—

**Genny**

You've got to see us—

**Jess**

Henry—I'm shaking in my Reebok's—I didn't know I'd be so scared.

**Gertrude**

The old boarding school's got Henry spooked—

**Jess**

I can face an audience, Henry, if you face the past.

**Genny**

Do you like my costume? (SHE TWIRLS.)

**Jess**

Where's your shit about harmony? Doesn't it work for you, Henry?

**Gertrude**

Them schools was fierce, Jess—

**Genny**

Don't argue—

**Jess**

Maybe your stories are just words—

**Henry**

I vowed I'd never go into a school again—

325

#### Gertrude
You're not enrolling, Henry—

#### Jess
Well then, maybe I don't have to go—why do I need this crap? Maybe I don't have to do what I don't want—

#### Gertrude
Jess—leave Henry alone. You don't know what those schools were like.

#### Henry
Do you?

#### Jess
I ain't been this scared—EVER. What am I doing here?—Acting in a fucking Columbus show. I'm an abandoned brat—no one ever wanted—

#### Genny
—You're the only one who plays the Columbus voice like you do.

#### Jess
—A stupid ventriloquist—

#### Gertrude
You won't be afraid once you start, Jess—

#### Jess
I got so much to say—

#### Genny
It'll come—

#### Jess
Henry—you tell me to bear the discomfort of school—

#### Henry
It won't be any harder than pulling Warren's car back with the truck.

#### Jess
You weren't much help with that—

#### Genny
Don't argue, Jess—you'll upset us for school—

#### Jess
I'm already upset.

#### Gertrude
Come on, Henry. I'll sit with you—

#### Henry
No— (HE DISAPPEARS IN THE WOODS. HIS DOG BARKS.)

#### Jess
(HE CALLS AFTER HENRY.) It feels a little like loaning money to someone who's not going to pay you back—

#### Gertrude
Let him go, Jess. He'll go talk to the squirrels. Warren always said— let Henry tell a story and he'll get over what's bothering him—

#### Genny
Come on, Jess. You can do what you're afraid of. Then you won't be afraid of it. Think of the Thunder Beings who help us. They thunder and give us courage. Once the Thunder Beings were scared of everything. They were so scared they couldn't talk. They were little invisible children behind their parents, the Lightning. So what did they do? They made noises. And the more noise they made, the more noise it sounded like they made. Part of their roar is in our imagination, Jess.

#### Jess
Is that one of Henry's stories?

#### Genny
Just start talking like Columbus, and they'll hear you sounding like Columbus—I think in his diary he was scared too—and maybe he felt like he didn't get what they owed him—

#### Jess
He was cruel to the natives, Genny. We should hang him from the mast—what do you want? Sometimes I try to talk to Henry, and all I get's a story.

#### Genny
He's talking to you. You just don't hear it yet.

**Jess**

I'm quivering inside, Genny. I want to run.

**Genny**

It's your energy trying to get out. The Thunder Beings are getting ready to swarm around you like the blackbirds. Come on, Jess. We're going to arrive in the New World—

# SCENE V

(THE BEAR AND ELK SPIRITS AND SOME BLACKBIRDS GATHER AT THE EDGE OF THE STAGE. THE CRANKERS OF THE SUN LIFT A SAIL OVER GERTRUDE'S CABIN, WHICH IS NOW COLUMBUS' SHIP. THEY HAVE TO CRANK THE SUN OUT OF THE WAY TO GET THE SAIL UP, WHICH THEY DO AWKWARDLY.)

#### Genny
*The reading of the Interpretation of the Diary of Christopher Columbus. His Return Voyage.* According to Jess Ortega and Genny Blue Eagle. Welllllllll folks here come the ships.

#### Jess
(SCARED AT FIRST.) Skip. Skip.

#### Genny
Where are we going?

#### Jess
Spain.

#### Genny
(SHE SQUEALS WITH DELIGHT.) OOOOOOOU!

#### Henry
(HENRY, SOMEWHERE IN THE WOODS, TALKS TO THE SQUIRRELS.) Tich. Tich. (JESS AND GENNY ARE AT SCHOOL. GERTRUDE, WHO IS WATCHING JESS AND GENNY, IS ALSO, AT THE SAME TIME, WITH HENRY. THERE'S NO BOUNDARY OF DISTANCE BETWEEN THEM. GERTRUDE, DIVIDING HER ATTENTION BETWEEN HENRY, AND JESS AND GENNY, MEASURES HENRY'S ARMS WITH A RULER.) In the boarding school, I was Columbus for Columbus Day. Someone made a blouse and Columbus-pantaloons for me. I had to learn a speech. I had trouble saying the words. (GERTRUDE MEASURES HENRY BETWEEN HIS UNDERARM AND WAIST. SHE STARTS TO MEASURE FROM HIS CROTCH TO THE KNEE. HENRY TAKES THE RULER. HE SPEAKS AS COLUMBUS.) In 1492 Columbus sailed the ocean blue— (HE LIFTS HIS HAND. HE WHACKS A RULER ACROSS HIS OWN KNUCKLES.)

#### Gertrude

Put your own words in your mouth, Henry. (MEANWHILE, JESS TRIES TO LEAVE THE STAGE. GENNY PULLS HIM BACK. THUNDER RUMBLES OFF STAGE. BOTH JESS AND HENRY HEAR IT.) Come on, Henry—boarding school's over. Can't you hear the squirrels? We're making dry ground out of the mud—

#### Henry

(HENRY WHACKS HIS KNUCKLES AGAIN.) I won't be afraid of these shadows.

#### Jess

(MEANWHILE AT SCHOOL, JESS BLOWS LIKE THE WIND.) Puf puf! Hurry back to Spain— (THE ELK AND BEAR SPIRITS CIRCLE HENRY AND JESS. THE BLACKBIRDS MOVE THEIR WINGS LIKE SAILS.)

#### Genny

Good-bye, Turtle Island. (SHE WAVES.) Good-bye earth that I knew.

#### Jess

*I'll have them talking about me.* (JESS STEERS. GENNY HOLDS TO THE SIDE OF THE SHIP.)

#### Henry

Columbus sailed his black ship over the sea—

#### Gertrude

Hold still, Henry. How will I get your costume made?

#### Henry

I'm so tired of water. So tired of wind flapping the masts of the caravel. (HENRY WHACKS HIS KNUCKLES ONE MORE TIME AND THE BLACKBIRDS TAKE THE RULER AWAY FROM HIM.)

#### Gertrude

I'll have you looking like a K-Mart seat-cover if you don't stand still, Henry.

#### Henry

I couldn't pass any island without taking possession.

#### Gertrude

Put a sail on it, Henry.

Henry
(HENRY RAISES BOTH HIS HANDS. THE ELK AND BEAR SPIRITS LICK
HENRY'S KNUCKLES.) A healing ceremony— (THE BLACKBIRDS
CIRCLE HIM WITH THEIR WINGS.)

Gertrude
Lets go to school and see Genny and Jess. We'll hear the voice of
the new Columbus. (SHE TAKES HIM BY THE HAND.)

Henry
Maybe we can rewrite history, Gert—when we get far enough away
from it.

Jess
(HE SPEAKS WITH CONVICTION NOW.)
*Admiral Don Christobal Colon.*
*Discoverer of the second world.*
*With the help of our Lord.*
(GENNY SWOOPS UP AND DOWN WITH THE BLACKBIRDS AND THE
WAVES.)
*Yes, I discovered the second part of the earth.*
*Was it ever the same after me?*
*I found pecados de oro for Isabel and Ferdinand.*
*Especeria for their bland mutton.*
*What did they know about being alone on the sea?*

Genny
Ooooouuu—(SHE CRIES NOW IN DISTRESS.)

Gertrude
That voice—(SHE COVERS HER EARS.)

Henry
It's Genny's voice, Gertrude.

Gertrude
It sounds like my daughter—

Henry
It's really your voice, Gertrude—that voice you hear. It's what the
squirrels say—it's what they tell me about you. When they come to
my cabin, and you're over at your place sweeping the porch—they
say, she seems happy, but underneath she's crying for her daughter, and the past she can't change. No matter how many rewrites
you put on it each day—your past happened. Get used to it, the

squirrels say. (THE BLACKBIRDS CIRCLE GERTRUDE. THE ELK AND BEAR LICK HER EARS.) The New World came, Gertrude. There's nothing we can do about it. Maybe it ain't so bad—but I don't see it yet. Neither do you. But I think there's ways to survive and not forget our past. Yep, Gert—you know it too. Sometimes I see you fly like a blackbird—higher than any of us.

### Jess

*I offered glass beads to the Indians.*
*I made them Christians!*
*I claimed the New World.*
(JESS AND HENRY DO A NEW WORLD STOMP-DANCE. THE BLACK-BIRDS FLAP THEIR WINGS IN UNISON NOW. GERTRUDE PULLS OUT A FEW OF THE FEATHERS AND PINS THEM TO HERSELF.)

### Henry

You look a little like your black bean chili, Gertrude, in those feathers. (THEY CIRCLE THE STAGE, THEN HENRY AS COLUMBUS DOES SOME FANCY DANCING ON HIS OWN.)

### Jess

Those blackbirds are doing some flapping with their wings! See the light of their eyes. The Pow Wow bustle on their tails. They'll win the traditional dancing—the fancy-dancing—the grass dancing! (HENRY, DRESSED AS COLUMBUS, DANCES AS HARD AS HE CAN. THE BEAR AND ELK SPIRITS ALSO DANCE. HENRY PINS A SIGN ON THE BEAR THAT SAYS "ELK" AND A SIGN ON THE ELK THAT SAYS "BEAR." GERTRUDE, DRESSED NOW ALSO AS A BLACKBIRD, SWEEPS THE SHIP'S DECK WITH HER BROOM. HENRY AS COLUMBUS DANC-ES AGAIN.) Yes. Before he started back to Spain—Columbus discov-ered America! He landed, thump, against the shore. He called us by the wrong name. Yndios. Well, shit happens, so they say. See the woods! See the rivers! He even discovered Oklahoma! Yes. Colum-bus discovered the Pushmataha Pow Wow! Look at Columbus dancing hard as he can. He's the best fancy-dancer the Pow Wow's ever seen.

### Genny

Now let's get to work here—

### Jess

Let's make waves, Gen. Let's hit it with what we got.
(THE DRUMS PLAY. THE SPIRITS DANCE.)

### Genny

OOOOOOH!!

#### Gertrude
Let's dance, Henry.


#### Henry
Okay, Chili-bean!


#### Jess
Here's some blackbird boogie. Now the drums—


#### Henry
Maybe an Indian flute—because the ladies like it.


#### Jess
Maybe a little bit of New Wave. Or Gertrude's K-Mart hard-country rock! See the ocean beating against the New World shore. We don't know where we're going. But we're going anyway. (EVERYONE CONTINUES THE POW WOW DANCE.) There's savages all around. And some of them are us. But we got this message from two Worlds and we're coming to our own. (JESS JERKS ON AN IMAGINARY SLOT-MACHINE HANDLE.) Yes, we're coming into Home.

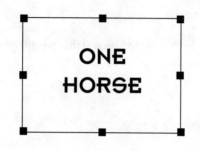

ONE
HORSE

(POW WOW ANNOUNCER HEARD ON THE CAR RADIO WHILE TRAVELING ACROSS NORTHERN WISCONSIN, JULY 19, 1992)

You don't want to miss the Grand Entry.

The flag bearers. Lead dancers. Royalty from Indian Country. Traditional dancers.

Drum. Drum. Drum. Drum.

How about a big round of applause. Yes. For the bells and jingles. Belling and jingling.

Way ha hey ho ya nah.

Bouncing like a 2-horse motor on a fishing boat pulled down a dirt road.

Woah.

All you dancers give us a toot.

Who whoa hoot hoot whooz whoop whoop.

Here comes th'girls bouncing.

Hey hey. Ugh ugh. A one a two. Some Indian polka.

Lead singers. Sing your flag song.

Sound engineer. Could you come up here, please? I'm picking up some noise.

Let's remember our Veterans.

When the ship first landed from the big waters, our Warriors were there. At the Little Big Horn. Wounded Knee. World War I and II. Korea. Vietnam. Respect our Warriors.

This song tells about the past and makes a path into the future.

Hey yo ho no ya he ha hey ya.

Drum. Drum. Drum. Drum.

Respect the Warriors. Now our Uncle will pray.

Aga sagag ay hey to um huyo to pa tah. Me gwetch.

Remember the benches are for dancers in costume.

The lost-and-found says they got two hair pieces. One is a thin one. It must go around the ears. Is the wind blowing hard for you? Maybe it's because you lost your hairpiece.

Ha ha.

You know there's a story behind everything. The Keeper of the Drum will tell the story of the Warrior's Staff and the Soldiers' Drum.

I don't like to speak in public. I'been having trouble talking in front of a lot of people. I'been having a difficult time, but I'll talk about the Warrior Staff. It had fallen into disuse. Some of the eagle feathers were gone. We didn't know what to do. Someone said we should go to the Vets. They gave us some of their power. They gave us their eagle feathers for the Staff. We're honored they give us their feathers. We're honored they trust us to keep the Warrior Staff.

Now the Soldiers' Drum, you know, it takes the hard feelings out.

You see one of the Grandmothers had a dream after WWI. She couldn't make sense of it. She went to the elders and finally a gourd-shaker on the reserve. He said her dream meant the war would end and the soldiers would come back. A drum should be made for the Vets to help them get over the war. You know to beat it. It cleans the hurts. The Spirit of War.

Then she dreamed the soldiers worried that if they died, they would be forgotten. That was their big worry in the war. Yes. All the soldiers from all the wars were afraid they'd be forgotten.

Would the bells and jingles be still?

Gash be gah.

All women wearing eagle feathers are mothers of Vets.

We remember our Vets and honor them.

Drum. Drum. Drum. Drum.
Drum. Drum. Drum. Drum.

Woha. That drum has been put to work. Take it easy for a while.

Now look at those custom-built fancy-dancers. Would all dancers come into the arena, please?

Are you awake yet? Benjoe's still counting his cards.

There's a lot of important people here. For a minute I thought I was at the Republican convention.

I got some of the head dancers mad at me. They think I forgot them. So they get a 2-dollar coin from the Mille Lacs casino. I got a fax machine up here, man. Messages get through all the time.

Are you ready?

Dancers into the arena, please.

A ho.

Some fine ponies out there in the parking lot.

Drum. Drum. Drum. Drum.

New vans and trucks. Firebirds and Benjoe's Pinto.

Ha ha.

We have our first lost child. Somebody help this little girl to find her mama or auntie or gramma.

Our raffle ticket prizes are a Marlin rifle. A Pendleton blanket. A car wash.

This is some celebration.

Seen any of Gilbert's sweethearts lately? He closed his eyes last night and sang his "Lonesome lovesick blues." He played his guitar and sounded like Hank Williams and got everyone so lonesome they went snagging, and when Gilbert opened his eyes he saw he was all alone up there on stage. Everyone had gone off together.

A ho.

DIANE GLANCY is Associate Professor at Macalester College in St. Paul, Minnesota, where she teaches Native American Literature and Creative Writing. Her first novel, *Pushing the Bear*, was published in 1996 by Harcourt Brace. A second novel, *The Only Piece of Furniture in the House*, was published by Moyer Bell, also in 1996. In 1995, TriQuarterly/Northwestern University Press published her third collection of short stories, *Monkey Secret*. A new collection of essays, *The West Pole*, is forthcoming from the University of Minnesota Press in 1997.